# AN INTRODUCTION TO LATIN AMERICAN POLITICS AND DEVELOPMENT

# An Introduction to Latin American Politics and Development

### Howard J. Wiarda
*University of Massachusetts and the Center for Strategic and International Studies (CSIS)*

AND

### Harvey F. Kline
*University of Alabama*

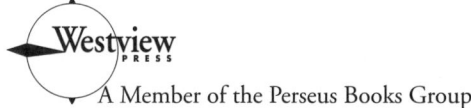

A Member of the Perseus Books Group

All rights reserved. Printed in the United States of America. No part of this publication may be reproduced or transmitted in any form or by any means, electronic or mechanical, including photocopy, recording, or any information storage and retrieval system, without permission in writing from the publisher.

Copyright © 2001 by Westview Press, A Member of the Perseus Books Group

Published in 2001 in the United States of America by Westview Press, 5500 Central Avenue, Boulder, Colorado 80301-2877, and in the United Kingdom by Westview Press, 12 Hid's Copse Road, Cumnor Hill, Oxford OX2 9JJ

Find us on the World Wide Web at www.westviewpress.com

Library of Congress Cataloging-in-Publication Data

Wiarda, Howard J., 1939–
  An introduction to Latin American politics and development / Howard J. Wiarda and Harvey F. Kline.
    p. cm.
  Includes bibliographical references and index.
  ISBN 0-8133-3770-4 (pbk. : alk. paper)
  1. Latin America—Politics and government.    I. Kline, Harvey F.    II. Title.

JL960.W515   2001
320.98—dc21                                                                 00-050358

The paper used in this publication meets the requirements of the American National Standard for Permanence of Paper for Printed Library Materials Z39.48-1984.

10   9   8   7   6   5   4   3   2   1

# Contents

List of Illustrations — vii
List of Acronyms — ix
Preface — xiii

1  The Context of Latin American Politics — 1
2  The Pattern of Historical Development — 13
3  Changing Political Culture — 31
4  Class, Social Structure, Social Change — 51
5  Interest Groups — 69
6  Political Parties — 111
7  Government Machinery, The Role of the State, and Public Policy — 131
8  The Struggle for Democracy in Latin America — 167
9  Conclusion: Democracy in Latin America — 201

Suggestions for Further Reading — 215
Index — 219

# Illustrations

| | | |
|---|---|---|
| Map 1 | Central and Middle America and the Caribbean | xvi |
| Map 2 | South America | xvii |
| Table 1.1 | Indices of Modernization in Latin America in the 1990s | 10 |
| Table 2.1 | Comparison of the Foundations of Latin American and North American Society | 18 |
| Table 3.1 | Social Attitudes in Various Latin American Countries | 47 |
| Table 3.2 | Attitudes Toward Politics in Various Latin American Countries | 48 |
| Figure 3.1 | Support for Democracy in Latin America | 41 |
| Figure 3.2 | Support for Democracy in South America and Mexico | 41 |
| Figure 3.3 | Support for Democracy in Central America | 42 |
| Figure 3.4 | Satisfaction with Democracy in Latin America | 42 |
| Figure 3.5 | Satisfaction with Democracy in South America and Mexico | 43 |
| Figure 3.6 | Satisfaction with Democracy in Central America | 44 |

# Acronyms

| | |
|---|---|
| AD | Democratic Action (Acción Democrática) |
| AD | Democratic Alliance |
| ADN | Democratic Action Party |
| ANDI | National Association of [Large] Industrialists |
| ANUC | National Association of Land Users |
| AP | Popular Action |
| APRA | American Popular Revolutionary Alliance (Alianza Popular Revolucionaría Americana) |
| APT | Asunción for All (Asunción Para Todos) |
| ARENA | National Renovating Alliance (Brazil) |
| ARENA | Nationalist Republican Alliance (El Salvador) |
| AUC | United Self-Defense Groups of Colombia |
| CACIF | Coordinating Committee of Agricultural, Commercial, Industrial, and Financial Associations |
| CFP | Concentration of Popular Forces |
| CIAN | Center for Anti-Narcotics Investigations |
| CNC | National Confederation of Peasants |
| CNOP | National Confederation of Popular Organizations |
| CNR | National Chamber of Representatives (Cámara Nacional de Representantes) |
| CNT | National Labor Command |
| COB | Bolivian Workers' Central (Central Obrera Boliviana) |
| CODEH | Committee for the Defense of Human Rights in Honduras |
| CONDEPA | Conscience of the Fatherland |
| CSTC | Syndical Confederation of Workers of Colombia |
| CTC | Confederation of Colombian Workers |
| CTM | Confederation of Mexican Workers (Confederación de Trabajadores Mexicanos) |
| CUT | Unitary Labor Central |
| DP | Popular Democracy |
| ELN | Army of National Liberation |

| | |
|---|---|
| EN | National Encounter Party (Encuentro Nacional) |
| ESG | Superior War College |
| EZLN | Zapatista National Liberation Army (Ejército Zapatista de Liberación Nacional) |
| FARC | Armed Forces of the Colombian Revolution |
| FEDECAFE | National Federation of Coffee Growers |
| FMLN | National Liberation Front of Farabundo Martí (Frente Farabundo Martí de Liberación Nacional) |
| FRAP | Popular Action Front |
| FSLN | Sandinista Front for National Liberation (Frente Sandinista de Liberación Nacional) |
| FSTSE | Federation of State Workers' Unions |
| FZLN | Zapatista Front of National Liberation |
| GDP | gross domestic product |
| GNP | gross national product |
| IADB | Inter-American Development Bank |
| ID | Democratic Left (Izquierda Democrática) |
| IMF | International Monetary Fund |
| ISI | import substitution industrialization |
| IU | United Left (Izquierda Unida) |
| MAS | Death to Kidnappers |
| MBL | Free Bolivia Movement |
| MDB | Brazilian Democratic Movement (Movimento Democrático Brasileiro) |
| MERCOSUR | Southern Common Market (Mercado Commun de Sudamérica) |
| MIR | Leftist Revolutionary Movement (Movimiento Izquierdista Revolucionario) |
| MNR | National Revolutionary Movement (Movimiento Nacional Revolucionario) |
| MRTKL | Tupaj Katari Revolutionary Movement of Liberation |
| NAFTA | North American Free Trade Association |
| NGO | nongovernmental organization |
| OAS | Organization of American States |
| PAN | National Action Party (Partido de Acción Nacional) |
| PCN | National Conciliation Party |
| PCP | Peruvian Communist Party |
| PCS | El Salvadoran Communist Party |
| PDC | Christian Democratic Party (Partido Demócrata Cristiano) |
| PDS | Democratic Social Party |
| PDT | Democratic Workers' Party |

| | |
|---|---|
| PFJ | Federal Judicial Police |
| PFL | Liberal Front Party |
| PLH | Honduran Liberal Party |
| PLN | Party of National Liberation (Partido de Liberación Nacional) |
| PLRA | Authentic Liberal Radical Party (Partido Liberal Radical Auténtico) |
| PMDB | Brazilian Democratic Movement Party |
| PNC | National Civilian Police |
| PNH | Honduran National Party |
| PPC | Popular Christian Party (Partido Popular Cristiano) |
| PRD | Democratic Revolutionary Party |
| PRD | Dominican Revolutionary Party |
| PRI | Institutional Revolutionary Party (Partido Revolucionario Institucional) |
| PRN | National Renovation Party |
| PRSC | Social Christian Reform Party |
| PSD | Social Democratic Party |
| PT | Workers' Party |
| PTB | Brazilian Labor Party (Partido Trabalhista Brasileiro) |
| SIN | National Intelligence System |
| SNA | National Agricultural Society |
| SOFOFA | Society for the Promotion of Manufacturing |
| UCS | Civic Solidarity Union |
| UDI | Independent Democratic Union |
| UDN | Nationalist Democratic Union (Unión Democrática Nacionalista) |
| UDP | Democratic Popular Unity (Unidad Democrática Popular) |
| UP | Patriotic Unity (Colombia—Unidad Patriótica) |
| USAID | U.S. Agency for International Development |
| UTC | Union of Colombian Workers |

# Preface

In the months that we have been working on this book, dramatic political happenings have occurred in Latin America. On the one hand, Argentina had a "boring" presidential election, far from the populism and military intervention of the past, and Mexico too had a relatively free presidential election, resulting in the defeat of the candidate whose party had been in power for over seventy years. On the other hand, Alberto Fujimori in Peru won a third term as president in elections that were of doubtful fairness and was then obliged to step aside, and Hugo Chávez in Venezuela carried out a constitutional reform that is likely to make it possible for him to stay in power for another twelve years. So far it is not clear whether democracy has finally arrived in Latin America or whether authoritarianism is simply hiding just below an artfully crafted democratic veneer.

Latin America has long been one of the world's most fascinating and interesting areas, offering everything a student of the area could hope for: vast social changes, rapid economic development, transitions to democracy, revolutions, a fractured history, repeated U.S. interventions (military and otherwise), class struggle, fascinating race relations, globalization and its effects, changing political culture, rapacious dictatorships, civil wars and conflicts, new experiments in public policy, an entire subregion of international relations, drug trafficking, migration—both legal and illegal—border conflicts, arms control, struggles to enter into the modern world, great baseball as well as great soccer, and a fascinating culture now having a major impact on the United States (think of Gloria Estefan, Ricky Martin, or Jennifer Lopez). What more could one ask for in looking for a region to study? If you can't find a topic that interests you in the list just offered, you shouldn't be reading this book!

Why are the United States and Latin America so different? Why is the United States so wealthy while Latin America seems so poor and undeveloped? Why has the United States been so stable and democratic and Latin America so torn by conflict and revolution? Why are there so many prejudices and resentments between the United States and Latin America? Why are so many Latin Americans now immigrating to the United States, and why is Latin America exporting so many drugs to the United States? Can the United States and Latin America ever get along, or will there always be anger as well as misunderstanding between the two cultures? Will Latin America eventually develop in accord with the U.S. economic and political model, or will these two main parts of the Western Hemisphere continue to go their own separate ways? These questions have long fascinated us, and in this book we will explore the differences between the United States and Latin America and ask ourselves why the two areas have gone in such separate directions.

Latin America is presently undergoing an earthshaking transformation as every element of the culture and society is being profoundly restructured. Values and beliefs are changing, vast social changes are under way, the economies of the region are being modernized, most of the countries are becoming democratic, and Latin America's traditional isolation is breaking down as the region joins the modern world. These changes have far-reaching implications, and they provide another reason for studying the area. In their basics, these changes are not unlike what other modern nations and regions—the United States, Europe, Japan—have gone through previously, but it is also clear that although Latin America is now joining the modern democratic world, it is doing so in its own way and in accord with its own culture and traditions. That makes Latin America a fascinating "living laboratory" of social and political change. We think it is a healthy sign that Latin America is developing and democratizing in accord with its own values and culture and not just as a pale imitation of the United States; this mature self-determination is not only a good sign for progress in Latin America but it is also intellectually stimulating for those who study the region. The study of Latin America thus speaks to important issues of diversity and multiculturalism in addition to providing fertile ground for the study of the comparative development of nations.

This book deals with these provocative issues and questions. It is intended as an introduction to Latin America: to the culture, economy, sociology, politics, and international affairs of the region. Our focus is particularly on the region's overall development—in all its dimensions.

The book is organized thematically. Chapter 1 considers the context of Latin American politics, and Chapter 2 deals with the patterns of historical development. Chapter 3 is concerned with changing political culture in the region, and Chapter 4 discusses class, social structure, and social change. Chapter 5 turns to interest groups and Chapter 6 to political parties. The themes of Chapter 7 are government machinery, the role of the state, and public policy. Chapter 8 considers the struggle for democracy in Latin

America, and Chapter 9 contains our conclusions about democracy and the future in the area.

Readers looking for a detailed country-by-country analysis should consult the companion volume to this book, the fifth edition of *Latin American Politics and Development,* edited by Howard J. Wiarda and Harvey F. Kline, which contains individual treatment of all the countries of the region by the country's leading Latin American experts. Indeed, we finished editing the fifth edition just before we wrote this book, so we were able to use that volume's expert analyses of individual countries to make our references to individual countries as accurate as possible. It is only appropriate, therefore, that we thank the following people for sharing their knowledge: Paul H. Lewis (Argentina), Iêda Siqueira Wiarda (Brazil), Paul E. Sigmund (Chile), Vanessa Gray (Colombia), David Scott Palmer (Peru), David J. Myers (Venezuela), Ronald H. McDonald and Martin Weinstein (Uruguay), Paul C. Sondrol (Paraguay), Donna Lee Van Cott (Bolivia), David W. Dent (Ecuador), Juan M. del Aguila (Cuba), Mitchell A. Seligson (Costa Rica), Richard Millett (Nicaragua), Tommie Sue Montgomery (El Salvador), Robert H. Trudeau (Guatemala), J. Mark Ruhl (Honduras), Anthony Peter Spanakos (Dominican Republic), Steve C. Ropp (Panama), and Georges C. Fauriol (Haiti).

This book was designed to be used as an introductory text in courses or seminars in Latin American politics, Latin American development, comparative politics, Third World politics, transitions to democracy, globalization, politics of developing areas, and social change. It can stand alone as a text or be used in conjunction with other texts.

We would like to thank Karl Yambert of Westview Press for his sound editorial advice and particularly for his vision in urging us to conceive of this *Introduction to Latin American Politics and Development* as a separate volume. As usual, we also wish to thank our wives for their forbearance while this book was in preparation while also absolving them of all responsibility for what follows—that rests with us alone.

*Howard J. Wiarda*
*Harvey F. Kline*

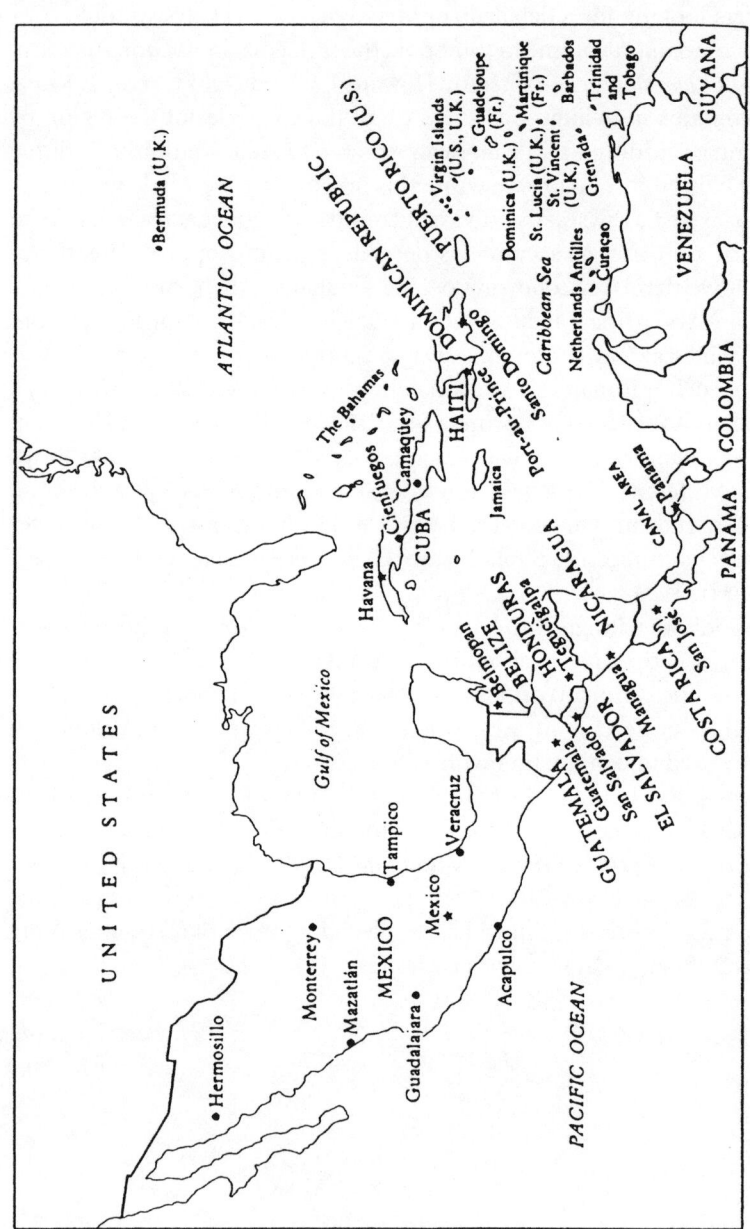

MAP 1   Central and Middle America and the Caribbean

MAP 2  South America

# 1

# The Context of Latin American Politics

Profound social, economic, cultural, and political transformations are sweeping through Latin America in the early twenty-first century, affecting all institutions and areas of life. Accelerated economic and social change, democratization, and globalization are having an impact on all countries in the region, but these processes are often incomplete and their impact is uneven. Latin America still has abundant poverty—malnutrition, disease, poor housing, and the worst distribution of income in the world; its economic and political institutions often fail to work well or as intended; and social and political reforms are still urgently needed. But at least some Latin American countries—generally those that are larger, more stable, and wealthier—are making what appears to be a definitive breakthrough to democracy and development, and many of the small nations are modernizing as well.

One should never speak of Latin America as if it were a single, homogeneous region, since in fact the area is exceedingly diverse. Indeed, because of this diversity we need to understand each country individually as well as common patterns. The Latin American countries share a common basis in law, language, history, culture, sociology, colonial experience, and overall political patterns that enable us to discuss the region in general terms, even while recognizing that each country is different and becoming increasingly more so. Unity amidst diversity is a theme that runs through this book.

Throughout Latin America's history its leaders and people have debated their heritage and future: Western or non-Western; feudal, capitalist, or socialist; First World (developed nations) or Third World (developing nations); evolutionary change or revolutionary change. Conflict over these issues has often delayed development.

Now at last a consensus seems to be emerging: democracy in the political sphere, a modern mixed economy, and greater integration with the rest of the world. Authoritarianism seems to be on the decline in Latin America, although when the economy weakens and instability results, the authoritarian temptation is still often present. Marxism-Leninism is similarly in decline, even while modern social democracy is still an attractive option for many political leaders. But more and more, Latin America is becoming middle-class and centrist. The old extremes are no longer attractive; the range of political and economic options has narrowed.

Driving these changes are democratization and globalization. Democracy is now the overwhelmingly preferred form of government in Latin America, even though it does not always work well or quickly enough, it often takes forms that are different from democracy in the United States, and it is still threatened by upheaval, corruption, and vast social problems. Globalization affects Latin America in all areas of life: culture (movies and television), society (behavioral norms), politics (democracy), and above all, economics. Latin America is now part of a global market economy. It has little choice but to open its markets to global trade and investment, even while recognizing that these changes impose hardships on some sectors of the population. With the Cold War over, there is little foreign aid, and Latin America can no longer play off the superpowers against each other. It must have private investment and become globally competitive or it will sink.

If a country deviates from the path of democracy or free markets, rejecting either an open economy or an open political system, then that all-important investment will simply go elsewhere, with dire consequences for the country affected. All political and economic leaders in Latin America now recognize these hard facts, even though they may still rail against them in populist fashion, try to soften the impact of globalization by implementing larger social programs, or disagree on the precise balance between authority and democracy, between statism and free markets, and between unfettered capitalism and social justice. The Latin American countries vary greatly in how they manage development policy, but they no longer have much choice when it comes to the basic model.

As Latin America has become more democratic and its economies more open, it has done so in ways balancing outside pressures with domestic and often traditional ways of doing things. Modernity and tradition often exist side by side in Latin America, where ancient agricultural methods and primitive slums reside alongside the latest in computer technology and skyscrapers of the newest design, reflecting the mixed, often transitional nature of Latin American society. Here patronage considerations often remain as important as merit and electoral choice, and as democracy has come to the area, it has often been a more centralized, executive-centered form of democracy in keeping with Latin American history, rather than one of separate and coequal legislative and judicial branches. At the same time, despite privatization and neoliberalism, the state has remained a strong force in the economy and social programs, closer to the European tradition than the U.S. laissez-faire model. Modernization in Latin America has represented a fascinating blend of U.S., European, and historic Latin American ways of doing things.

## A Quick Snapshot

For the purposes of this book, Latin America consists of eighteen Spanish-speaking countries, one Portuguese-speaking country (Brazil), and one French- or patois-speaking country (Haiti). Including South America, Central America and Mexico, and the Caribbean islands, Latin America encompasses 8 million square miles (21 million square kilometers), about one-fifth of the world's total land area. Its population is approaching 500 million, almost twice that of the United States. The former or present British, Dutch, and French (other than Haiti) territories or colonies in the area are also interesting and worthy of study and are part of the geographic region of the Americas, but they are not, for the most part, culturally, socially, religiously, or politically "Latin" (Iberian) American and therefore they are not included in this book.

The social and racial composition of Latin America is exceedingly diverse and complicated. At the time of Columbus's "discovery" of America in 1492, large numbers of indigenous people lived in what is now Mexico, in parts of Central America, and in the western area of South America; even today the assimilation and integration of indigenous people into national life remains one of the great unsolved problems of these countries. In areas where the climate was right for plantation agriculture but where few Indians had lived even in precolonial times, or where the Indian population had been decimated by the ravages of conquest and disease, such as the Caribbean islands, northeast Brazil, and some coastal areas, European colonists brought in large numbers of African slaves to cultivate the land.

Throughout the area, White Europeans formed the upper class while Indians and Blacks were slaves, peasants, and subsistence agriculturists. Once the Indians had disappeared, social and race relations in the Caribbean islands and northeast Brazil would be written in terms of the relations between Whites and Blacks; on the mainland the major socio-racial components were White and Indian. The cultures of the Spanish colonies in the

Caribbean and the Portuguese colony in Brazil, because of the African influence, were different from those in the other Spanish-speaking countries. In some countries, all three major racial strains, Indian, Black, and White, are represented; today they are joined by Asian and Middle Eastern peoples.

In contrast to the North American colonists who took their wives and families along to settle and farm, the conquistadors of Latin America viewed colonization as a military campaign, with no women, at least initially. Widespread miscegenation between Whites and Indians, Whites and Blacks, Blacks and Indians, and all of their offspring took place right from the beginning. Hence a mulatto (White and Black) element emerged quickly in the Caribbean and Brazil and a mestizo (White and Indian) element appeared in the mainland countries of the Spanish empire, with endless gradations based on color, hair, and facial features.

There is racial prejudice in Latin America, but because of the many variations and gradations, Latin Americans tend not to typecast people as "Black" or "White" or "Indian" based solely on color, as North Americans do. Indeed, in many of the Central American and Andean countries people are *indios* or *indígenas* only if they dress like Native Americans and speak a language other than Spanish. If such a person were to move to a city, wear Western-style clothes, and speak Spanish or Portuguese, he or she would probably no longer be called an Indian, even though of course there would have been no change of ethnic background. In the United States a person who is mulatto, or of mixed Black and White racial background, is usually characterized as Black. But in Latin America there are many designations between Black and White, such as *café au lait* (coffee with cream), and between Indian and White, such as *Ladino* or *cholo*—a person of Indian background who has assimilated into White, European culture. Even though such a person may still look Indian to North American eyes, in Latin American culture, assimilation means that a person has put the Indian background in the past and is no longer an Indian. Rather, the person is now in between and often becomes a part of the growing middle class in Latin America.

Racial identity in Latin America is generally more fluid and permeable than it is in the United States; in addition, higher education, wealth, and Western clothing and comportment tend to make one "whiter." But since being viewed as whiter is pragmatically seen by most Latin Americans as being easier and/or better, it has long been hard to launch Indian or Black rights or power movements, although this is changing as well. Endlessly fascinating, socio-racial relations in Latin America are very different from those in the United States.

In his book *Latin American Societies in Transition*, Richard C. Williamson suggests that in the 1990s, in broad ethnic terms, the countries of Latin America can be classified into four major groups:

1. Countries in which a mestizo population dominates;
2. Countries overwhelmingly European in character;
3. Countries with conspicuous Indian groupings, generally inhabiting the highlands; and
4. Countries dominated by African admixtures.[1]

The first group of countries includes the South American countries of Venezuela and Colombia, as well as Honduras, Nicaragua, El Salvador, and Panama in Central America, and Mexico. The predominantly European countries are Argentina, Chile, Uruguay, and Costa Rica, and the countries with large Indian groups are Guatemala, Ecuador, Peru, Bolivia, and Paraguay. Finally, the countries dominated by African admixtures are Brazil and the Caribbean countries of Cuba, the Dominican Republic, and Haiti.

Many countries have regional variations. For example in Colombia the mestizo culture is predominant, but there are parts of the country that are more Black-White dominated (the Pacific coast and the Valle del Cauca and Chocó departments), parts that are an admixture of Blacks and Indians (the Atlantic coast), and even parts that have large numbers of the mixtures of all three racial strains (the Antioquia region, where the Spanish encountered significant numbers of Indians and brought slaves for gold mining). Indeed, the Mexican intellectual, José Vasconcelos referred to the latter as the "cosmic race."

The economies of Latin America are similarly diverse, largely because of the variety of natural resources in the region. A few countries, notably Argentina, Brazil, Uruguay, and Venezuela, have vast, rich agricultural lands comparable to the U.S. Midwest; in most of the other countries subsistence agriculture has predominated. Because of the tropical climate in much of the region, only the southernmost countries can grow the kinds of grains found in Europe and the United States—corn, wheat, barley, and so on. In other countries, sugar, coffee, cacao beans, and tropical fruits have predominated. Mexico and the larger South American countries have considerable mineral wealth and some have oil, but others have few natural resources and are likely to remain poor, whether they call themselves capitalist or socialist.

Because of their resources, some countries—generally the bigger ones with large internal markets such as Argentina, Brazil, Chile, and Mexico—

are making it in the global economy and becoming competitive with the most efficient countries. Another group of Latin American countries is doing moderately well economically and improving their condition. But a handful of countries, Bolivia, Ecuador, Haiti, Honduras, and Nicaragua, are not doing well at all and are ranked among the world's poorest nations.

The Latin America countries differ not only in terms of people and economics but also in terms of geography. The continent contains the world's second highest mountain range, the Andes, which soars to over 20,000 feet and runs like a vertical spine up and down the Pacific Coast, separating the Pacific countries from the interior and Atlantic ones. Latin America also has some of the world's largest river systems, including the Amazon, the Orinoco, and the Plate, but few of these connect major cities with agricultural areas or provide the kind of internal transportation networks formed by the rivers and Great Lakes of North America. In many countries, mountains come right down to the sea, leaving little coastal land for settlement and agricultural development; much of the interior land is similarly unsuitable for cash crops. And while some countries have iron ore, few have coal, making it difficult to produce steel, one of the keys to early industrial development. Again, although nature has been kind to Latin America in some resources, it has been stingy in others; and while a few countries are resource-rich, others are stunningly poor.

One of the most startling features of South America is the vast Amazon basin, stretching nearly two thousand miles east and west and north and south. Largely uninhabited until recently, the Amazon rain forest produces upwards of 40 percent of the world's oxygen supply. Environmentalists seek to preserve this environment, while Brazil and other countries on its perimeter see the Amazon's resources as the keys to their future development. As Map 2 illustrates, most of South America's great cities are located on the ocean coast; only in recent decades have efforts been made to populate, develop, and exploit the vast interior.

Geographically, Latin America is a land of extremes: high mountains that are virtually impassable, lowlands that are densely tropical and difficult to penetrate, and extremes of heat, rainfall, and climate that make living and working difficult. Latin America largely lacks the resources that the United States had during its great march to modernization in the nineteenth century, and this has been one of the key reasons the region lagged behind its neighbor to the north. The mountainous, chopped-up terrain has also made internal communications and transportation difficult, dividing Latin America into *patrias chicas,* or small, isolated villages, and making national integration extremely difficult. Only now, with the advent of modern communications and transportation, have the Latin

American countries become better integrated and begun to develop their vast potential.

## The Economies

The Latin American economies were founded on a basis that was rapacious and exploitive. Under the prevailing economic theory of mercantilism, the colonies of Spain and Portugal existed solely for the benefit of the mother countries. The considerable gold, silver, and other resources of the colonies were drained away by the colonial powers. Ironically, Latin America's precious metals benefitted the mother countries not at all but flowed through Spain and Portugal to England and Holland, where they helped launch the Industrial Revolution. As was to be the case in the Americas, the north of Europe then forged ahead while the south fell further behind.

The most characteristic feature of colonial Latin America was the feudal or semifeudal estate, patterned after the European model, with Spaniards and Portuguese as the overlords and Indians and Blacks as peasants and slaves. Even after independence, Latin America remained mainly feudal; only slowly did capitalism and an entrepreneurial ethic develop. Under feudalism, the land, wealth, and people were all exploited; there was almost no effort to invest the profits from the land into development or to raise living standards. In accord with the feudal ethic and prevailing values, the total social product was fixed; people had to accept their station in life. Then as now, land, cattle, and peasants were symbols of status to the wealthy elites and were not necessarily used for productive purposes. However, economic conditions varied considerably among the colonies: in the Caribbean islands and northeast Brazil large-scale sugar plantations dominated the economy, while Mexico, Central America, Colombia, Peru, Bolivia, and other areas of Brazil were valued for their mineral wealth. Argentina, Uruguay, and other farm areas were settled later because at the time there were better ways than agriculture to get rich quick.

Few areas in Latin America were founded on the productive, family-farm model of the New England colonies; Costa Rica comes closest. The vast territory of Latin America was divided up among the Spanish and Portuguese conquerors into huge estates that were often the size of U.S. states or counties and resembled medieval fiefdoms. Along with the land, in the system called the *encomienda*, came the right to exploit the Indian labor living on the land. Each Spanish and Portuguese conquistador could live like the feudal nobility: haughty, authoritarian, exploitive, avoiding manual labor. These large estates were largely self-sufficient, often with their own priest, political authority (the landowner himself), and social and economic life. In theory, the landowner was to care for the Indians, including their instruction in the Christian faith.

It was only in the last half of the nineteenth century that these feudal estates began to be converted into more capitalistic enterprises, producing more intensively for a world market as well as home consumption. Sugar and tobacco in the Caribbean, bananas and coffee in Central America and Colombia, rubber in Brazil, beef, hides, and wool in Argentina and Uruguay were the new crops now being produced for profit. The old feudal estates began to modernize and become export-oriented enterprises. Foreign investment, first from Great Britain and later from the United States, stimulated this conversion process. Latin America went through the first stages of economic development, but in the process many Indians and peasants were exploited even more than in the past or pushed off their communal lands into the infertile hillsides. The result was class polarization and, in Mexico, a violent revolution in 1910.

Production for the export market resulted in an economic quickening throughout Latin America that led to further growth later on, and it also brought Latin America into the world economy for the first time, with both positive and negative consequences. Greater affluence led to new economic opportunities and greater political stability in most countries from roughly the 1880s to 1930, but dependence on exports also made Latin America subject to global economic forces over which it had no control. In some countries, 60 percent or more of the export earnings depended on one crop (sugar, coffee, bananas), and if that crop suffered a price decrease on world markets, the entire national economy could go into a tailspin. That is precisely what happened in virtually every price fluctuation and especially in the 1929–1930 world market crash, when not only did the bottom drop out of all the Latin American economies but their political systems collapsed as well. Almost every country of the area, with the exception of Colombia and Mexico, experienced a military coup d'état associated with the Depression.

Large-scale industrialization began in most Latin American countries in the 1930s precisely because, during the Depression, they had no export earnings with which to purchase imported manufactured goods and therefore had to produce them on their own. Most of the heavy industries—steel, electricity, petroleum, manufacturing—were established as state-owned industries, reflecting the weakness of private entrepreneurialism and the history of mercantilism. The system is called state capitalism to distinguish it from the laissez-faire or free market capitalism of the United States. This was the beginning of Latin America's large, but often bloated, inefficient, and patronage-dominated state sector.

During World War II and the postwar period, Latin America developed rapidly on the basis of what was called the import substitution industrialization (ISI) model. But instead of decreasing the need to export primary goods, ISI increased that need, since exports were needed to pay for machinery for the new industries, which had to be imported. In addition, growing demands for new social programs outstripped many countries' ability to pay for them. Then came the massive oil price increases of the 1970s, which divided the Latin American countries into two groups: the oil exporters (Venezuela, Mexico, and Peru) and the oil importers (all the other countries). The importing countries found it more difficult to fund development because more and more resources were being used to pay for petroleum. The exporting countries borrowed against their oil profits to pay for imports of manufactured goods; some accumulated vast debt and found themselves unable to pay back the loans. As a result, during the debt crisis of the 1980s Latin America was unable to pay its obligations and many countries slipped into near bankruptcy. From the 1960s to the 1980s, economic downturn again helped produce political instability, as it had in the 1930s.

In the 1990s the Latin American economies began to recover. The growth was often anemic and uneven and debt continued to be a burden, but there was recovery throughout the region and many countries began to reform and modernize their economies. In an effort to become competitive in the global economy, many countries sold off inefficient public enterprises, opened previously protected economic sectors to competition, emphasized exports, decreased tariffs, and sought to reduce or streamline inefficient bureaucratic regulation. They tried to diversify their economies internally and also sought a wider range of trading partners. All of these reforms are summed up in the term "neoliberalism." But neoliberal reform efforts often produced mixed results; although reducing state size was rational economically, it conflicted with the entrenched systems of political patronage by which friends and supporters were rewarded with cushy state jobs. Also, industries that had long been protected by tariffs during the ISI period often found they could not compete during the neoliberal period. They went out of business, hence increasing unemployment.

As shown in Table 1.1, Chile, Argentina, Brazil, and Mexico were the chief leaders and beneficiaries of the new, free market economic policies. Several other countries did moderately well, but some remained poor and backward.

## Conclusion

Over the course of five hundred years Latin America has changed from a feudal and mercantilist system to more modern, capitalist, or mixed economies. In most Latin American countries, agriculture and mining are

TABLE 1.1   Indices of Modernization in Latin America in the 1990s

|  | GDP per capita (US$) 1997 | Average Annual GDP Growth 1990–97 | Life Expectancy 1999 | Percent Urban 1997 | Rate of Inflation 1998 |
|---|---|---|---|---|---|
| Argentina | 6512 | 4.3 | 73.1 | 86.8 | 0.7 |
| Bolivia | 942 | 2.0 | 61.4 | 60.5 | 4.4 |
| Brazil | 3239 | 0.5 | 67.9 | 82.8 | 2.5 |
| Chile | 3957 | 6.9 | 75.2 | 88.2 | 4.7 |
| Colombia | 1738 | 2.5 | 70.9 | 74.8 | 16.7 |
| Costa Rica | 2063 | 1.3 | 76.8 | 49.8 | 12.4 |
| Dominican Republic | 1057 | 2.2 | 71.0 | 67.1 | 7.8 |
| Ecuador | 1392 | 1.5 | 69.8 | 62.4 | 43.4 |
| El Salvador | 1293 | 3.3 | 69.4 | 49.6 | 4.2 |
| Guatemala | 990 | 1.4 | 64.2 | 45.0 | 7.5 |
| Haiti | 214 | −6.1 | 58.4 | 32.4 | 7.4 |
| Honduras | 670 | 0.4 | 69.8 | 49.4 | 15.7 |
| Mexico | 3347 | 1.0 | 72.4 | 75.3 | 18.6 |
| Nicaragua | 491 | −0.5 | 74.1 | 75.3 | 8.1 |
| Panama | 2702 | 3.7 | 74.0 | 55.8 | 1.4 |
| Paraguay | 1489 | 0.0 | 69.7 | 52.8 | 14.6 |
| Peru | 2209 | 2.7 | 68.3 | 71.3 | 6.0 |
| Uruguay | 3437 | 3.6 | 72.8 | 86.8 | 8.7 |
| Venezuela | 3267 | 1.7 | 72.8 | 94.8 | 29.9 |
| Latin America | 3205 | 1.6 | 70.0 | 77.7 | 10.3 |

Sources: Inter-American Development Bank, "*Economic and Social Progress in Latin America (IPES98): Facing Up to Inequality in Latin America.*" Online. Available at: http://www.iadb.org/oce/ IPES98_eng/. October 6, 2000. Comisión Económica para América Latina, "*Estudio Económica de Américo Latina y el Caribe, 1998–1999.*" Online. Available at: http://www.eclac.cl/espanol/ Publicaciones/estudio99/eee99/indice99.htm. October 6, 2000.

still important to the economy, but now industry, manufacturing, telecommunications, construction, tourism, and other services have become important as well. Most of the countries in the region are no longer single-crop economies, and with a few exceptions, wealth and the standard of living have increased as well. Mexico is now second only to Canada in trade with the United States, and quite a number of the Latin American countries (e.g., Argentina, Brazil, Chile) have become major global economic actors. But the growth is still uneven and most of the smaller countries lag behind, with few resources and limited internal markets. By forming free trade areas such as the North American Free Trade Association (NAFTA) and the Southern Common Market (MERCOSUR), the Latin American countries have sought to forge increased trade and larger markets.

## Note

1. Robert C. Williamson, *Latin American Societies in Transition* (Westport, CT: Praeger, 1997), p. 127.

# 2

# The Pattern of Historical Development

The United States was founded in the seventeenth and eighteenth centuries, when the first stirrings of modernization were just occurring—capitalism, liberalism, pluralism, representative government, the Enlightenment, the Industrial Revolution. Latin America, in contrast, was founded in an earlier time when feudal and medieval practices and institutions still held sway. If the United States was "born free," Latin America was "born feudal," and these differences still account for many of the contrasts between the two areas. To a degree unknown in the United States, Latin America has long been dominated by a political, social, and economic structure that has its roots not in modernity but in medievalism. Much of Latin America's recent history involves the efforts and struggle to overcome or ameliorate that feudal past. Because this feudal legacy remains so strong, because the heavy hand of ancient history hangs so oppressively over the area, we must come to grips with Latin America's past in order to understand its present and future.

## The Conquest

The conquest of the Americas by Spain and Portugal was the extension of a reconquest of the Iberian Peninsula that had been under way for the preceding seven centuries. In the eighth century A.D., the armies of a dynamic, expansionist Islam had crossed the Straits of Gibraltar from North Africa and conquered most of present-day Spain and Portugal. In the following centuries the Christian forces of Spain and Portugal had gradually retaken these conquered lands until the last of the Islamic Moors were driven out in 1492, the same year that Columbus discovered America. Because of the long military campaign against the Moors, which was also a religious crusade to drive out the Islamic "infidels," Spanish and Portuguese institutions tended to be authoritarian, intolerant, militaristic, and undemocratic. The political system was autocratic and top-down; there was no separation of powers or checks and balances as had already emerged in England. Spain and Portugal carried these same autocratic and medieval practices and institutions to Latin America.

The conquest of the Americas was one of the great epic adventures of all time; its impact was worldwide. The encounter with the New World vastly expanded humankind's knowledge and pushed back the frontiers of exploration, initiated the first real anthropological studies of non-Western peoples, led to a period of prolonged European world dominance, and helped stimulate the Industrial Revolution. It also led to the brutalization, isolation, cultural destruction, and death of much of the indigenous population. Spain and Portugal are still trying to live down the legacy of this colonial past in Latin America.

At the time of Columbus's landing there were only about 3 million indigenous people in all of North America but some 30 million in Latin America. In addition, the Indians in Latin America were often organized into large civilizations—Aztec, Maya, Inca—of five to seven million persons each, whereas most North American Indian groups were organized on a smaller, tribal, nomadic basis. In North America, the Indians were often eliminated or pushed farther west and eventually confined to reservations, and much the same policy was followed in some parts of Latin America, such as Argentina and northern Mexico.

However, in other parts of Latin America the large numbers and organization of indigenous groups called for a different strategy. The Spanish tactic was usually to capture or kill the Indian chiefs, replace them with Spanish overlords, and rule and enslave the Indians by dominating their own power structure, meanwhile seeking to Christianize, Hispanicize, and eventually assimilate them to European ways. That has been the strategy for over five hundred years, but recently Indian groups in such countries as Mexico, Guatemala, Colombia, Ecuador, and Bolivia have been raising the issue of indigenous rights and seeking new degrees of autonomy or self-government from the nation-states that Spain and Portugal left in their wake.

The degree of colonial influence in Latin America varied from place to place. The first area to feel the impact of Spanish colonial rule was Hispaniola, an island in the Caribbean that later was divided between the two independent countries of Haiti and the Dominican Republic. Here Spain carried out its first experiments in colonial rule: a plantation economy, using first Indian and then African slave labor; a two-class and caste society; an authoritarian political structure; and a church that served as an arm of the conquest. Spain's feudal and medieval institutions were thus transplanted to the New World. But Hispaniola had little gold and silver and, as the Indian population was decimated, largely by disease, Spain moved onto more valuable conquests.

Next came Cuba and Puerto Rico, but when the scarce precious metals and Indian labor supply were exhausted here too, Spain moved on to conquer Mexico and explore Florida and the North American Southeast. The conquest of Mexico by Hernán Cortez was fundamentally different from the earlier island conquests: First, in Mexico Spain found not small Indian tribes but a huge Indian civilization, the Aztecs, with immense quantities of gold and silver and a virtually unlimited labor supply, and second, Mexico's huge mainland territory finally convinced the Spaniards that they had found a new continent and not just scattered islands on the outskirts of Asia. Mexico therefore became a serious and valuable colony to be settled and colonized by Spain, not just some way station on the way to somewhere else.

From Mexico, Cortez's lieutenants fanned out to conquer Central America and what is now the southwestern region of the United States. Meantime Vasco Núñez de Balboa had crossed the Isthmus of Panama to gaze out upon the Pacific, and other Spanish conquistadors had sailed along both the Atlantic and Pacific coasts of South America. In the 1530s the Pizarro brothers, using the same methods Cortez had used in Mexico, moved south from Panama to conquer the vast Inca empire that stretched from southern Colombia in the north, through Ecuador and Peru, to Chile in the south. Other Spanish explorers spilled over the Andes from Peru to discover and subdue Bolivia and Paraguay and sailed all the way downriver to present-day Buenos Aires, which had been explored in the 1530s but was not settled until the 1580s. Meanwhile Chile, where the Indian resistance was especially strong, was conquered in the 1570s, and other previously unconquered territories were now explored and subdued. Portugal had discovered Brazil in 1500 and gained a foothold along the northeastern coast. In the Treaty of Tordesillas (1494), the pope drew a north-south line through the heart of South America, separating the Spanish from the Portuguese territories.

In less than a hundred years from the initial discovery in 1492, therefore, Mexico, the Caribbean, Central America, and all of South America, east to west and north to south, had been conquered. Spain had most of the territory, Portugal had large Brazil. It was a remarkable feat of conquest and colonization in a short period of time, especially if one considers that it took the North American colonists almost three hundred years to cross the continent from the Atlantic to the Pacific.

## Colonial Society: Principles and Institutions

The institutions that Spain and, less aggressively, Portugal brought to the New World reflected the traditions that had grown up in the mother countries during their centuries-long struggles against the Moors and their efforts to form unified nation-states out of disparate social and regional forces. These institutions included a rigid, authoritarian political system; a similarly rigid and hierarchical class structure; a feudal, statist, and mercantilist economy; an absolutist church; and a similarly closed and absolutist educational system.

In the New World, the Spanish and Portuguese conquerors found abundant territory that they could claim as feudal estates, great wealth that enabled them to live like grandees, and a ready-made "peasantry," the indigenous Indian population or imported African slaves, that they could exploit for labor. Many of the men who accompanied Columbus and other explorers to the New World were the second and third sons of the emerging Spanish and Portuguese gentry, who under Spanish law were prohibited from inheriting their father's land, which went to the first son. But in the New World they could acquire vast territories and servants and live like feudal overlords. The oligarchies of Latin America, then as now, were haughty, aloof, authoritarian, and disdainful of both manual labor and those forced to work with their hands. This aristocratic ethos and the feudal system remain a very powerful force in Latin America even to this day.

The political institutions established by Spain and Portugal in Latin America reflected and reinforced the medieval system of the mother countries. At the top was the king, who claimed absolute power; his authority stemmed from God (divine-right monarchy) and was therefore unquestionable. Below the king was the viceroy (literally, "vice king"), who with similar absolute power served as the king's agent in the colonies. Below the viceroy was the captain-general, also absolute within his territorial sphere of influence; next came the landowner or *hacendado,* who likewise enjoyed absolute power within his own estate.

The economy was feudal and exploitive; in accord with the prevailing mercantilism, the wealth of the colonies was drained off to benefit the mother countries and was not used for the betterment of the colonies themselves. Similarly the social structure was basically feudal and two-class: a small group of Spaniards and Portuguese at the top, a large mass of Indians and Africans at the bottom, and almost no one in between.

Democracy could not develop in such a strict two-class structure, in which one's status was determined not only by social and economic standing but also by race.

The Roman Catholic Church reinforced royal authority and policy in the colonies and was similarly absolutist and authoritarian. Its role was to Christianize and pacify the indigenous population and thus serve the Crown's assimilationist policies. Some individual clergy sought to defend the Indians against enslavement and maltreatment, but the Church was primarily an arm of the state. Intellectual life and education, monopolized by the Church, were scholastic, based on rote memorization, deductive reasoning, and unquestioned orthodoxy.

It is not surprising that Latin America was founded on this feudal-absolutist basis in the early sixteenth century; that was before the onset of modernization and democratization, and most countries were still organized on that basis. What is surprising is that this system lasted so long—through three centuries of colonial rule, only slightly modified by the Latin American independence movements, and on into the twentieth century. Most Latin American countries are still struggling to overcome this feudal past.

The founding principles and institutions of Latin America were essentially medieval, pre-1500. In contrast, by the time the North American colonies were established fully a century and more later, the back of feudalism had been broken in England, and hence the thirteen colonies that would later form the United States were organized on a more modern basis. For by that time the idea of limited, representative government had emerged to replace absolutism, the Protestant Reformation had destroyed the older religious orthodoxy and given rise to religious and political pluralism, the Industrial Revolution was under way, mercantilism was giving way to commerce and entrepreneurship, reason and the scientific revolution were breaking the hold of the old scholasticism, and a new, multiclass social structure was beginning to emerge. Founded on these principles and the possibilities for change, North American society was modern from the start, whereas Latin America continued to be plagued by feudalism. That also explains why the United States was destined to forge ahead while Latin America lagged behind. Table 2.1 summarizes these contrasting foundations of U.S. and Latin American society.

Spanish and Portuguese colonial rule lasted for over three centuries, from the late fifteenth through the early nineteenth century. It was a remarkably stable period with few revolts against the colonial system, a testimony to its efficiency if not its justice. But in the late eighteenth century the first serious cracks began to appear in this monolithic colonial structure. Under the impact of the eighteenth-century Enlightenment, ideas of

TABLE 2.1 Comparison of the Foundations of Latin American and North American Society

| Institutions | Latin America, 1492–1570 | North America, Seventeenth Century |
| --- | --- | --- |
| Political | Authoritarian, absolutist, centralized, corporatist | More liberal, early steps toward representative and democratic rule |
| Religious | Catholic orthodoxy and abslutism | Protestantism and religious pluralism |
| Economic | Feudal, mercantilist, patrimonialist | Emerging capitalist, entrepreneurial |
| Social | Hierarchical, two-class, rigid | More mobile, multiclass |
| Educational and intellectual | Scholastic and deductive | Empirical |

liberty, freedom, and nationalism began to creep in, and the examples of revolutions in the United States (1776) and France (1789) caused tremors in Latin America. In addition, a rising Latin American commercial class sought to break the monopolistic barriers of Spanish mercantilism in order to trade freely with other countries. Another main source of independence sentiment was the growing rivalry between Creoles (persons of Spanish background born in the colonies) and *peninsulares* (Spanish officials sent by the Crown to govern the colonies). The Creoles had growing economic and social influence, but the *peninsulares* monopolized all administrative positions. Denied the political power to go along with their rising prominence, many Creoles began to consider doing away with the inconvenience of Spanish colonialism and moving toward independence.

These were the long-term causes of Latin American independence, but the actual and immediate stimulus to independence was precipitated by events in Europe. In 1807–1808 the forces of Napoleon Bonaparte invaded the Iberian Peninsula, occupied both Spain and Portugal, ousted the reigning monarchs, and installed Napoleon's brother Joseph on the Spanish throne. The Latin American Creoles opposed this usurpation of royal authority by Napoleon's army and, operating under longtime medieval doctrine, moved to hold power until the legitimate king could be restored. This was in effect an early declaration of independence. A few years later Napoleon's forces were driven from the peninsula and the Spanish and Portuguese monarchies restored. However, when the Spanish king initiated some liberal policies, limited the role of the Church, and agreed to accept checks on royal authority, the conservative Creoles in Latin America moved for independence.

The independence struggles in Latin America waxed and waned for nearly two decades before succeeding in the 1820s. The first revolt in Argentina in 1807 was quashed by Spanish authorities, but independence sentiment was also growing in Colombia, Mexico, Venezuela, and other countries. Independence sentiment waned for a time after 1814 when the Spanish monarchy was restored but resumed again in 1820 as a result of the king's shortsighted policies.

Simón Bolívar, the "George Washington of Latin America," led the struggle against Spanish forces in Venezuela, Colombia, and Ecuador. José de San Martín liberated Argentina, then crossed the Andes to drive the Spanish forces from Chile. The key to the independence of the rest of South America was to be Lima, Peru, one of the key Spanish viceroyalties and home of a sizable Spanish garrison. Bolívar came south overland, San Martín came north by ship, and in the key battle of Ayacucho in 1824, the royalist forces were defeated, thus ending Spanish authority in South America. By 1821, independence forces were also in control in the other main Spanish viceroyalty, Mexico City. Once Mexico was freed, Central America, as part of the same viceroyalty, was liberated without much actual fighting. By the mid-1820s almost all Spanish forces and authority were removed from mainland Latin America. The exceptions were the islands of Cuba and Puerto Rico, which remained Spanish colonies until 1898. Throughout the nineteenth century their nationalism was frustrated by the lack of independence, which would also shape twentieth-century politics in the two islands.

Haiti and Brazil were also special cases. In Haiti a successful slave revolt in 1795 drove out the French colonial ruling class, destroyed the plantations, and established Haiti as the world's first Black republic, unloved and unwelcomed by the rest of the world (including the United States), which still practiced slavery. Haiti's economy went into decline, and its political system since then has alternated between repressive dictatorships and chaotic upheavals.

Brazil was a different story. When Napoleon's troops occupied Portugal, the royal family fled to Rio de Janeiro, making the king, Dom João, the first reigning monarch to set foot in Latin America. In 1821 Dom João was called back to Lisbon, but he left his son Pedro in charge of the separate kingdom of Brazil. The following year Pedro was also called back to Portugal, but he refused to go and declared Brazil an independent monarchy. Thus Brazil gained independence without the upheaval and destruction experienced by the other countries. It was ruled as a monarchy until 1890; the country thus escaped the tumult that soon enveloped its Spanish-speaking neighbors.

Unlike the revolutions in the United States and France, the independence movements in Latin America had almost all been conservative movements of separation from the mother countries rather than full-scale social or political revolutions. Led and directed by the White, aristocratic Creole elite, these movements were aimed at holding power for the deposed monarch and in defense of the old social hierarchy. After they became movements for full independence, they retained their elitist, conservative orientation. Whenever social revolution raised its head during these independence struggles, it was either isolated and despised as in the Black revolt in Haiti or brutally repressed as in Mexico, where large-scale Indian protest had been part of the independence struggle.

The same conservative orientation was present in the laws, constitutions, and institutions established in the new republics. Despite provisions for the separation of powers and lists of human rights, the new political systems in Latin America were not democratic. The franchise was extremely limited: only literates and property owners (less than 1 percent of the population) could vote, if and when there were elections. Feudal landholding and the class system were kept intact, before and after independence. The Church was given a privileged position, and Catholicism in most countries remained the official religion. But now a new, similarly conservative power force was added; the army replaced the Crown as the ultimate authority and became in effect a fourth branch of government. Although Latin America adopted constitutions modeled after that of the United States, checks and balances, civil liberties, and separation of powers existed largely in theory only. The laws and constitutions of the new Latin American states enshrined the existing elitist power structure and perpetuated paternalistic, top-down, elite rule.

During the three hundred plus years of colonial rule, Latin America had gained no experience with self-government, had developed little infrastructure, and had built none of the "webs of sociability," the neighborhood, community, religious, civic, and social groups, that nineteenth-century theorist Alexis de Tocqueville identified with U.S. democracy. The struggles for independence also caused the Latin American economies to fall into decline and severely disrupted the social structure. It should not be surprising, therefore, that after independence Latin America fell into chaos and that the disintegrative forces set loose by independence continued. The former viceroyalty of New Granada split into the separate nations of Colombia, Ecuador, and Venezuela; the viceroyalty of Río de la Plata divided into the separate countries of Argentina, Paraguay, and Uruguay; and the Central American Confederation disintegrated into the small "city-states" of Guatemala, El Salvador, Honduras, Nicaragua, and Costa Rica, all with economies that were too small to be viable. Within the new nations, further fragmentation and confusion occurred. Only Brazil under its monarchy and Chile under a stable oligarchy escaped the divisive, disruptive, disintegrative forces that were common early in the post-independence period.

Deprived of their Spanish markets but still lacking new ones, many of the countries slipped back to a more primitive barter economy and living standards plummeted. Similarly, although the old Spanish/Portuguese socio-racial and class categories were formally abolished in most countries, they were resurrected informally; at the same time, the levels of education and literacy and the rates of integration and assimilation were so low that pluralist and participatory democracy seemed only a distant dream. In many countries the majority of the population did not speak the national language, participate in the national economy, or even know that they were a part of a nation-state.

In the absence of political parties, organized interest groups, or well-established institutions of any kind, the Latin American countries sank into either dictatorship or anarchy, usually alternating between the two. And internationally Latin America was isolated and cut off from the modern, Western world. Hence the immediate post-independence period, from the mid-1820s until the mid-1850s, was in most countries a time of turbulence and decline.

### Early Stirrings of Modernization

By the 1850s a degree of stability had begun to appear in many Latin American countries. Leaders had resolved some of the more vexing questions of early independence—sovereignty and borders, federalism versus unitarianism, the structure of government, and church-state relations. By this time also the first generation of post-independence military dictators, including Juan Manuel de Rosas in Argentina and Antonio López de Santa Anna in Mexico, had passed from the scene. Agriculture began to recover; a degree of order returned.

Along with increased stability at midcentury came foreign investment and greater productivity. The first banks in the region were chartered. British capital was invested in the area, providing a major stimulus to growth. New lands were opened to cultivation and new exports such as sugar, coffee, tobacco, beef, and wool began to restore national coffers. The first highways, railways, and port facilities were built to transport the exports to foreign markets. Telephone and telegraph were introduced. The land and opportunities available in Latin America began to attract immigrants from Europe, who often brought knowledge and entrepreneurial skills with them. They opened small shops and started farms and prospered; often this new wealth intermixed with older, landed wealth through family and business connections. As Latin America's prospects thus began to improve, the area attracted other investors: France, Germany, Italy, and most importantly the United States, which began to replace England as the largest investor in the area.

These changes, beginning at midcentury but accelerating in the 1870s and 1880s, represented the first stirrings of modernization in Latin America after nearly four centuries of stagnation. They brought prosperity for the landed and business elites and stimulated the growth of a small middle class, but often peasant and Indian elements were left behind or had their lands taken from them for the sake of greater production for global markets.

Economic growth also increased political stability, although not in all countries. Three patterns may be observed. The first, present in Argentina, Brazil, Chile, Peru, and other countries, involved the consolidation of power by an export-oriented landed oligarchy whose leaders rotated in the presidential palace over a thirty- to forty-year period. Power changed hands only among the elites; the majority of the population was excluded from political participation. The second pattern, evident in Mexico, Venezuela, and the Dominican Republic, involved the seizure of power by strong authoritarian dictators—no longer the simple "men on horseback" who gained power after independence but leaders who provided both long-term stability and development. These leaders provided order, attracted new investment, and built up the national infrastructure, but their accomplishments came under dictatorial auspices.

A third pattern emerged slightly later, in the first decades of the twentieth century, in the smaller, weaker, resource-poor countries of Central America and the Caribbean. In Haiti, Cuba, the Dominican Republic, Nicaragua, and Panama, this pattern involved U.S. military intervention and occupation, with the Marines carrying out many of the same policies as the order-and-progress oligarchs and dictators: pacification, infrastructure development (roads, communication, port facilities), and overall nation-building. The Marines and the U.S. intervention and occupation were resented by nationalist elements in these countries, but the stability, order, and development they brought provided a foundation for future growth.

Two subperiods are discernible here. The first, from 1850 to 1890, saw greater stability, more banks, increased investment, population growth, rising exports, and infrastructure development. All of these established the preconditions for the second period, which lasted from 1890 to 1930. During this time the region experienced an economic takeoff and enjoyed the most stable and prosperous conditions yet in Latin American history. Under more stable regimes and with economies that for the first time were exporting to a world market, Latin America began its development process—not at the rapid rate enjoyed by the United States and Europe during the same period, but slowly and unevenly.

Although Latin American development at this time was often impressive, it occurred under nondemocratic leadership: oligarchs, order-and-progress dictators, and U.S. military occupations. Hence the potential for future problems was also present even amidst the growing prosperity. In three countries, the political and economic applecarts were upset even before the 1930s market crash and global depression soon caused the entire edifice to come crumbling down. In 1910 the order-and-progress dictator Porfirio Díaz was overthrown in Mexico, precipitating a bloody ten-year social revolution out of which Mexico's present political system emerged. In 1912 in Argentina and in the early 1920s in Chile a rising middle class challenged the old oligarchs, eventually gaining the right to vote and wresting political power away from the elite. These changes, which took place in some of the more advanced countries of Latin America, provided a foretaste of what would occur in other countries in later decades.

## Upheaval and Restructuring

When the market crashed in the United States in 1929 and Europe the following year, the effects were global. The bottom dropped out of the market for Latin American exports, sending the region's economies into a tailspin and undermining their political systems as well. Between 1930 and 1935 governments were overthrown in fourteen of the twenty Latin American countries; these were not simply the usual substitution of one colonel for another but real transforming revolutions.

The immediate causes of this collapse were economic, but deep-rooted social and political issues were also involved. By this time Latin America had a business class, a middle class, and a small though restless trade union movement, but power was still monopolized by the old landowning oligarchs. Something had to give. The chasm between the traditional powerholders and the new social and political forces clamoring for change had grown wider; the new forces were demanding reform and democratization while the older elites clung onto their privileges at all costs. The 1930s Depression was the catalyst that collapsed the prevailing political as well as economic structure.

Once Humpty Dumpty (the old, elite-based Latin American political systems) had fallen off the wall, the question was, how to put it together again? A variety of solutions was tried; this would prove to be an important turning point in Latin America's political evolution. Some countries, after a brief interruption and instability in the early 1930s, reverted to reaction by restoring oligarchic rule. In other countries new, tough dictatorships, such as those of Fulgencio Batista in Cuba, Anastasio Somoza in Nicaragua, Rafael Trujillo in the Dominican Republic, and Jorge Ubico in Guatemala, brought the new business and middle classes into power and stimulated development, but again under authoritarian auspices. (It is getting ahead of the story only a little bit to note that all these countries that had brutal right-wing dictatorships produced left-wing revolutions later on.) In Mexico the old regime was replaced with a one-party authoritarian/corporatist regime that monopolized power for the next seventy years.

The regimes of Juan Perón in Argentina and Getúlio Vargas in Brazil borrowed some semifascist features from Mussolini's Italy in an effort to bring labor unions into the system even while imposing strict controls over them. During the Depression and into the war years, quite a number of countries borrowed selectively from European corporatism and semifascism while maintaining a democratic facade. Populism, or rule by a charismatic leader who instigates programs for the long-forgotten lower classes, was another option, and yet another was democracy—seen in Chile and Uruguay followed by Costa Rica, Colombia, and Venezuela. Socialist and Communist parties were organized; the revolutionary alternative, as in Cuba, came later.

The 1930s were thus, in David Colliers and Ruth Berins Colliers's term, a "critical juncture" in Latin American history, a period in which a variety of alternative developmental models—authoritarian, quasifascist, populist, single party, democratic, socialist, radical—were tried out or came to power in the various Latin American countries. Some countries rotated between several of these options or tried to combine them. Many countries are still strongly shaped in terms of their party systems and political institutions by the choices made and the directions taken during this period. The Depression years of the 1930s and the later war years of the 1940s were thus a time of both uncertainty and upheaval; although the old, stable, oligarchic order was disintegrating or had come crashing down, what would replace it was not altogether clear and is still not clear in quite a number of countries seventy years later.

As the demand for Latin American products rose again during World War II, industrialization expanded and the Latin American economies began to recover from the devastation of the Depression. In the postwar period this gradual economic growth continued, enabling some countries to move toward greater prosperity and democracy while others continued under dictatorship. Although modest economic growth was occurring throughout the region in the 1940s and 1950s, stimulating further social change, the political systems of Latin America remained divided, conflictual, and often unstable. Dictatorship was the prevailing pattern; although Chile, Costa Rica, and Uruguay functioned as democracies, other countries oscillated between authoritarianism, populism, and more liberal regimes.

A key turning point in the region and in U.S.–Latin American relations was the Cuban Revolution of 1959. Cuba became the first openly socialist country in Latin America, the first to ally itself with the Soviet Union, and the first to openly turn its back on the United States. Domestically, the revolution initiated improvements in health care, education, and other social programs, although over time its economic policies proved a failure and its political system was hardly democratic.

For our purposes, we are more concerned with the broader regionwide impact of the revolution in Cuba. First, Cuba added a new political model, a new option, to the Latin American landscape, one that stood for armed revolution and a Marxist-Leninist political structure. Second, the Cuban Revolution divided reform groups into pro- and anti-Castro factions and thus hurt the prospects for democratic development and social reform in Latin America. Whereas the older struggle had been between conservative oligarchic groups (Church, army, landowners) and newer reform elements (middle class, business, labor, peasants), the new struggle introduced the tactic of using revolution instead of the ballot box to achieve power, and thus deeply divided the change-oriented elements.

Third, while the Cuban Revolution forced the United States to pay closer attention to Latin America (which it did through programs like the Peace Corps and the Alliance for Progress), it skewed U.S. policy by focusing it almost exclusively on the prevention of "another Cuba" (i.e., another country that was Marxist-Leninist and allied with the Soviet Union, that sponsored revolutions in other Latin American countries, and that housed missiles aimed at the United States). This was called the "lesser evil doctrine": When faced with the choice between a usually wobbly Latin American democracy that believed in freedom even for leftists and a tough, anti-communist military regime, the United States government almost always supported the military regime. The policy polarized Latin America even more, undermined numerous fledgling democracies, and led in the 1960s and 1970s to a series of civil conflicts and wars that tore several countries apart.

There was a brief democratic interlude in the late 1950s and early 1960s in Argentina, Brazil, the Dominican Republic, and Honduras, but by the late 1960s and through the 1970s Latin America had succumbed to a new wave of militarism. By the mid-1970s, fourteen of the twenty countries were again under military-authoritarian rule, and in three others, the military was so close to the surface of power that authoritarianism ruled even though civilians were still technically in office. Only Colombia, Costa Rica, and Venezuela were democracies, and even they were elite-directed regimes.

The domestic causes of this throwback to military authoritarianism were basically economic and political. By the 1960s the Latin American economies had become less competitive in global markets, the ISI strategy was not working, the terms of trade had turned unfavorable, that is, it cost Latin America more exports of sugar, bananas, coffee, and so on to pay for its manufactured imports than before, and the economies of the area could not pay for all the social programs its citizens were demanding. Politically, the 1960s was a period when workers, peasants, and left-wing guerrillas were all mobilizing; the traditional elites, feeling threatened by the mass mobilization, thus turned to the military to keep the lower classes in check. This is called "bureaucratic authoritarianism"—or rule by the institutional armed forces and their civilian supporters, as distinct from the man-on-horseback leaders of the past. Meanwhile at the international level it was the height of the Cold War, and the lesser evil doctrine generally pushed the United States to opt for anti-communist authoritarianism over unstable democracies.

By the late 1970s the steam had gone out of most of these military regimes and Latin America began to reverse course and return to democracy. The armed forces had often proved just as corrupt and inefficient at running governments as their civilian predecessors. They were notorious human rights abusers and thus despised by their own people, and the international community, led by the United States, pressured them to return to the barracks. By this time the United States had concluded, again with the Cuban example in mind (dictator Batista ousted by communist Castro), that maybe human rights and democracy were better guarantees of stability and anti-communism than abusive authoritarianism. There followed one of the most amazing transformations in all of Latin American history; by the turn of the millennium, nineteen of the twenty Latin American countries were ruled more or less democratically, with Cuba as the lone holdout. Latin America was the main arena of the "third wave" of democratization, a phenomenon that affected the entire world and that was surely one of the most significant events of the late twentieth century.

Many of these new democracies are still weak and not very well institutionalized. They lack strong and independent legislatures, judiciaries and court systems, bureaucracies, political parties, interest groups, and local governments. They are often not very effective in carrying out public policies. They are referred to as "electoral democracies" (formal elections are held), but not "liberal democracies," in the sense of being open, pluralistic, and egalitarian. Many regimes in the area are still partial or limited democracies, designations that indicate links to Latin America's authoritarian past. Nevertheless even partial democracies are better than no democracies at all; no one doubts that an important breakthrough has been made, and certainly the human rights situation in virtually every country is far better now than it was a decade or two ago.

## A Framework for Thinking About Change

The 1930s were a key turning point, maybe *the* key turning point in Latin American history. For in that period, give or take a decade or two depending on the country, Latin America's old, oligarchic, feudal, and medieval social, economic, and political structure began to collapse—in some cases collapsing altogether, in others hanging on but in attenuated form. This was really the "twilight of the Middle Ages." Finally, after four hundred and fifty years of stagnation, Latin America seemed on the road to change and modernization. What replaced the old order was in the 1930s still uncertain, often unstable, frequently alternating between one type of regime and another. But it is clear that Latin America had begun a profound transformation leading to modernization. What finally seems to be emerging now, after decades of confusion and upheaval, is a system of democracy and freer markets. This process is still incomplete and fragile, and it shows many continuities with Latin America's feudal past.

As we begin to probe more deeply into Latin America's political institutions and processes, readers should keep in mind the following framework for assessing the changes that are now occurring. How much has changed in each county and in the region as a whole? What are the emerging patterns? What outcomes are likely? Not only will that give us a deeper understanding of Latin America, but it is also fundamental to the overview and interpretive analysis that are at the heart of this book.

### Changes in Political Culture

The term "political culture" (discussed in more detail in Chapter 3) refers to the core beliefs, values, assumptions, and ideas (including religious ideas) that people in different countries and cultures have about politics. As we have seen, until the 1930s Latin American political culture was often feudal and medieval. But now education has increased, literacy expanded, and radio, television, satellite dishes, cell phones, and VCRs have brought new ideas even to the most isolated areas. The old fatalism and passivity began to fade, people were mobilized, new and challenging ideas such as democracy and socialism arose. The Catholic Church, long a supporter of the traditional political culture, began to change; Protestantism as well as secular ideas made strong inroads. The fundamental beliefs, ideas, and orientations by which people order their lives are changing. So in each country and for the region as a whole we will want to know: Among which groups are these ideas changing? How deep and extensive are the changes? What impact has a more democratic and participatory political culture had on institutions and policy?

## Economic Change

Latin America's economies are now more diversified, including business, industry, services, manufacturing, tourism, mining, and agribusiness—no longer limited to the subsistence and plantation agriculture of the past. The national economies are larger, more complex, and more fully integrated into world markets. Most of them are now moving away from the statism and mercantilism of the past toward a system of open markets, freer trade, greater efficiency, less corruption, and other neoliberal policies. These changes are creating greater affluence, creating new jobs and opportunities, and giving new dynamism to the regional economies. But there are also lags—uneven development and maldistribution of wealth, with some groups and countries doing much better than others. Peasants, the poor, and marginal peoples often get left behind. And all of these changes, the positive and the negative, carry important political and policy implications, which vary from country to country.

## Social Change

The economic changes just outlined have also accelerated social change. The old landed oligarchy is giving way to a more diverse panoply of business, industrial, commercial, banking, and other new elites. A sizable middle class has grown up in every country, ranging from 20 to 40 percent of the population, and the size and political orientation of this constituency will help determine whether democracy survives. Labor unions have been organized, peasant groups are mobilizing, urban unemployed slum dwellers are becoming politicized. In addition there are new women's groups, community organizations, social movements, and indigenous movements. Some of the older groups, like the Church and the military, are also undergoing change, becoming more middle class and less elitist in orientation, and Roman Catholicism is being challenged in many countries by Protestant evangelicalism, which often implies quite different values, attitudes toward work, and ideas about the role of the family. Meanwhile in a forty-year period the Latin American population has gone from a rural majority to two-thirds urban. All of these social changes and the far greater social pluralism that results force us to ask if political pluralism (which usually means democracy) can be far behind.

## Changes in Political Institutions

Along with the politico-cultural, economic, and social transformations in Latin America have also come changes in political institutions. First, political parties in many countries tend to be better organized, with a real mass base and real programs and ideology, as compared with the small, personalist, and patronage-based parties of the past (which still exist in some countries). Second, there are many more interest groups than ever before, and greater civil society, reflecting the greater societal pluralism. These groups enjoy more independence from the state, and their agendas need to be satisfied—although U.S.-style lobbying is still seldom practiced in Latin America. Third, government agencies and institutions are being forced to modernize, increase efficiency, reduce corruption, and deliver real goods and services. Elections have become more honest and are recognized as the only legitimate route to power, and legislatures, court systems, the police, local government are all being modernized in various ways.

## Changes in Public Policy

Along with Latin American political processes and institutions, public policy programs are also modernizing. In the past, governments in Latin America had few functions, but now government is being called upon to provide a host of new public policy programs: agrarian reform, family planning, education, economic development, the environment, housing, health care, and dozens of others. Moreover, a more politically mobilized population is demanding these programs as a matter of course, and governments in this new era of democracy have to deliver or they will be voted out. Rather than jobs, patronage, and handouts, public institutions in Latin America are called upon to provide real public goods and services.

## Changes in the International Environment

For centuries Latin America was isolated from the world, but now it is becoming closely integrated into the global community—politically, culturally, and economically. Politically, Latin America is becoming democratic; if a country deviates from that course, the full weight of international sanctions may come down on it. Culturally, Latin America is being swept up in the global culture of jeans, rock music, Coca-Cola, and consumerism, and as a result, political values in the region, especially those of young people, are becoming more like those everywhere else: democracy, less authoritarianism, less religious, less traditional. Economically, Latin America is now a part of the global economy, with mostly good consequences (increased trade, more commerce, jobs, and affluence) but with some negative consequences (unstable currencies, fluctuating market demands, austerity measures, hardships for the poor). But since foreign aid is meager and no other country is about to bail it out, Latin America can no longer choose among other options: It must join the global economy, compete with everyone else, and adopt neoliberal economic policies. It must do so not only because outside pressures force it to but also because its own business leaders, middle classes, and governments also recognize they have no other choice. Latin America cannot avoid these hard choices, but it can do things to ameliorate the pain that some groups suffer.

All of these long-term modernizing changes have had a profound effect on Latin America, but they vary throughout the region—among countries and within institutions and even individuals—which continue to show complex mixes of traditional and modern attitudes and practices. So as Latin America begins a new millennium, we will want to know just how democratic the region in general and individual countries in particular are. Have Latin American societies modernized enough to provide a firmer basis for pluralism and democracy? How successful are the new reforms in favor of free trade and open markets, and will they pay off in improved living standards? How strong are political parties, interest groups, and government institutions? Now that the Cold War is over, can U.S.–Latin Americans relations progress on a normal, more mature footing? And what of Latin America's relations with the rest of the world? These are some of the crucial questions that this book tries to answer.

# 3

# Changing Political Culture

Although men and women everywhere often have remarkably similar goals and aspirations—peace, freedom, justice, self-advancement, personal and family well-being, and the like—they differ markedly in how they think about these concepts, what categories they use, what values and assumptions they bring to these deliberations. Those of a Confucian background, for example, will tend to use one set of categories and beliefs, Hindus another, Muslims a third, Christians still a fourth, and so on. For instance, while those raised in a Confucian background tend to emphasize societal, communal, and group values, those brought up in a Buddhist context are more individualistic. Moreover, the differing value systems carry with them important political considerations. These differences in how people think, in the values they hold, in their belief systems, are what political culture is all about.

Political culture comprises the basic values, ideas, beliefs, and behavioral patterns that predominate in a given society, and it helps us to distinguish one political society from another. Political culture is an important explanatory factor in helping us understand differences between countries. All of us, even if blindfolded, know immediately when we cross the border into Mexico that we are no longer in Chicago; we know that Japan operates very differently from Haiti. The sights, sounds, smells, and way of behaving are very different. While peoples around the globe may have similar dreams, their cultures are often very different. And when those differing cultural values and beliefs impact politics, we call it "political culture" to distinguish it from other forms of culture such as music, dance, and the like.

Political culture represents a composite view of a country's own societal beliefs and operating norms as found in or based on its dominant religion, historical experiences, values and ideology, and standard behavior. Political culture can be analyzed and described by examining a country's literature, beliefs, folklore, philosophical assumptions, and behavior. An understanding of political culture comes when we get a genuine "feel" for a country, understand it as citizens of that country do, acquire genuine empathy for its people, and see the country on its own terms rather than through our own rose-colored glasses. Developing such empathy is crucial, but nowadays political culture can best be understood and presented by using public opinion surveys.

In thinking about political culture and its importance, we want to avoid stereotyping as well as cultural, ethnic, or racial prejudice. We do not want to say, for instance, all Germans are this, all Latinos are that, all Chinese are something else. Rather, we are interested in the overall patterns that exist, and we need to express these in "tendency statements." So rather than saying, for example, that "Latin Americans support authoritarianism," (inaccurate), we can use public opinion surveys to say that historically, for reasons to be elaborated below, Latin Americans have *tended* to have a stronger preference for strong government than would be the case in the United States.

Used carefully, political culture can be an important explanatory tool. For although it is relatively easy to change from authoritarian to democratic institutions, it is much harder to change the values and beliefs, the political culture that lies underneath the institutions. But if the basic values and beliefs do not change, then the institutional changes are likely to be quite ephemeral and easily reversed.

Measuring this kind of change can be a complex task. Political culture usually changes more slowly than do institutions, with significant change often requiring two or three generations or more. Furthermore, the definition of political culture may be open to interpretation, since the surveys are based on samples of the population rather than the entire population. In addition, any single nation may have two or more political cultures, based for example on social class or race or liberal versus conservative ideology, and differing interpretations of these political cultures may be in conflict. Although political culture thus changes slowly, it does change; it is also constantly undergoing reassessment and reinterpretation.

## Historic Latin American Political Culture

Whereas the political culture of the United States, at least since the Civil War and in many respects even much earlier, has been mainly liberal (with belief in representative government and the classic freedoms of the Bill of Rights), democratic, and committed to egalitarianism and the rule of law, the political culture of Latin America has historically been more elitist, authoritarian, hierarchical, organic-corporatist, and patrimonial. Whereas the United States as a society was in a sense "born free"—that is, without a feudal or medieval past—Latin America, as we saw in the previous chapter, was "born feudal"; its roots and main institutions were a product of the Middle Ages and medievalism, and the heavy weight of that history and the institutions it bequeathed still hang ponderously over the area. Let us examine each of these traits in turn.

## Elitism

Elitism in Latin America stems from the idea that people are *not* born equal, that only the elites should rule. This idea goes back to Plato and Aristotle and the notion that society should be governed by educated philosopher kings and not by the masses. These early political theorists observed that people differed in terms of intelligence and physical attributes, and therefore they believed that those who displayed the greatest intelligence and physical beauty should form the ruling class. Absent were notions of egalitarianism, equality of opportunity, or capacity to rise above one's background. Aristotle even justified slavery by describing a "natural slave class," an argument that Spain revived when it discovered the indigenous peoples of Latin America.

Latin American elitism also stems from the Spanish/Portuguese tradition of nobility, from the feudal landholding system, from racism (Europeans at the top of the social pyramid, Indians and descendants of African slaves below), and from a long history of Iberian and Latin American political theory that justified elite rule. Elitism is still found throughout Latin America in the haughty attitudes of the ruling class, their disdain for manual labor *and* for those who work with their hands, and the sense of superiority that separates the White elites not only from Blacks and Indians but also from mulattos and mestizos. We have interviewed many representatives of the elite class in several Latin American countries, and it is clear from these interviews that many members of the elite are still not convinced that Indians and Blacks also have "souls," are human people, and therefore have to be treated with some measure of dignity and respect.

How then can you have democracy if the elites do not really believe in equality or in the principle of one person, one vote? How can you democratize or change political institutions fundamentally if the political culture of elitism persists, with the elites assuming haughty airs, treating the lower classes with disdain, and expecting special treatment from presidents and government agencies? Indeed, how can any real political change be expected if the elites expect their class always to be in control as a "natural right?" Democracy is hard to establish in a setting where elitism is so strong a part of the political culture. In their defense, the elites often cite the lack of development in Latin America, the vast and "wild" empty spaces, the weakness of civil society and institutions, and the "primitive" character of the indigenous populations, all of which presumably justify elite rule. But these are not serious arguments in the modern age, although objectively it is easy to see why such pervasive elitism can be used to justify widespread undemocratic practices.

## *Authoritarianism*

Authoritarianism in Latin America stems from many of the same sources as elitism. First, there is the Iberian tradition of strong, macho "men on horseback." Second are the conditions in Latin America that seem to require a strong hand at the till—the difficult terrain, the vast empty interior, the primitive indigenous tribes, the weakness of grassroots society and institutional infrastructure, and the persistent underdevelopment. Third, and stemming from the first two, is the long practice of executive dominance of all institutions. A fourth reason for Latin American authoritarianism is the persistence of elite rule and the perceived need to keep the lower classes in their place using strong methods.

In recent decades authoritarianism in Latin America has given way to more democratic practices. But even now, (1) the executive power in most countries remains overwhelmingly predominant; (2) the temptation to revert to authoritarianism in times of trouble remains strong; and (3) many Latin American regimes—including those of Hugo Chávez in Venezuela and Alberto Fujimori in Peru—exhibit curious hybrid forms of democracy, such as open elections coupled with authoritarian practices.

## *Hierarchy*

The notion of hierarchy stems from many of the selfsame justifications and societal conditions as do elitism and authoritarianism. Hierarchy is a very difficult concept for North Americans, with their strong sense of egalitarianism, to grasp, let alone treat with any measure of objectivity.

The idea of hierarchy goes back to Graeco-Roman and Christian conceptions of "natural" or "God-given" inequalities among people, and to the belief that every being should be secure and happy in his or her station in life. These conceptions resulted in the medieval notion of the "chain of being," a notion that was still deeply rooted at the time of Columbus and his contemporaries. At the top of this hierarchical chain are God, archangels,

angels, and so on through the heavenly bodies. Then come men, but only certain types of men. First are kings or rulers, who receive their mandates from God, not from such modern methods as democratic elections. Then come nobles or oligarchs, who similarly receive their status, land, power, and peasants from on high. Next come soldiers, artisans, craftsmen, eventually workers and peasants, and finally animals, vegetation, and inert substances—all of whom must accept their station in life. To rebel would be to challenge God's immutable law. Members of each layer in this hierarchy are expected to perform the functions to which they are "naturally" best suited and not to try to rise above their proper position.

Note that Africans and Indians are not even mentioned here. That is because this system of hierarchy, developed by Aristotle and put in Christian form by Saint Thomas Aquinas, was fashioned before Latin America was discovered. So after Columbus, the theologians and jurists in Spain and Portugal had to decide where Indians fit: Were they humans, with souls? If so, they had certain basic or minimum rights even if they belonged at the lower end of the human chain. Or were they among the higher forms of animals, with no souls and no rights, who could therefore be enslaved? After a long debate, Spain and Portugal determined that Indians were indeed human, but in the meantime Europeans in the colonies had already forced the Indians into a form of slave labor.

A hierarchical society, reinforced by race, is very rigid. People are locked into their station in life. Social mobility is impossible. There is no possibility to get ahead and therefore ambition is futile; your future is decided by God or fate, not by your own intelligence, hard work, or merit. It is not hard to see why the hierarchical, inegalitarian societies of Latin America would for many centuries stifle change, development, and democracy.

## *Organicism and Corporatism*

Organicism also has strong roots in ancient political theory, historic Catholicism, and the feudal past. Organicism suggests that society and government, like the human body, should be "organic," with all the parts unified and interconnected. From this concept, together with a lack of organizational infrastructure and a fear of chaos, comes the strong emphasis on unity in Latin American politics, the desire to integrate and tie all the parts together. From this we can see why separation of powers, checks and balances, and strong local government have seldom been present.

Corporatism is a related concept; it refers to the state regulation and control of the nation's interest groups and their organization by functional or group categories rather than on the basis of individualism or freedom of association. The main corporate groups in Latin America have been the Church, armed forces, and oligarchy; more recently the business sector, middle class, trade unions, peasants, women, and indigenous elements have also been organized in this way. The state organizes official groups to represent each social sector as a way of integrating the society and also of preventing more radical, nonofficial groups from gaining a foothold. Groups are incorporated into the system if they agree to play by the rules of the game; they also receive from the state recognition and tangible benefits such as jobs and entitlements.

Corporatism implies a state-structured, controlled, even monopolistic system of interest groups. As such it is inimical to a liberal, pluralist, and democratic system of free, unfettered interest groups. When we couple the Latin American states' control of interest groups with the often mercantile-like control of economic activity, it becomes clear that we are not dealing with liberal, democratic, pluralist, and free political or economic systems. Further, corporatism in Latin America is part not only of institutional life but of the political culture itself, in that group solidarity often predominates over individual rights.

## *Patrimonialism*

Another continuing feature of traditional Latin American political culture is patronage or patrimonialism. Historically, Latin America has been based on a system of mutual obligations—a favor for a favor. This is another quasifeudal concept, with its roots in Greek and Christian philosophy as well as everyday practice: If you give me a gift or do me a favor, then I owe you one in return. Political patronage in Latin America manifests itself in various ways: votes in return for gifts or money, votes in return for a government job, friends or relatives rewarded with government contracts, special access to government decisions for friends of the officeholder, sometimes whole programs or government agencies doled out to a party or group in return for political support. At high levels, patronage verges on and is corruption; at low levels it constitutes the "grease" that keeps the machinery of government working.

Most Latin American countries have only weak civil service laws to protect government workers in their jobs, and the president has vast power to appoint friends and supporters to any job, from cabinet minister to janitor. Sometimes a savvy president will also give patronage posts to his enemies as a way of keeping them in his pay, indebted to him, and in his sight. Patronage also works for aspiring *politicos*: If I attach my name to that of a rising political star and he attains office, then he is likely to take me along with him into high office. Patronage is thus all-pervasive, but there are also degrees of patronage, versus merit. And while patronage often provides the cement that holds Latin American government together, it is not very conducive either to democracy or to good public policy.

These features of historic Latin American political culture—elitism, authoritarianism, hierarchy, organicism and corporatism, and patrimonialism—remained largely intact for most of the three centuries of Spanish and Portuguese colonial rule. Over this long period these ideas and beliefs became deeply ingrained in the thinking and behavior patterns of Latin Americans. In somewhat modified form, they are still present in all the countries of the region.

## The Change Process

Beginning around the middle of the eighteenth century, a split developed in the Spanish and Portuguese "soul" or political culture, and by extension also in the political culture of Latin America. On one side of the split, the majority remained Catholic, conservative, traditional, and oriented toward the political culture values outlined in the previous section. On the other side, a small minority was more liberal and rationalist, was attracted to the ideas of the Enlightenment, and believed in some of the classic freedoms, including freedom of religion and trade.

This split in the political culture also had a geographic and sociological base. Traditional Latin American political culture was strongest in the rural areas and among landowners, peasants, the Church, and eventually the army. More liberal Latin American political culture was mainly concentrated in the capital cities among intellectuals, students, business and commercial elements, and the middle class. One can thus see that political culture was closely interrelated with geographic factors and class or sociological factors. This split in the soul of Latin America is often important for understanding politics, even today.

Following independence in the early nineteenth century, this split deepened and widened. In quite a number of countries the liberals came to power briefly immediately after independence, only to be replaced shortly by conservative oligarchs and "men on horseback." Thereafter, throughout most of the nineteenth century and even beyond, liberals and conservatives vied constantly, fought numerous civil wars, and alternated in power; or else, authoritarianism alternated with confusion and chaos. The single, unified, conservative political culture of earlier years was now challenged by another, the political culture of opposition liberalism.

By the middle of the twentieth century a third political culture, socialist or social democratic, had taken root in Latin America, competing with the other two. The three main political cultures—conservative, liberal, and socialist—were so far apart that they pertained to quite different worlds: feudal, capitalist, and socialist. The divisions between these political cultures were so deep in some countries that no compromise was possible. The political culture was fragmented, torn apart. In countries like Argentina, Brazil, Chile, and Uruguay the three political cultures were almost equally divided among the electorate, producing conflict, polarization, fragmentation, and eventual breakdown. The term "conflict society" is used to describe this kind of nonconsensual political system.

Meanwhile, profound changes were also occurring in Latin American society and in the economy, with major implications for the political culture. Among the changes were the following:

1. Latin America was becoming more literate and educated, which served to weaken the traditional political culture.
2. Latin America was becoming more urban, which again weakened the traditional society and strengthened the liberal, populist, and socialist groups.
3. Latin America was becoming less religious and less Catholic, and since much of the traditional conservative political culture was based on historic Catholic beliefs, that also weakened the traditional political culture.
4. Latin America became more industrialized and economically developed, and that too weakened the traditional political culture.
5. Latin America was more closely integrated into world markets, trade, and the global political culture of rock music, Coca-Cola, blue jeans, television, and consumerism.

These forces all served to undermine the traditional political culture and to introduce new values and ways of behaving.

The cumulative impact of all these changes was powerful. The traditional "sleepy," semifeudal societies and landholding systems of Latin America began to give way. After some four hundred and fifty years, feudalism and medievalism began to fade from the area. New and deep cracks appeared in the pillars holding up the edifice of the "old" Latin America; at the same time, new political parties, interest groups, and social movements sprang up that represented a more modern region. (These are covered in more detail in later chapters.) A whole way of life, an entire traditional political culture that had been stable for centuries, began to yield to newer conceptions. In other words, Latin America began a process of modernization not entirely unlike the process that other, more developed countries had already gone through.

And yet, even with all these changes Latin America's traditional political culture remained strong. The traditional values of elitism, authoritarianism, hierarchy, organicism and corporatism, and patrimonialism remained influential even though they now alternated or mixed with more modern and democratic values. The result was still a great deal of confusion and often conflict between old and new, traditional and modern. Or the presence of conflicting traditional and modern values could even operate at the same time, within the same institution, within the same individual. To this day much of Latin America has not yet reached a happy consensus on what its future directions should be.

## Current Attitudes Toward Democracy and Authoritarianism

From the 1930s to the 1950s, precisely the period when all the changes mentioned above were taking place, Latin America was a deeply conflicted society. A brief opening to democracy in the late 1950s and early 1960s was followed by reaction and a reversion to authoritarianism in the late 1960s and 1970s, and in the 1980s by a series of quite remarkable transitions to democracy. By the 1990s and continuing to today, nineteen of the twenty countries were governed by regimes that could be described as more or less democratic.

When the Soviet Union collapsed in 1989–1991 and the Cold War ended, most of the Marxist guerrilla movements and political parties in Latin America dissolved or changed their ideological colors as well. That had the effect of largely removing the violent revolutionary alternative from the list of Latin American political options, although the social democratic option remained. With the earlier discrediting of authoritarianism and now the collapse of Marxism-Leninism, democracy and free markets seemed to be the only option left. Indeed, during the 1990s that formula formed what is called the "Washington Consensus," an agreement between the United States and Latin America that the best political economy strategy is democracy, free trade, and open-market economies.

The questions now are, Is Latin America prepared for full democracy? Does it have the experience in self-government to make democracy work? Does it have the literacy levels needed for voters to make sound choices? Does it have the base, the institutions (e.g., courts, legislatures, local government, experienced bureaucrats, rule of law, open political systems, transparency in budgetary matters), the infrastructure, and the deep web of associational life at grassroots levels that are required if democracy is to function?

Immediately after the overthrow of authoritarianism in the late 1970s and 1980s, support for democracy was extremely high throughout Latin America. With only slight variations among countries, public support for democracy was measured in the 85, 90, or 95 percent range. Voter turnout in most countries was also high, often reaching 80 percent (as compared with 50 percent in the United States). Democracy seemed to be the only legitimate form of government; coups, authoritarianism, and Marxism-Leninism were thoroughly discredited and without popular support.

This early enthusiasm, even euphoria, for democracy was based more on expectations than reality, however. Authoritarianism had been vanquished, democracy was new and exciting, elections were being held in many countries for the first time in two or three decades. People were swept up in the euphoria of the moment and the polls reflected that enthusiasm for democracy. But at that moment democracy still consisted mainly of vague promise. It had not yet delivered very much in the way of economic development or new social programs. The enthusiastic support for democracy in this period was based on its promise, not yet its reality.

Over the course of the 1990s considerable disillusionment with democracy set in. In most countries democracy has not delivered on its promises. Probably those promises were inflated; democracy, after all, is a way of choosing political leaders, not a magic formula for solving deep-rooted social and economic problems. Nevertheless many Latin Americans *expected* democracy to deliver real and immediate social and economic benefits, and when it did not, disillusionment set in and support for democracy was eroded. Our next step in analyzing the current political culture is to ask another question: Is this decline in support for democracy simply an adjustment to new realities, or does it reflect a serious threat to democracy itself?

Fortunately we have good public opinion poll data to help us answer this important question. Here we can use contemporary, scientific poll data to support and give greater precision to the more interpretive analysis of Latin American political culture presented earlier. First, recall that in the 1980s support for democracy was in the 80–90 percent range. Now look at Figure 3.1, which shows that the support for democracy in Latin America as a whole (measured as the percentage who agree that democracy is preferable to all other forms of government) was by 2000 down in the 60 percent range, falling by 20 to 30 percent from that of a decade earlier. Moreover, although the difference is slight, support for democracy has dropped between 1998 and 2000 and may continue to drop.

Now let us look at the data on individual countries. Figure 3.2 shows the support for democracy in Mexico and the South American countries. The bars next to each country indicate support in each of four time spans: 1996 on the bottom, then 1997 and 1998, with 1999–2000 on the top. Figure 3.3 shows the support for democracy in Central America (with the bars going left to right from 1996 to 1999–2000).

Several features are notable in these figures. First, in the countries that seem to have the best institutions and infrastructure for democracy—

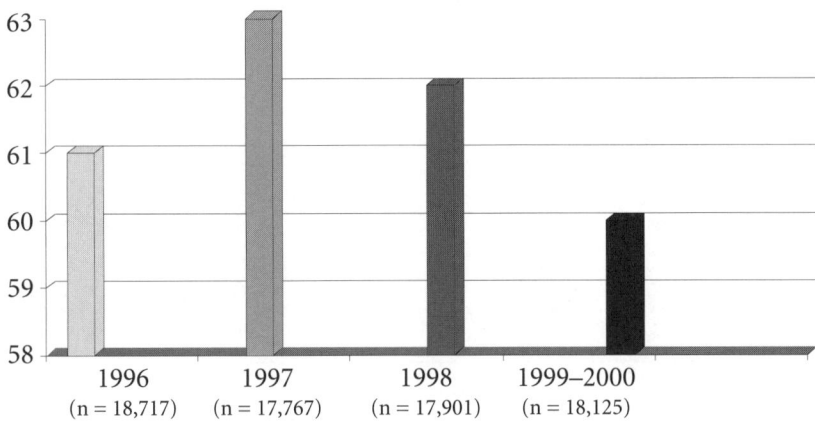

FIGURE 3.1  Support for Democracy in Latin America*

*Source:* Latin obarómetro: Opinión pública Latinoamericano, "Democracia es preferible." http://www.Latinobarometro.cl/00Graf2.htm. October 10, 2000.

*Percentage of survey respondents agreeing with the statement: "Democracy is preferable to all other forms of government."

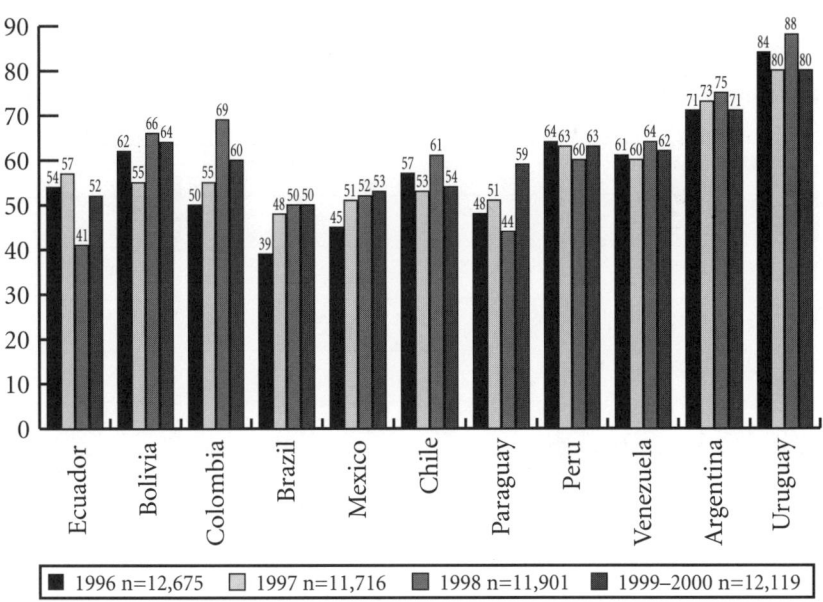

FIGURE 3.2  Support for Democracy in South America and Mexico*

*Source:* Latino Barómetro: Opinión pública Latinoamericano, "Democracia es preferible." Online. Available at: http://www.Latinobarometro.cl/00Graf2.htm. October 10, 2000.

*Percentage of survey respondents agreeing with the statement: "Democracy is preferable to all other forms of government."

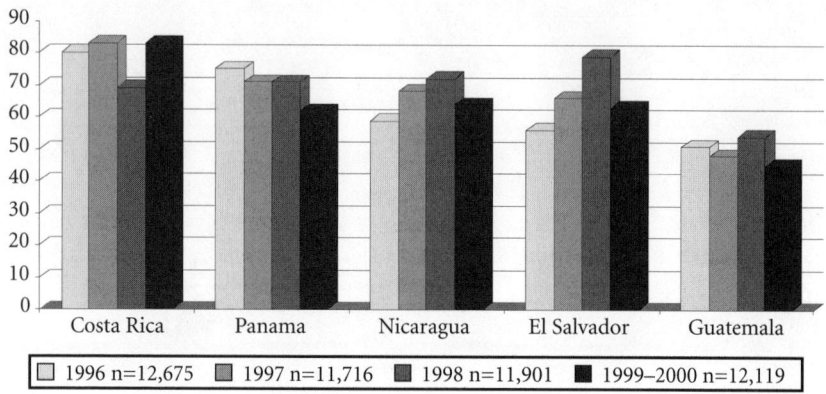

FIGURE 3.3  Support for Democracy in Central America*

*Source:* Latino Barómetro: Opinión pública Latinoamericano, "Democracia es preferible." Online. Available at: http://www.Latinobarometro.cl/00Graf2.htm. October 10, 2000.

*Percentage of survey respondents agreeing with the statement: "Democracy is preferable to all other forms of government."

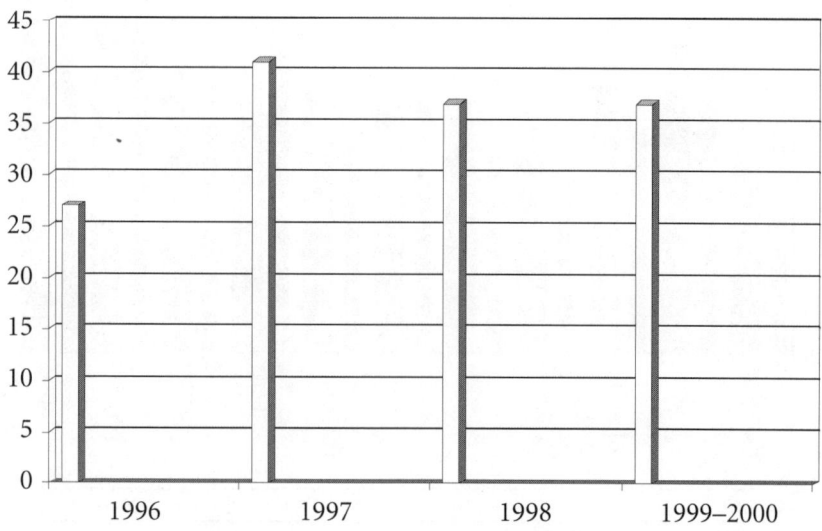

FIGURE 3.4  Satisfaction with Democracy in Latin America*

*Source:* Latino Barómetro: Opinión pública Latinoamericano, "Democracia es preferible." Online. Available at: http://www.Latinobarometro.cl/00Graf2.htm. October 10, 2000.

*Percentage of survey respondents who state that they are "very satisfied" or "moderately satisfied" with the functioning of democracy in their own country.

Argentina, Costa Rica, Uruguay, and Chile—the publics are most strongly supportive of democracy. The only exception is Chile, where the public is surprisingly in the middle of the pack in its support of democracy. Second, in quite a number of countries but with several exceptions, support for democracy seems to be falling. Generally, support has declined by only a few percentage points per year, but this decline will be important if it continues. Third, there are shockingly low levels of support for democracy in Colombia, Brazil, Mexico, Paraguay, and Guatemala. Support in all these countries is measured at 50 percent or lower. One might predict that when a country falls below the mark of 50 percent in its support for democracy, then democracy is in serious trouble and a coup or authoritarian solution may be eminent. In Mexico, faith in democracy has been elevated with the election of opposition leader Vicente Fox.

Figures 3.4, 3.5, and 3.6 offer even more cause for alarm for democracy supporters. These figures measure the public's *satisfaction* with democracy. In other words, is democracy delivering what people expect it to deliver?

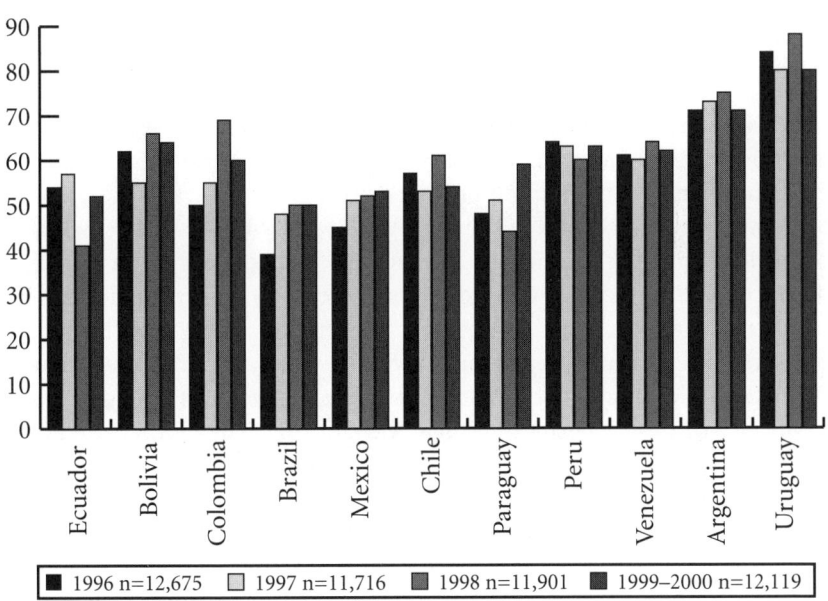

FIGURE 3.5  Satisfaction with Democracy in South America and Mexico*

*Source:* Latino Barómetro: Opinión pública Latinoamericano, "Democracia es preferible." Online. Available at: http://www.Latinobarometro.cl/00Graf3.htm. October 10, 2000.

*Percentage of survey respondents who state that they are "very satisfied" or "moderately satisfied" with the functioning of democracy in their own country.

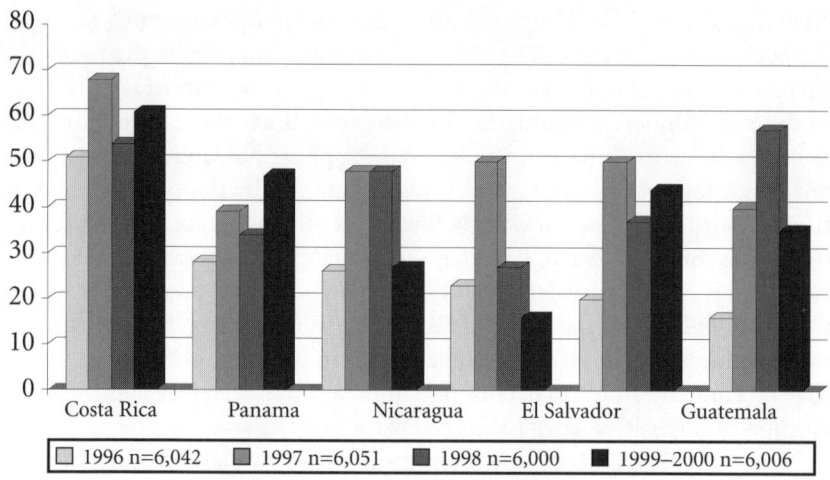

FIGURE 3.6    Satisfaction with Democracy in Central America*

*Source:* Latino Barómetro: Opinión pública Latinoamericano, "Democracia es preferible." Online. Available at: http://www.Latinobarometro.cl/00Graf3.htm. October 10, 2000.

*Percentage of survey respondents who state that they are "very satisfied" or "moderately satisfied" with the functioning of democracy in their own country.

Several features in these figures stand out. The first is the low level of satisfaction with democracy in *all* the countries, with the Latin American average hovering in the high 30 percent range. Only two countries, Costa Rica and Uruguay, consistently show levels of satisfaction with democracy over 50 percent. The second feature echoes the data measuring support for democracy: Satisfaction with democracy seems to be on the decline in most countries. And third, once again there is shockingly low (below 20 percent) satisfaction with democracy in several countries—Paraguay, Brazil, and Nicaragua. We can safely say that in these countries and in quite a number of others besides (Bolivia, Ecuador, El Salvador, Guatemala, Honduras, Peru, Venezuela—by this time we are up to half the countries of Latin America) democracy and democratic legitimacy are in deep trouble. Indeed, in several of these low-satisfaction countries, support for authoritarianism is now stronger than support for democracy.

To add to this discouraging picture, support for many of democracy's essential ingredients—political parties, congresses or parliaments, and labor unions—is even lower than the support for democracy itself. In almost all countries in the region, support for these political institutions is in the 20 percent range or lower. Once again, those countries with strong democratic institutions where support for and satisfaction with democracy are high also tend to look more favorably on parties, unions, and legislatures, but in the countries with already low support for democracy, support for these essential supporting institutions of pluralist democracy is often in the teens or even lower. Bear in mind that the measure of support for these institutions includes *all* parties and the entire party system and organized labor *in general*, not only one individual party or union. But can you have democracy where support for these democratic institutions is so low? Many Latin Americans, recognizing these trends, are starting to talk about democracy without parties or parliaments. But is that still democracy?

The trends are clearest in Venezuela and Peru, although they are present in other countries as well. In Venezuela, after forty years of free but often corrupt democracy, former paratrooper Hugo Chávez, who had earlier tried to seize power in a coup, won election to the presidency in 1999. He sent the National Congress packing, intervened in the justice system, discredited the old parties, and wrote a new constitution, giving himself virtually unlimited power. Chávez called himself a "Rousseauian democrat"; in contrast to the U.S. systems of representative democracy, he proposed to rule through direct democracy, speaking directly to the people and thus bypassing political parties and the legislature. Chávez was elected, but he had concentrated so much power in his own hands that people soon started calling him an autocrat. He did remain popular, especially with the lower classes. By operating in this way, Chávez was close to the mainstream of Venezuelan public opinion, which favors populism, direct democracy, and strong government and is critical of the old parties and institutions, and he therefore had widespread public support. But can this sort of unchecked strongman rule still be democratic?

The case of President Alberto Fujimori of Peru is similar. He was elected in 1990 but soon dissolved the Congress, coerced the judiciary into submission, and destroyed the old political parties. He ruled as an autocrat but an effective one—restoring the economy and defeating the violent Shining Path (Sendero Luminoso) guerrilla movement—and his poll numbers, like Chavez's, also remained high, especially with the lower classes. He was reelected in 1995 and then again in 2000 in what many believed was a tainted election. Again the regime's solution was direct, Rousseauian "democracy" or strong government without the institutions usually considered necessary for democracy—an independent legislature, a free press, and political parties. The regime was so autocratic, even authoritarian, that, despite the elections, it was hard to call it democratic anymore. By the year 2000 the regime had been discredited and change was in the air.

Although Peru and Venezuela are the two most obvious cases, similar trends are occurring throughout much of Latin America. That is, many regimes that are at least formally democratic, with regular elections, are in fact becoming more autocratic and authoritarian. The tendency is toward strong presidents who govern without much popular participation, interest group activity, or political party pluralism and competition. Paraguay and Ecuador have both had coups d'état, although in both a facade of constitutionalism has been maintained; the dominant pattern does not go so far as to install full-scale military rule. It allows democratic elections, but then once the elections are over, political power is dominated by strong executives who govern largely without pluralism, parties, or congress, becoming de facto autocrats.

Two interpretations of this tendency are possible. One is to wring one's hands, lament that democracy is in decline, and urge governments of the area to return to democratic purity. This is probably the dominant response in policy circles in Washington and among Latin American intellectuals.

The other interpretation, perhaps less morally satisfactory but certainly more realistic, builds on the analysis presented in this chapter. It points out that Latin American political culture has not, historically, been very supportive of liberal democracy and that Latin America's prior experiences with democracy have often been short and unsatisfactory. Democratic institutions are still weak; the infrastructure, economies, social base, and associational networks of the region are still often fragile and underdeveloped; and civil society and pluralism are in their early stages of development. In that context, we cannot expect full-blown democracy to develop overnight or in pristine forms.

One of the reasons that democracy remains weak and not well institutionalized in Latin America is that a lack of trust persists in the political culture. Lack of trust can also be measured by using public opinion data. Marta Lagos has measured three items that shed light on the dearth of interpersonal trust in Latin American political culture; her results are illustrated in Table 3.1. As the first column shows, only in Uruguay did at least one-third of the respondents believe that one can "trust most people," while that measurement falls to one out of nine in both Venezuela and Brazil. The second column illustrates that once again Uruguay leads all of the countries in levels of trust, with only one-third stating that their compatriots were dishonest. That figure reaches as high as 64 percent in Mexico and 65 percent in Chile. Finally, the third column illustrates that Uruguay once again leads the countries, with the lowest percentage of respondents who think that their compatriots break the law.

This lack of interpersonal trust, Lagos argues, may be at the heart of the problem of low confidence in institutions. If people cannot be trusted, nei-

TABLE 3.1   Social Attitudes in Various Latin American Countries

| Country | Interpersonal Trust[1] | Lack of Honesty[2] | Lawbreaking[3] |
| --- | --- | --- | --- |
| Uruguay | 33 | 33 | 50 |
| Argentina | 23 | 59 | 82 |
| Colombia | 23 | 61 | 68 |
| Paraguay | 23 | 41 | 63 |
| Mexico | 21 | 64 | 72 |
| Ecuador | 20 | 58 | 77 |
| Chile | 18 | 65 | 66 |
| Bolivia | 17 | 72 | 79 |
| Peru | 13 | 85 | 88 |
| Brazil | 11 | 62 | 87 |
| Venezuela | 11 | 57 | 74 |

Source: Marta Lagos, "Latin America's Shining Mask," *Journal of Democracy* 8, no. 3 (July 1997): 128.

[1] Percentage of respondents who answered "I can trust most people" to the question, "Generally speaking, would you say that you can trust most people or that you can never be too careful when dealing with others?"

[2] Percentage of respondents who answered either "a little" or "not at all" to the question, "Do you think that the [nationals] are very, quite, a little, or not at all . . . honest?"

[3] Percentage of respondents who answered either "a little" or "not at all" to the question, "Do you think that the [nationals] are very, quite, a little, or not at all . . . law-abiding?"

ther can institutions (with the possible exception of the Roman Catholic Church). Further, when high distrust is built into public and private institutions, democracy stands on shaky ground.

The data in Table 3.2 demonstrate that Latin America's subject political culture, characterized by generally passive acceptance of the political system, little tendency to communicate opinions or desires to the political elite, and little willingness to participate, overshadows its civic or participatory political culture, in which people have confidence in their ability to influence the political system. With the exception of the efficacy of voting, all of the variables suggest that Latin Americans are not likely to think that they can influence the outcome of political events by becoming involved.

Lagos suggests that we evaluate these results in two manners: in comparison with other countries of the world and in contrast with the history of Latin America. As she concludes,

> Held up against the template of Western civic culture and established democracy, Latin America appears gray and troubled. Held up against the template

TABLE 3.2  Attitudes Toward Politics in Various Latin American Countries

| Country | Efficacy of Voting[1] | Openness About Politics[2] | Equality of Political Opportunity[3] | Efficacy of Politicians[4] |
|---|---|---|---|---|
| Paraguay | 70 | 24 | 60 | 9 |
| Nicaragua | 69 | 42 | 42 | 41 |
| Uruguay | 67 | 34 | 73 | 10 |
| Argentina | 63 | 38 | 42 | 6 |
| Brazil | 61 | 35 | 38 | 6 |
| Panama | 59 | 41 | 44 | 6 |
| Ecuador | 58 | 27 | 55 | 40 |
| Peru | 52 | 31 | 30 | 8 |
| Venezuela | 49 | 32 | 35 | 9 |
| Chile | 49 | 29 | 42 | 12 |
| Mexico | 46 | 32 | 31 | 10 |
| Costa Rica | 45 | 33 | 59 | 16 |
| Colombia | 43 | 41 | 39 | 6 |
| El Salvador | 42 | 25 | 29 | 16 |
| Guatemala | 38 | 21 | 21 | 17 |
| Honduras | 37 | 25 | 32 | 19 |

*Source:* Marta Lagos, "Latin America's Shining Mask," *Journal of Democracy* 8, no. 3 (July 1997): 131.

[1] Percentage of respondents who agreed with the statement, "The way you vote can change the ways things will be in the future," rather than, "No matter how you vote, things will not improve in the future."

[2] Percentage of respondents who answered, "Most people say what they think" to the question, "When people are asked to express their political opinion, do you think that most people say what they really think, or that most people do not say what they really think?"

[3] Percentage of respondents who answered, "same opportunity as others" to the question, "Do you think that the political tendency you support has the same opportunity as others to get into power, or that it does not have the same opportunity?"

[4] Percentage of respondents who answered, "a lot" of "quite a lot" to the question, "As things are today, would you say that politicians are offering a lot, quite a lot, a few, or no solutions to the problems of the country?"

of the region's past, however, democracy appears as the only collective idea besides Catholicism to have defied the odds of the culture-loaded dice. From this vantage point, it can be predicted that every Latin American country, whatever might be its individual difficulties, will strive mightily to remain at least as democratic as it has been so far.[1]

Therefore, we may for now have to settle for something less than full democracy in most countries. This seems a reasonable response given Latin

America's political culture, which shows a mix of democratic and authoritarian beliefs and values, as well as its current lack of trust and the weakness of its political institutions. Instead of embracing democracy in its pure and most developed form, as we might wish, Latin America seems to be tending toward a mixed system that may be a fairly accurate reflection of its own current realities. Latin America has to find its own equilibrium, probably somewhere between autocracy and full democracy, that reflects its own history, culture, and social, economic, and institutional development. Some of these hybrids may be called limited democracy, controlled democracy, or executive-centered democracy. Although we may lament that democracy in many countries of Latin America is not yet present in its pure and pristine forms, that can still be the goal that we set for the area.

## Note

1. Marta Lagos, "Latin America's Shining Mask," *Journal of Democracy* 8, no. 3 (July 1997): 137.

# 4

# Class, Social Structure, Social Change

Latin America was for a long time organized on the basis of a rigid, fundamentally two-class, quasifeudal social structure. The class structure was reinforced by racial criteria: Whites at the top, Indians and Blacks at the bottom. This two-class system was long viewed as immutable and God-given; the system went on unchanged for centuries because to rebel against it was to violate God's "natural order" and risk eternal damnation. The rigid two-class social structure was reinforced by the feudal landholding system, the mercantilist state, and the system of top-down, authoritarian political control.

Although changes in this two-class system began during the late nineteenth and early twentieth centuries, in recent decades the changes are occurring more rapidly. Now, in addition to a business-commercial class, a middle class, and labor unions, others have begun to mobilize—women, peasants, and indigenous elements. New social movements and elements of civil society have come into existence.

A large middle class and a more pluralist society are widely thought of as part of the essential foundations for successful democracy. To the extent that Latin America has a strong middle class and a pluralist society, its possibilities for democracy are enhanced. And yet, as we will see in this chapter, the middle class remains weak, pluralism is limited, many aspects of the old two-class society are still present, and the social basis for democracy is still fragile. The result is often a mixed or hybrid political culture and society and a persistently precarious democratic government.

## Historical Background

The men who accompanied Columbus and later Spanish and Portuguese explorers across the Atlantic to the New World were military adventurers, mainly the second and third sons of the lesser nobility. They were neither of the high nobility, who already had land and peasants in Spain, nor of the peasant class. Under the Spanish and Portuguese laws of primogeniture, whereby the first son inherits the land, these second and third sons were unable to acquire land and peasants at home. That is why America looked so enticing: it seemed to have unlimited land there for the taking, as well as a ready-made "peasantry" in the native Indians. By participating in the conquest, every conquistador could hope to live like a grandee, with vast gold and silver, huge landed estates (the size of a U.S. state or county), and a large number of peasants. These elite or aristocratic status considerations were paramount in the Spanish-Portuguese conquest and settlement of the Americas, and they go a long way toward explaining Latin America's elite behavior even today.

In the Americas, the Spaniards and Portuguese encountered a large Indian population, upwards of 30 million people. The Indians were unevenly distributed throughout Latin America and their cultures represented a variety of levels of organization and sophistication, and we need to take these factors into account in assessing the different countries of the area. In the Caribbean Islands and on the eastern or Atlantic side of South America, the Indians were relatively few in numbers and were organized, for the most part, in small-scale tribes and civilizations. But in Mexico, Central America, and the Andean region (present-day Ecuador, Peru, and Bolivia) the conquistadors found large-scale Indian civilizations (Aztec, Mayan, Incan) of approximately 5 to 7 million persons each. So the possibilities for using indigenous Indian ("peasant") labor varied considerably depending on (1) the availability of laborers and (2) their willingness to work.

Spain and Portugal set out not only to conquer and enslave but also to Christianize and thus to pacify and assimilate the Indians. Millions of Indians died, first from the conquest, then from forced labor, mainly as a result of the diseases that the Spaniards carried and for which the Indians had no immunity—small pox, influenza, and tuberculosis. They also died from the culture shock that came from seeing their gods and civilizations defeated, humiliated, and destroyed by the conquistadors.

In those areas where the Indian labor was thin or died off and where temperature, land, and rainfall made the land suitable for plantation agriculture (the Caribbean Islands, northeast Brazil, the mainland Caribbean coast), African slave labor was brought in to do the manual work. From this time on, social and race relations in the Caribbean and Brazil would mainly involve the interrelations of Europeans and Blacks, whereas in the rest of the mainland the primary ethnic groups were Europeans and Indians. Although slavery was clearly an evil institution in all its forms, it is generally conceded that the Portuguese in Brazil were less cruel and rigid about it than were other Europeans in the Caribbean (the Spanish and eventually the English, French, and Dutch).

On top of the hierarchical social and class structure that was inherited and brought over from medieval Spain and Portugal was now superimposed a racial system of human classification. Initially this was simple: White, European Spaniards and Portuguese were at the top of the socio-racial pyramid, Indians and Blacks at the bottom. But recall that the conquistadors, unlike the North American colonists, had not brought wives or families along, so right from the beginning racial miscegenation among the three racial groups occurred. Hence already in the first generation there were mulattos (mixtures of Whites and Blacks) and mestizos (mixtures of Whites and Indians); by the second and third generations there were also mixtures of Blacks and Indians, mestizos and Whites, mulattos and Whites, mestizos and Indians, mulattos and Blacks, mestizos and mulattos, and so on. The Spanish devised a name and racial category for each offspring, down to 128 parts. This was not an egalitarian society; each racial category had distinct work obligations as well as distinct rights under the law. At the same time one could move up in the social scale through cultural assimilation as well as "lightening."

For the most part, however, Blacks and Indians were consigned to the lowest rungs of the social ladder as slaves or peasants. They were forced to work in the mines or on the plantations established by the Spanish and Portuguese. It was difficult, backbreaking, often deadly work; many died or were ground down by the experience. Some managed to escape; others retreated to the mountains or inaccessible jungles to get away from the cruelty of the colonial system. White civilization and Indian or Black civilization developed together, but apart; they often occupied the same geographic space but their lifestyles, cultures, and economic levels were so far apart as to be totally unbridgeable. This is not a formula for democracy or for forming future nation-states; in many countries of Latin America the problem of integrating Blacks and Indians, who may constitute a majority of the population, into social, economic, and political life is still the great national problem.

The *hacienda* (*fazenda* in Portuguese), or large estate, was the classic institution of the colonial period, found throughout Latin America. Haciendas were immense in territory and largely self-sufficient. The hacienda consisted of a manor house where the landowner (*hacendado*) and his family lived, and a servants' or slaves' quarters. Many haciendas included a priest and a chapel as well, to serve the religious needs of the hacendado and his family and to help Christianize the Indians. The estate produced enough for home consumption plus some for sale. But the enterprise was more feudal than capitalistic; status considerations—knowing one's place and performing one's expected functions—were more important than implementing intensive cultivation to make a profit, which was frowned on in Catholic theology. The owner exercised absolute power over the estate—economically, socially, religiously, politically—another link in the chain of absolutism that stretched from king to viceroy to hacendado.

This rigid system of class and caste lasted for centuries; its formal-legal aspects were eventually abolished after independence, but informally many aspects of this unyielding social structure remain present today. Nevertheless, by about the mid–eighteenth century a few changes had begun to appear. In the cities a business-commercial class had begun to grow up that wanted to break the Spanish and Portuguese colonial monopolies and be free to trade with other countries such as France, England, or Holland. The division between native-born Europeans (Creoles) and officials sent from Spain (*peninsulares*) was widening at this time and would eventually be a main factor in independence. A considerable number of mulattos and mestizos had bought or been granted freedom and, while it would be a stretch to call them middle class, they did often serve as middlemen between the European and the Indian and Black communities.

After independence in the 1820s and under the influence of republicanism, most Latin American countries formally abolished the Iberian caste system. But that did not mean that racial and ethnic prejudice or the system of social inequalities disappeared. In most countries, slavery continued after independence, any hint of social revolution that accompanied independence (as in Mexico) was brutally repressed, and the lives of Indians and Blacks did not improve.

If anything, life got worse for the poor with the disruption and chaos that accompanied independence and new nationhood. Property and literacy requirements excluded Indians and Blacks from political participation; they were kept locked in the peasant class and in subservient status and were denied the full rights of citizenship. There were two exceptions: in Haiti there was a successful slave revolt (1795–1805) that threw out the White (in this case French) ruling class and ushered in the world's first Black republic, and in Mexico in the 1850s an Indian reform movement came to power for the first time.

Later in the nineteenth century, as much of Latin America entered the economic take-off stage, greater social change began to occur. A new business-commercial class, often formed by immigrant families, emerged alongside the traditional landed elite and frequently intermarried with it. This stimulus to economic activity also gave rise to a new middle class, which for the first time occupied many government positions and began to demand the right to vote and participate. In the more advanced countries, Argentina, Chile, Mexico, and Uruguay, a small trade union movement emerged for the first time. As more significant and large-scale industrialization eventually came to Latin America in the 1920s and 1930s, trade unions developed in the other countries as well.

After World War II and throughout the rest of the twentieth century, other social groups began to mobilize. In the 1950s and 1960s peasants were organized and mobilized for the first time, through political parties, peasant leagues, and even guerrilla movements. In the 1970s and 1980s, under the influence of the global women's movement, Latin American women began to organize. And in the 1990s we witnessed the rise of indigenous movements and their assertion of Indian rights. By now, virtually all groups in Latin America have been mobilized and organized, although the process is very uneven and some groups are better organized than others.

Other profound social changes have meanwhile been taking place throughout Latin America in the years since the 1950s. First, the literacy rate has risen from about 30 to 70 percent; much of Latin America is now better educated and more politically aware than before. Second, radio and television have had a profound impact, conveying images of modern life to a previously traditional countryside. Third, in two generations the Latin American population has shifted from 70 percent rural to 70 percent urban; Latin America is no longer "sleepy" and agricultural. Fourth, millions of Latin Americans have carried their migration one step farther by immigrating to the United States and other countries. In other words, Latin America is now a far different society than it was in the feudal past: more dynamic, more mobilized, more multiclass, more pluralistic, more affluent, more involved.

## Regional and National Variations

To this point we have been mainly treating Latin America as a single area. But in fact the differences between the several countries, in terms of class structure, social relations, and political systems, are wide and getting wider. Let us look at some of the patterns these differences form.

In terms of class structure, Argentina, Chile, Costa Rica, and Uruguay have relatively large middle classes. In these countries, depending somewhat on how one counts, 30–40 percent of the population may be considered middle class. These are also the countries that, by most measures, are the most economically developed and the most democratic, thus implying a correlation between democracy, development, and the size of the middle class. By contrast Haiti, which has only a small middle class and is among the least developed countries in the world, is among the least democratic of the Latin American countries. Most of the other countries in the region fall somewhere in between these examples.

A second pattern is revealed when we examine ethnic integration. The countries with the largest indigenous ethnic groupings—Bolivia, Ecuador, Guatemala, Paraguay, and Peru—are also among the countries that have had difficulty achieving both economic development and democracy. In a number of these countries, the major national issue for some two hundred years has been how to integrate their Indian groups, which may number from 40 to 80 percent of the total population, into the national life—socially, economically, linguistically, politically.

The United States has major problems integrating its minority population, which numbers from 15 to 20 percent of the total, into its national life; imagine, then, the problems of having to integrate *50 percent* or more of your population into national life, especially when the steps required for integration are much more basic than they are in the United States: speaking the national language, being part of a money economy, or even identifying with the existing nation-state as compared with an indigenous grouping. These fundamental gaps between the mainstream and the minority populations constitute severe problems of social integration that have historically hindered several of the Latin American countries from achieving development and democratization goals.

A third and often related pattern is found in the degree of class difference. In Brazil, Colombia, and Mexico the gaps between rich and poor are among the widest in the world. But other Latin American countries also have this problem of *huge* class, income, and also racial differences between the elites and the rest of the population. It is difficult to construct democracy when such vast differences exist. Class and racial conflict may be endemic, rather than the degree of egalitarianism that is necessary for democracy.

A fourth pattern appears when we examine the cultural makeup of individual countries. It is significant that the Latin American countries that are most European in character—again, Argentina, Chile, Costa Rica, and Uruguay—are also among the most developed and the most democratic. That is not to ascribe some innate racial superiority to these countries—although that was frequently done in earlier explanations and is still often done by the peoples of these countries themselves. Instead, this difference has to do with the fact that these countries had a broader background in European institutions, including both the economic institutions for development and the political institutions for democracy, and that they did not have large minority populations, and so largely avoided the problems of integration into the national life described above. So it is not "Europeanness" in a racial sense that accounts for these countries' relative success but the fact that by virtue of their institutions and their historical background, they were in a position to take advantage of developmental opportunities.

There are also predominantly mestizo and mulatto countries, including Colombia, Cuba, the Dominican Republic, El Salvador, Guatemala, Honduras, Mexico, Nicaragua, Panama, and Venezuela. These are often "in-between" countries: they have class and racial differences that are significant but not so extreme as in some other more racially polarized countries; they have developed and democratized but not as successfully as some others; and they have achieved considerable ethnic integration but still have not become fully integrated. On the other hand, these may be among the most multicultural and multiethnic countries in the world and, with their sizable mestizo and mulatto populations, offer hope for greater integration, development, and democratization in the future.

## Major Social Groups

In this section we look at the major social groups in Latin America—the elites, the middle class, industrial workers, the peasantry, the lumpen proletariat, women's groups, and indigenous groups. Here we examine the social background and attitudes of these groups; in Chapter 5 we will look at their organized political expression as interest groups.

There are far fewer interest groups in Latin America than in the United States, and Latin Americans tend to belong to fewer such groups than do people in the United States. In the United States, individual citizens are often members of many groups—religious bodies, scouts, unions, school groups, community groups, business associations, sports groups, and so on. Their memberships in these groups tend to prevent them from developing a fierce, undivided loyalty to any one of them. But that is not true in Latin America. First, the number of interest groups in individual countries tends to be quite small, often a dozen or even fewer major groups in the small, poorer, less institutionalized countries. Second, there are fewer cross-cutting memberships and loyalties. Hence a person tends to go "all out" for his or her group, and the intense commitments are not ameliorated by multiple group associations. In this way Latin American society can almost be seen as a society made up of "stock types": the oligarch, the military officer, the student, the worker, the peasant. And this characteristic often makes compromise and the art of getting along much more difficult.

## The Elites

The White, aristocratic, often haughty, landed oligarchy was long the most powerful group in Latin America's past, often pilloried for its resistance to change and development. But that description made sense only as long as Latin America consisted of rural, backward, agricultural countries, and today the situation is much more complicated.

In most Latin American countries, the landed oligarchy is still a powerful influence and often still a reflection of the old, Spanish and Portuguese aristocratic ethos of disdain for manual labor and for those who do the labor. In many countries, too, the oligarchy has moved to the cities, diversified its wealth and influence into banking, commerce, and industry, and intermarried with new, rising, often foreign-born entrepreneurs.

But the traditional image of this oligarchy monopolizing economic, social, and all political power now needs to be modified, if not rejected. For one thing, the oligarchy is now better educated and technically skilled than before, meaning that its better elements survive while its losers are consigned to oblivion. Second, the oligarchy is now much more diverse than before, involving multiple centers of economic activity involving many different groups—Jewish, Asian, Arab, European, American. Third, in many countries the elites have had to compromise with the rising mestizo and mulatto middle class, thus diluting their power somewhat. And fourth, the elites now have to deal with both democratization and globalization. Democratization (one person, one vote) implies a certain diminution of elite power, even though the elites are usually well connected in whatever government comes to power. Globalization forces elites to compete on a global basis with everyone else, which means they must become as efficient and pragmatic as everyone else. The result is that the elites are still powerful in Latin America but they now must operate within a more pluralist, competitive, and democratic context.

## The Middle Class

Even in colonial times, Latin America had a small middle class, consisting of handfuls of artisans, craftsmen, soldiers, and bureaucrats. But the growth of a sizable middle class did not begin until the late nineteenth and early twentieth centuries when economic development stimulated significant middle sector growth. Today the middle classes of Latin America are much more diverse and much larger, ranging from 20 percent of the population in the less developed countries to 35–40 percent in the more developed countries.

The trouble was that this emerging middle class was deeply divided along economic, social, racial, and political lines and did not constitute the stable, consensual, middle-of-the-road basis for democracy that exists in western Europe and the United States. Some members of the middle class were relatively liberal, but others were even more conservative than the oligarchs and either sided with the military to prevent democratic and reformist regimes from coming to power or overthrew them once in power.

The attitudes of the middle class have changed considerably since then. Today the middle class dominates such key groups as the military officer corps, the church hierarchy, small and medium-size business, university student bodies, trade union and political party leadership, and the bureaucracy, so it is important to know where it stands. There is vast evidence that this important group, whose primary interest is stability, now sees democracy as the best way to maintain that stability, and no longer prefers military authoritarianism. Of course the middle class is still diverse, still often divided, still often insecure in its position. But it is also becoming more centrist and pragmatic, and in today's world that means support for the rule of law, democracy, and constitutionalism.

## *Industrial Workers*

Because Latin America was predominantly agricultural and rural for so long, the development of an industrial working class always lagged behind Europe and the United States. When industrialization did finally come to Latin America, it was focused on the agricultural or raw materials export sectors; hence, the first groups of organized workers were often the sugar workers, tin miners, copper workers, banana workers, cane cutters, meat packers, and stevedores.

Today at least some countries in Latin America have large-scale and heavy industry, and in Argentina, Brazil, Mexico, Chile, and Venezuela the metallurgists, autoworkers, and other industrial unions are influential and a voice to be reckoned with. But in most countries the industrial sector remains quite small, even while these countries have diversified into tourism, commerce, assembly plants, telecommunications, agroindustry, and the service sector. The result of these trends is that the industrial proletariat remains generally small, not well organized, and weak politically. In most countries organized workers make up only between 5 and 12 percent of the workforce, a group that is large enough to demand attention but not large enough to destabilize or overthrow the system through strikes or revolution. Further, with globalization, the percentage of unionized workers has decreased in many countries. In addition, the labor movement is often deeply divided between communist, social democratic, Christian democratic, and more conservative and independent unions, further diminishing their influence.

At least for now, therefore, it seems unlikely that we will soon see organized rival political parties that are based on the basic political split characteristic of the developed European countries—that between the middle class or bourgeoisie and the working class or proletariat. Instead Latin American politics will remain more fluid, with populist politicians and appeals rather than strictly class-based ones.

## *The Peasantry*

"The peasantry" has long been a vague, catchall term that covers such diverse groups as small landowners, tenant farmers, and agricultural workers on large estates. Up to thirty years ago, this was by far the largest social group in Latin America, but politically the weakest.

In recent decades the countryside has experienced extensive social and economic transformation, but the political weakness of the peasantry has been little affected and may even have been made worse. The main factors in this development are urbanization and emigration: Latin America as a whole has gone from 70 percent rural and agricultural to 30 percent rural and agricultural. This means that the peasantry no longer constitutes the majority of the population; rather the majority is now to be found in the cities.

Part of the explanation for this shift is that the countryside itself is changing, from small holdings and subsistence agriculture to large-scale agroindustry. Labor-intensive agriculture is being replaced by bigger, more mechanized agriculture utilizing fewer seasonal workers. Seeing little future in the countryside, vast numbers of peasants have migrated to urban areas or abroad to look for jobs and a better life. The relative decrease in their numbers means that politicians and governments pay them and their problems even less attention than before.

The irony is that in absolute terms the numbers of rural peasants remain high or even higher than before, and their problems of poverty, malnutrition, disease, and lack of regular employment are still present. What has diminished is not the number of peasants, but their predominance as a percentage of the total population, making peasants a weaker group. In addition, most peasants are only weakly organized, so their political clout remains slim. So while the number of peasants remains high, their political influence seems to be eroding still farther.

## The Lumpen Proletariat

One result of the movement of peasants to the cities has been a tremendous growth in the urban populations of Latin America, the enormous swelling of big-city slums, and the inability of government services to keep pace with all the new migrants and their needs. Cities like Buenos Aires, Argentina; São Paulo, Brazil; and Mexico City, Mexico, are approaching populations of 20 million each; they are among the largest cities in the world and are all but unmanageable. The poverty is overwhelming; we have all seen pictures of children from the big-city slums scavenging for food and other necessities in the dumps of these cities. In all the capital cities of Latin America and many secondary cities as well, the rapid urbanization has given rise to crises of basic needs: water supplies, electricity, housing, education, social services, jobs, health, nutrition, and health care. Crime and violence are also reaching epidemic proportions.

The recent arrivals to the urban slums are often highly motivated to prosper and are angry about their plight; if they were still traditional "sleepy" peasants, they wouldn't have migrated to the cities in the first place. As people who have moved from the familiarity of the countryside to the frightening newness of the city slum, they are also disoriented socially, and often become the new recruits of the rapidly growing Protestant Evangelical groups that offer not only salvation but hope for upward mobility. But migrants are usually only minimally organized and politicians seldom pay them much attention. Most are unemployed or underemployed, which is why they are described with Marx's term, "lumpen," or "almost," proletariat, and few of them are members of unions or political associations.

Given their miserable conditions, the lumpen proletariat are often vulnerable to extremist, demagogic, and populist appeals, even though they seldom become members of political parties or other organized groups in civil society. This is a volatile group, some of whose members are responsible for rising crime and looting while others build new rooms or porches onto their slum homes, lobby politicians to bring them electricity and water, and thus acquire a stake in the system. This is an "in-between" element, part of neither the rural peasantry nor the urban proletariat but stuck in between these two. The one other thing we know about them: once they've tasted city life, they rarely go back to the poor countryside from which they came.

## Women's Groups

In Latin America's historically Catholic societies, women as women were not supposed to participate directly in the political process; the basic unit of society was seen as the family, and women were expected to play a political role mainly through their husbands. At the same time, women were cast in the image of the Virgin Mary—pure and idealized, placed on a pedestal; the worship of Mary (Marianismo) provided a female ideal that was counterpart to the male ideal of machismo (masculine power and strength). For a long time, the result of these expectations was the lack of an independent vote for women and only a very few women officeholders.

The next stage of the history of women in Latin America saw the extension of the suffrage to women, the appearance of women's sections in the main political parties, and a gradual increase in the number of women holding office, mainly in traditional "women's positions" such as health and education. Now the old myths about women's subordination are giving way and more women in Latin America hold advanced degrees, work in professional fields, and occupy political positions. There have been women presidents, women vice presidents, and many women cabinet members and legislators. Quite a number of political parties now have quotas to ensure that more women run for office.

Despite women's better education, professional achievements, and increased political role, politics is still often seen as unladylike. Politics is usually thought to be too aggressive for all but a few women to participate in. The women's movements in Latin America are thus often split between those women who are professionally trained and educated and want to either get ahead in their professions or serve in traditional women's capacities such as teaching, health care, and social services, leaving men to compete in hardball electoral politics, and those who wish to pursue more aggressive ideological, gender, and political agendas. Now for the first time professional Latin American women can have both careers and a family life, but the political career is still fairly unusual for women. And because few women serve in low-level political positions like town council, mayor, and congressional representative, in the near future it remains unlikely that many women will be found at higher levels.

## *Indigenous Groups*

In addition to bringing death and destruction, the conquest of the Americas by Spain and Portugal was such a culture shock to Indian peoples in Latin America that many retreated or were forced into the jungles and mountains, refusing to participate in European civilization. Hence many of the Latin American countries with large Indian populations remained unintegrated, and this hindered both economic development and efforts at democratization. There were Indian uprisings historically in Bolivia, Mexico, and Peru and some efforts by a handful of political parties and reformers to extend rights to the Indians, but in general the Indian, like the peasant (the two were often synonymous), remained the forgotten person of Latin American politics.

In the last two decades Indian groups have increasingly organized and mobilized. They are demanding full rights as citizens and, in some cases, a measure of autonomy or self-government for their ethnic group. Some of the demands for territorial sovereignty, however, cross present-day national frontiers and encompass the lands of the ancient pre-Columbian Indian civilizations of the Americas—the Aztec, Mayan, and Incan empires. They thus arouse the ire of the military, political, and nationalist leaders of individual countries. Like the other groups surveyed here, therefore, Indian groups are often split between those who want to use politics as a way of getting more benefits for themselves within the existing power structure (the co-optation option) and those who want genuine autonomy and real political power for themselves (the radical option). We discuss these options more fully in Chapter 5.

## State-Society Relations

As the above analysis makes clear, Latin America has become increasingly pluralist over the last several decades. But it is still a system of limited pluralism in which only a relatively small number of groups compete in the political process. Moreover, some groups are clearly more powerful than others. In Latin America generally it is the elite groups, the business community, and the upper middle class that have the most power, with the armed forces often waiting in the wings as the ultimate arbiter of political affairs. By contrast, the trade unions, the peasantry, the lumpen proletariat, women's groups, and indigenous groups—by far the majority of the population—are usually disorganized, divided among themselves, and without power in the overall political system. It is obvious that pluralist democracy cannot function when social power is so imbalanced and when some small elite groups have such a disproportionate amount of power compared to the large mass of the population.

That power imbalance is reflected in Latin America's system of state-society relations. "State-society relations" refers to the ways and systems by which social groups relate to the state or government and through which the state in turn manages the growing pluralism of social groups.

There are three forms of state-society relations: (1) totalitarianism, in which the state totally subordinates all social groups to its control and the groups are mere creatures and agents of the state; (2) liberal pluralism, in which social groups enjoy free association with no or limited control over them by the state, as in the United States and other democracies; and (3) corporatism, a hybrid solution in which the state structures and controls some social groups while allowing freedom for others. Corporatism has long been the dominant pattern of Latin American state-society relations, but now, with democracy, the trends are shifting toward a system that combines corporatism with liberal pluralism.

In Latin America there are a number of corporatist interest groups; historically the most important have been the Church and the army, both of which received special privileges and immunities from the state and acted as fourth and fifth branches of government. But as social change accelerated in the twentieth century, the state often stepped in to structure and control the political participation of new social groups—principally labor unions, peasant associations, and indigenous movements. The state did this by creating official, state-run organizations for these groups or by using its power to grant official recognition to some favored groups while withholding it from others. Later in the book we will describe in more detail how these groups were either co-opted into the state structure, on the one hand, or repressed and prohibited from participating, on the other. Clearly this corporatist system of state-society relations, involving significant control by the state over interest groups, was not very liberal or democratic, but it was not fully totalitarian either.

In some countries corporatism was extended to include corporate or group representation in government as well. That is, in such government agencies as the parliament or council of state (a high-level advisory body like a cabinet), groups such as the Church, the army, the bureaucracy, the universities, and major economic associations were represented *as groups* rather than on the basis of one person, one vote. In another alternative, this form of group or corporatist representation would be combined with geographic representation, as in the U.S. Congress.

In addition, the all-important system of labor relations was organized in a corporatist fashion. Some unions were suppressed, but others were created by or received the official blessing of the state. Employers were then forced to implement wage and benefits policies that were mandated by the government rather than attained by a system of collective bargaining or liberalism.

The high point of corporatism in Latin America was reached in the 1930s and 1940s. But even after World War II the corporatist form of state-society relations persisted in many countries, particularly in the area of labor relations and in the process by which trade unions, peasant associations, and indigenous movements were absorbed into the political system under state control. Under the military or bureaucratic-authoritarian regimes that returned to power in Latin America in the 1960s and 1970s, corporatism was solidified, often with a vengeance—that is, using more repression than co-optation.

However with the return to democracy in the 1980s and 1990s, many of the older corporatist institutions and practices were abandoned or modified. In other words, the transitions to democracy that Latin America has experienced in the last two decades involved not only holding elections and instigating better human rights observance, but also the liberalization and democratization of interest group activity. For example, the older corporatist restrictions on trade union activity were abolished or reformed in many countries, direct collective bargaining between labor and employers was now permitted, without the heavy hand of the state, and interest groups were permitted to organize freely without the state determining whether they were allowed to participate.

The result in most Latin American countries is still a mixed, often overlapping system of corporatism and liberal-pluralism. Although some corporatist state controls over interest group activity have been abolished, others remain in place, especially those concerned with labor union activity. Many countries want to be fully pluralist, free, and democratic, but they are afraid to give up all corporatist or state controls lest chaos or fragmentation result. So some degree of corporatist representation remains. Even in democratic Chile, for example, the armed forces are still guaranteed eight lifetime seats in the Senate and are thus able to protect their special place in society. Similarly in Mexico, although the country now enjoys considerable freedom and recently held democratic elections in which for the first time the opposition won, the interest group system remains a complex mix of corporatist and liberal-pluralist influences.

The system of state-society relations is a critical arena in Latin America, but it is often ignored. For although almost all the Latin American countries now have regular democratic elections and their human rights records are better than before, their interest group system is still often a hybrid: partly free and pluralist as in the United States and partly corporatist and controlled by the state. It is fair to say that interest groups in the United States are strong and the state or government is often weak; but in Latin America it is the state that is strong (at least in aspirations, for many Latin American governments are unable to even implement their own laws effectively), and interest groups are usually weak, subordinate, and often controlled by the state.

## Economic and Social Change

Economic and social change goes on inexorably, regardless of the government in power. Of course some governments are more development-oriented than others and the distribution of wealth is obviously affected by the nature of the government in power, but usually some form of change occurs whether the government in office is military or civilian, authoritarian or democratic. Change is ubiquitous.

We emphasize this point because economic and social change continues to go forward and is even accelerating in many Latin American countries. For example, while some countries still lag behind, many have now recovered from the economic doldrums and debt crises of the 1980s and are experiencing increased growth, they are attracting larger amounts of investment capital, their exports and earnings are increasing, jobs are being created, and freer markets are opening up. Latin America as a whole is adjusting to globalization. Likewise, in most countries, literacy rates continue to increase, urbanization continues, and life expectancy is rising. These broadscale economic and social changes have important, ongoing political effects as well.

Among the transformations spawned by continuing socioeconomic change are those in the political culture. As Latin America becomes more urban and developed, the old, traditional values are being challenged or ignored. The old assumptions about social hierarchy are giving way to a stronger sense of egalitarianism, especially among young people. The old assumptions about race and caste are similarly undergoing change, even though racism is still present. The old sense of fatalism, the belief that change will come only if God or the fates will it, is similarly breaking down as people take charge of their own lives: The flight of tens of millions of former peasants to the cities provides ample evidence of greater social mobility and less fatalism. You cannot convince workers or peasants anymore that they must be forever poor and their children malnourished because God, the saints, or the "natural order of the universe" have willed it that way. Thus as people's ideas and beliefs about the social order change, so do their expectations about civil society and government.

Because of these shifts in political culture, as well as overall social and economic modernization, political institutions and practices are changing as well. Political parties in an era of democracy, for example, are now often mass-based and have a mass appeal, rather than just appealing to elites. Interest groups are better organized and more oriented toward more modern issues—the environment, education, health care, good government, pollution, city services—than toward the issues of the past. Government is being called upon to deliver real services—schools, medical care, water supplies, regular electricity—and not just patronage positions. And if government is not responsive to these issues, it can be voted out of office in the next election. The current challenge for many political leaders is to be responsive to these demands by providing real programs and services while still fulfilling necessary patronage obligations.

The issues that people in Latin America are concerned with have also changed as a result of social and economic change. For instance, given Latin America's rural character and its inequitable landholding pattern, it was once thought that agrarian reform was absolutely necessary to solve the region's problems; for a time, agrarian reform was seen as almost a cure-all panacea for the ills of the area. But now, even though agrarian reform may still be necessary, the massive migration of peasants to the cities has shifted the attention of politicians and government agencies from rural problems to urban problems. Besides, who would want to try to eke out a meager substance on a small plot of rural land that no longer offers a future? In this sense Latin America is little different from U.S. farm states where young people are leaving the rural areas in droves because they see no future in the family farm, and the bright lights of Denver, St. Louis, Minneapolis, Chicago, and other cities seem to offer better opportunities.

Globalization and accompanying increases in trade and integration are also having profound effects. For one thing, because of globalization/integration, countries now almost have to have a democratic system of government because if they don't, trade and investment will quickly dry up and economic sanctions will probably be imposed, with disastrous consequences that no country can afford. Globalization also demands an honest and efficient government, one that educates its people for the new economy, provides real social services, and is transparent in handling public funds and awarding contracts. If a government is not honest and efficient or does not fulfill these functions, investment will simply go elsewhere, again with calamitous consequences. Significantly, change is now initiated, not simply through pressure from outside actors such as the United States, the World Bank, or the International Monetary Fund (IMF), but because Latin America's own business communities and professional classes recognize these new realities, and they themselves pressure the governments to reform.

## Conclusions and Implications

Latin America has changed enormously in recent decades. It has gone from an essentially two-class and semifeudal society to a much more modern, multiclass, and pluralist society. It has also become more open, more mobile, and more free. Although many legacies from the past remain—such as elitism, hierarchy, and patronage politics—the current changes have made Latin America a much different society than it was in 1960 or 1970.

Social change has also altered the nature of Latin America's corporatism and fundamentally transformed the structure of state-society relations. In addition, a host of new organizations collectively known as civil society—community groups, human rights organizations, good-government groups, neighborhood associations, social movements of peasants and others—have sprung up alongside the traditional social groups. In Chapter 5 we look specifically at how all these social changes have affected the interest group system; in subsequent chapters we trace their effects on political parties, governance, democracy, and public policy.

# 5

# Interest Groups

As suggested in Chapter 4, interest groups in Latin America are involved in the region's current transition from a corporatist, historic past to a newer system based on pluralism and democracy. Over the past decade there has been a conflict between two different views of what the political rules of the game should be. On the one side are the new forces that desire majority rule, human rights, and freedom of association. On the other side are those who favor traditional ways of doing things: creating an administrative state above party and interest-group politics in which such agencies as the Church, the army, the university, and perhaps even the trade unions are often more than mere interest groups, rather forming an inseparable part of the state system itself.

The degree of government control over interest groups is of particular importance in that conflict. While traditionally, state-society relations have ranged from almost complete control by the government (totalitarian) to almost complete freedom (liberal pluralism), the usual pattern has involved considerably more state control over interest groups' corporatism than in the United States. As a result, interest groups in Latin America have generally behaved differently than those in the United States.

Among the nations at the government-control end of the continuum we find Mexico, where, after the Revolution of 1910, a party apparatus grew up that incorporated all of the major interest groups. Labor was part of the Institutional Revolutionary Party (PRI) through the Confederation of Mexican Workers (CTM), and peasant groups were co-opted through the National Confederation of Peasants (CNC). Any other organized group could affiliate with the National Confederation of Popular Organizations (CNOP)—and most did. While business and commercial groups never became officially part of the PRI, they informally entered into the governing coalition. In the end almost all relevant political groups were part of that coalition, leading eventually to a situation of near stalemate among interest groups.[1]

The Mexican case was the extreme but, as Charles Anderson has argued, before the 1980s no country in Latin America experienced a definitive democratic revolution—that is, a struggle resulting in agreement that elections would be the only legitimate way to obtain public power.[2] In the absence of such a consensus, political groups did not necessarily work for political power by seeking votes, garnering the support of political parties, or making contacts with elected representatives. The groups might instead seek power through any number of other strategies, including coercion, economic influence, technical expertise, and controlled violence.

Any group that *could* mobilize votes was likely to do so for electoral purposes. But since elections were not the only legitimate route to power, the result of any election was tentative. The duration of any government was uncertain, given the varying power of the competing groups and the incomplete legitimacy of the government itself. Without a definitive term of office for any government, political competition became a constant, virtually permanent struggle and preoccupation.[3]

Further, group behavior in Latin America was conditioned by a set of unwritten rules, called by Anderson the "living museum" effect. Before a new group could participate in the political system, it had to demonstrate tacitly both that it had a power resource and that it would respect the rights of already existing groups. The result was the gradual addition of new groups under these two conditions but seldom the elimination of the old ones. The newest, most modern groups coexisted with the oldest, most traditionalist ones.

A related factor was the choice between co-optation and repression. Co-optation worked like this: As new groups emerged as potential politically relevant actors, already established actors (particularly political parties or strong national leaders) sometimes offered to assist them in their new political activities. The deal struck was one mutually beneficial to both: The new group gained acceptance, prestige, and some of its original goals, and the established group or leader gained new support and increased political resources. The established group generally required that the co-opted group drop some of its original goals, leading many observers to criticize the system for not allowing enough change. But those leaders and observers who preferred stability to more fundamental change saw the co-optation system as beneficial to the political system. The uncertainty of such a system was shown in the late 1960s and early 1970s in Colombia, where, during the presidency of Carlos Lleras Restrepo, peasants got some representation through the National Association of Peasant Users (ANUC). This group did not fit with the more conservative ideology of the subsequent president, Misael Pastrana Borrero, and consequently the

ANUC lost all the power and perquisites that it had achieved during the Lleras presidency.

The only other option in this system was to reject co-optation and face repression. In some circumstances, new groups, often more radical, rejected the rules of the game and refused to be co-opted. Instead, they took steps indicating to established groups and leaders that they might act in revolutionary fashion against the interests of the established elites. In the case of a group that violated the ground rules by employing guerrilla tactics or mass violence, for example, an effort would be made by the established interests to repress the new group, either legally, by refusing it legal standing, or through the use of military or police violence. Most commonly, such repression proved successful, and the new group, at least for the time being, disappeared or atrophied, accomplishing none of its goals. The general failure of groups that rejected co-optation and faced repression made co-optation seem more desirable to new groups, since obtaining some of their goals through co-optation was preferable to being repressed.

## The Latin American Revolutions

While co-optation and repression succeeded in maintaining the "living museum" in most cases, there were four cases of revolution, or the elimination of power contenders, as Anderson defines it: the Mexican Revolution of 1910–1920, the Bolivian Revolution of 1952, the Cuban Revolution of 1959, and the Nicaraguan Revolution of 1979. Cases of the reverse process, whereby violence and repression were used to eliminate the newer challenging groups and to secure in power the more traditional system, include Brazil in 1964 and Chile in 1973. Both led to the elimination of independent political parties, student associations, and labor and peasant unions as power groups.

### *The Mexican Revolution*

The Mexican Revolution lasted almost a decade, and as a result Mexico in 1920 had 1 million fewer residents than it had in 1910. Porfirio Díaz, who had been in power since the 1870s, stole the 1910 election, leading to an uprising led by Francisco Madero that toppled the dictatorship and left Madero in the presidency. A right-wing coup ended Madero's term in 1913 and plunged the country into a revolution. Then a newly emergent Constitutionalist movement in the north, led by Venustiano Carranza, gathered an army composed of defecting federal troops and Madero loyalists. This force defeated elements of the old order. In the end, liberal reformers lost control to radicals, who dominated the writing of the nation's new fundamental law, the 1917 Constitution.

The principle articles of the constitution provided that the state offer free, universal, secular education; stipulated that the oil, natural gas, and other subsoil minerals belonged to the state, which could restrict private ownership of these resources; authorized the division of huge estates into small holdings; required protection of workers' rights, including maximum workdays, equal salaries for men and women, and the right of workers to form unions and to strike; empowered legislatures to limit the number of priests in their states and denied the Roman Catholic Church the right to hold property and involve itself in politics; and broached a plethora of approaches—private, public, cooperative, and communal—to economic development.

## *The Bolivian Revolution*

The conflict in Bolivia was essentially between the oligarchy, made up of tin barons and the landed elite, and the new reformists. Although the Bolivian Revolution did not occur until 1952, the process leading to it began in 1940 with the founding of the National Revolutionary Movement (MNR). Attempting to expand its base beyond its middle-class origin, the MNR entered into alliances with the Quechua and Aymara Indians and with the country's largest union, the Bolivian Workers' Central (COB), founded by mine workers in 1944. Both the Great Depression and the Chaco War, in which Bolivia lost extensive territory to Paraguay, allowed the MNR to harness disaffection to a program of nationalism and populism that challenged the dominance of the tin-mining oligarchy, which had already been weakened by the decline of tin prices in the 1930s. The oligarchy also lacked a strong military partner, weakened as the army was by its defeat in the Chaco War.

The increasing militancy of organized labor destabilized the military government between 1946 and 1952. In 1951 the military prevented the MNR candidate from assuming power, despite a landslide victory. Hence in April 1952 the MNR armed Indians and workers and overthrew the military government. The subsequent MNR reforms swept away the old political order based on the alliance between tin barons and the landed elite, imposing in its place a system dominated by a rising urban middle class of professional politicians. This destruction was carried out by eliminating the oligarchy's economic base—the mines and the large landed estates.

The MNR took Mexico's PRI as its model, seeking to channel and moderate the popular social forces unleashed by the revolution. The MNR rewarded peasants for their support and co-opted their vote by giving the vote to illiterates, ending traditional mandatory work for peasants, and by founding a system of unions.

## *The Cuban Revolution*

Fidel Castro came to power in Cuba in January 1959, after a three-year guerrilla war against military dictator Fulgencio Batista. Over the next several years, three things occurred simultaneously: Under Castro the new government developed as a dictatorship, rather than as the democracy that many thought he would bring; Castro shifted gradually from dependence on his guerrilla fighters—the Twenty-sixth of July Movement—to reliance on the Communist Party; and there was a parallel shift from close relations with the United States to amicable relations with the Soviet Union.

In the years that followed, the Castro Revolution completely changed the island. The private property of rich Cubans and foreigners was nationalized, including that of U.S. multinational corporations. Health care and education became free for all. Housing was constructed for the poor, and limits were put on rents charged. Certain groups—including prostitutes, gays, and intellectuals as well as the wealthy—were excluded from the process. A country was constructed that increased the quality of life for the poor, but that in so doing lost all vestiges of democracy.

The Castro Revolution also became the mortal enemy of all U.S. governments from Eisenhower to Clinton. CIA-trained Cuban exiles attempted to overthrow the revolution through the Bay of Pigs invasion of 1961. The Soviet Union placed surface-to-surface missiles in Cuba in 1962, leading in October of that year to the Cuban missile crisis. The Cuban government also assisted revolutionaries throughout Latin America—and even in parts of Africa.

While at this writing the Cuban Revolution still exists and Fidel Castro is in power, the experiment has been less than a complete success. Castro himself called the country a "nation of bums" in the 1980s, simply because Cubans were not working any more than they had to in order to purchase scarce consumer goods. Attempts to industrialize and diversify the economy failed, leading the country to depend on sugar exports more than ever. And then in the late 1980s, when the Soviet Union fell, Cuba lost the massive amounts of Soviet foreign aid that it had grown to depend on.

## *The Nicaraguan Revolution*

A Marxist guerrilla movement, the Sandinista Front for National Liberation (FSLN), had been in existence in Nicaragua since the early 1960s, but in the mid-1970s it began to attract support from wider elements of society. When opposition newspaper editor and political leader Pedro Joaquín Chamorro was murdered in early 1978, popular discontent exploded. Political and economic pressures exerted by business leaders, with some support from the Carter administration, failed to oust President Anastasio Somoza Debayle, and national and international support increasingly coalesced around the Sandinistas. After a prolonged and bloody struggle, the revolutionaries forced Anastasio Somoza Debayle into exile and occupied the capital in July 1979.

Sandinista leaders initially convinced non-FSLN politicians and business leaders to cooperate with the FSLN in forming a broad-based government. But it soon became clear that real power lay with the nine-member Sandinista National Directorate, which was intent on creating a controlled economy, supporting other Central American insurgency movements, and establishing close ties with Cuba and the Soviet Union. Internal political conflict increased, and with the inauguration of the Reagan administration in 1981, the United States began to support armed resistance to Sandinista rule. Known as *contras,* these forces inflicted significant economic damage on the Sandinista regime but were never able to seriously challenge its power.

Elections were held in 1984, but major elements of the internal political opposition boycotted the process, claiming that the political environment created by the regime made effective participation impossible. The FSLN used these elections to consolidate control, installing party leader Daniel Ortega as president and adopting a new constitution that incorporated the aims and principles of a socialist revolution. But a combination of factors—the costs of the ongoing contra war, the impact of a U.S. economic boycott, and the FSLN's own economic mismanagement—ultimately devastated the economy and undermined FSLN efforts to consolidate their control.

That there were only four cases of revolution in an area of twenty nations shows that revolution was not the usual case. Overall, the system of co-optation and repression worked, beginning after independence with a limited traditional oligarchy and continuing until the 1990s with the addition of other social groups.

## The Traditional System

In Latin America today, the traditional system of power contenders and power capabilities is being replaced with liberal democracy. Since some individuals and groups favor the new system while other people and organizations prefer the historical one, throughout Latin America there is conflict between the supporters of the new democracy and the supporters of the traditional system. To further describe that conflict, below we begin by talking about the groups that existed before the transitions to democracy that have occurred since 1980. We then present the newer groups.

After independence, three groups, often referred to as the "nineteenth-century oligarchy," were predominant: the military, the Roman Catholic Church, and the large landholders. Through the process of economic growth and change, new groups emerged: first, commercial elites and later, industrial elites, students, and middle-income sectors; secondly, industrial labor unions and peasants; and most recently, groups representing indigenous people, women, consumers, non-governmental organizations (NGOs), and many others. Particularly since the end of the nineteenth century, the United States has been a politically relevant force in the domestic politics of the Latin American countries. During the Cold War years of conflict with communist countries, the U.S. government seemed most interested in keeping Latin America out of the enemy camp; today, in the absence of international enemies, U.S. governmental concerns have more to do with democracy, human rights, and drugs. Other foreign countries and international actors are now active in Latin America as well.

*The Armed Forces*

During the wars for independence, the Spanish American countries developed armies led by a great variety of individuals, including Creoles, priests, and people of more humble background. The officers did not come from military academies but were self-selected or chosen by other leaders. Few of the officers had previous military training, and the armies were much less professional than the armies we know today.

Following independence, the military sector continued as one of the most important power groups. The national army was supposed to be preeminent, and in some countries national military academies were founded in the first quarter-century after independence. Yet the national military was challenged by other local or regional armies. The early nineteenth century was a period of considerable chaos and limited national integration, with the *patrias chicas*, or regional subdivisions of individual countries, often dominated by local landowners or *caudillos*, "men on horseback," who had their own private armies. This struggle between the central government and its army on the one hand and the *patrias chicas* and local caudillos on the other, with the former winning out in most cases, continues to be a central factor in Latin American development. One of the unanswered questions about Latin American politics, even now, is the extent to which outlying areas of the countries, in the mountains or jungles, are effectively covered by the laws made in the national capitals.

The development of Brazil varied somewhat from the Spanish American norm because Brazil was colonized by Portugal and because it avoided a violent struggle for independence. The Brazilian military first gained prominence in the Paraguayan War (1864–1870). Until 1930, the Brazilian states had powerful militias, some as strong as the national army.

Although nineteenth-century Latin American militaries varied in many ways, our study of them reveals two related themes. First, a variety of militaries, including the national armed forces, became active in politics. At some times they were regional or personal military organizations; at others, they were the military arms of political parties that were taking part in the civil wars frequently waged between rival factions. Second, the national military often played the role of a moderating power—staying above factional struggles and preferring that civilians govern, but taking over power temporarily when the civilians could not effectively rule. This moderating power of the national military emerged in most countries, especially in Brazil, where with the abdication of the emperor in 1889, the military became the chief moderator in the system.

As early as the 1830s and 1840s in Argentina and Mexico, and later in the other Latin American countries, national military academies were established. Their goal was to introduce professionalism into the military, requiring graduation rather than elite family connections for officer status. These academies were for the most part successful in routinizing entry and promotion in the officer corps, and by the 1950s a Latin American officer was promoted to general, with potential political power, only after a career of some twenty years.

This kind of professionalization was designed to make military service a highly specialized career that taught the skills for warfare but eschewed interest in political matters. Officership would supposedly absorb all the energy of its members, and this functional expertise would be distinct from that of politicians. Civilians were theoretically to have complete control of the military, which would stay out of politics. Yet this model of professionalism, imported from western Europe and the United States, never took complete root in Latin America. Usually in the absence of strong civilian institutions, the military continued to play politics, to exercise its moderating power, and to carry out coups d'état.

Latin American countries varied vastly in the importance of their militaries in politics. Three examples, Haiti, Paraguay, and Colombia, will help reveal the range of difference. In the case of Haiti, consolidation of political power in the hands of strongmen made the armed forces the institutional pillar of society. Born out of revolutionary violence and later suffering socioeconomic destruction, Haiti never succeeded in constructing the structures of a civilian society capable of minimizing the rule of force. Part of Haiti's history is the competition between mercenary bands and peasant groups fighting a ragtag military. The deinstitutionalization that has marked portions of the nation's experience was reversed during the U.S. occupation after 1915. Ironically, the most visible product of this period turned out to be the Garde d'Haiti—later transformed into the army. The armed forces remained by default the only organization with a national political reach and a semblance of institutional cohesion.

In Paraguay the military was also deeply involved in politics—culminating with a general who had power for over thirty years. Elected president on August 15, 1954, Alfredo Stroessner of Paraguay was to rule through reelections until February 3, 1989—the longest rule of any leader in the Western Hemisphere until Fidel Castro broke his record in 1995. Stroessner constructed a dictatorship built upon the Colorado Party and the military, with Stroessner as caudillo over both institutions. Unlike most of his South American contemporaries, Stroessner secured a popular base for his dictatorship by bringing the traditional Colorado Party under his formal control. The party was the primary instrument of patronage, and the Stroessner regime penetrated society via a national network of party branches and wards. The Colorados acquired official status, sponsoring Stroessner's eight successive presidential candidacies, building a personality cult for the dictator, and providing a mass base to counterbalance the military. By 1967, Stroessner's purges had made the Colorado Party a monolithic image of Stroessner. The party had immense grassroots support, and was one of Latin America's most powerful, best organized political movements. Stroessner's master plan was to exceed the limitations of Colorado Party ideology. Inspired by Stroessner's authoritarian style and a demagogic, populist tone, *Stronismo* meant loyalty to Stroessner as president and support for an anti-communist National Security Doctrine.

The military was the other key pillar and ultimate guarantor of the system in Paraguay. Loyalty to Stroessner by the officer corps formed the basis of *caudillismo*: personalist rule supported by loyal retainers, rewarded with wealth, power, and patronage. Among officers who could not be bought, Stroessner adroitly appealed to their corporate interests by reorienting their role and mission, assuring them they were needed to guarantee the regime against insurgency. High military spending and public acclaim from General Stroessner added institutional luster to the armed forces. Unlike leaders of neighboring military regimes in the 1960s and 1970s,

Stroessner also shielded the Paraguayan military from controversy, leaving most tasks of repression and human rights abuses to the plainclothes secret police. The Stroessner regime continually utilized the menace of "Communist subversion" to move in preventive fashion against any sign of growing militancy among social groups (peasants, students, workers, the Church) before these could directly challenge the regime. Documentation from the regime's intelligence agencies, discovered in 1992, reveals how pervasively the dictatorship penetrated almost all social institutions and uncovers Stroessner's collaboration with neighboring dictatorships. This evidence belies the stereotypical notion that Stroessner's was simply an old-fashioned, poorly organized personalist tyranny.

In 1988 Stroessner won his eighth reelection to the presidency. The aging dictator's health-related detachment from day-to-day decisionmaking, a growing succession crisis, and a worsening economic situation (growing unemployment and rising inflation) all served to discredit the regime. Paraguayans themselves had also changed. They were a more mobilized, expectant population, less overwhelmingly rural and atomized, and simply less willing to accept political restrictions. Emerging business elites, long tolerant if not supportive of Stroessner's dictatorship as a bargain for peace and prosperity, began to demand a more impartial, more rational, and less politicized bureaucracy and legal system.

The international context had also changed, and Paraguay remained an island of authoritarianism surrounded by new democracies in Argentina and Brazil. These factors triggered divisions in the once monolithic Colorado Party, threatening its symbiotic relationship with the military. A militant faction remained fanatically devoted to Stroessner and ultimately to his son, Air Force Colonel Gustavo Stroessner. The traditionalist Colorados argued for a nonpersonalist transition after Stroessner to ensure continued Colorado Party dominance. A violent coup d'état in early 1989—led by military rebels loyal to traditionalist General Andrés Rodríguez, father-in-law of the dictator's younger son—deposed Stroessner, sending him into exile in Brazil.

Colombia's history is quite different; the Colombian military has been one of the least interventionist and most civilian-controlled in Latin America, and Colombia had only four years of military government in the entire twentieth century. Before the turn of the century there was little professionalism in the armed forces, with a national army supporting the party in power and another army associated with the opposition party. Only in 1907 were army and navy academies founded, with a war college following two years later.

Colombian presidents cannot, of course, ignore the military, which jealously guards the integrity of the military institution and its share of the national budget (although that share has traditionally been one of the lowest per capita in Latin America). Moreover, the Colombian president must take care not to upset the prerogatives of the military. During the first term of President Alfonso López Pumarejo in the 1930s, the president transferred military officers who opposed him to remote posts and promoted those who supported him; during his second term, he was briefly taken prisoner in a coup attempt. During the Conservative years between 1946 and 1953, both Presidents Mariano Ospina Pérez and Laureano Gómez took steps toward making the army an arm of the Conservative Party, a process that politicized the military more than ever and very likely helped precipitate the military coup of 1953, the most recent by the Colombian military against a civilian president.

Throughout Latin America, a change occurred in the role of the military by the late 1950s and early 1960s. The success of guerrilla revolutions in China, Indochina, Algeria, and Cuba led to a new emphasis on the military's role in counterinsurgency and internal defense functions. In addition, Latin American militaries—encouraged by U.S. military aid—began to assume responsibility for civic-action programs, which assisted civilians in the construction of roads, schools, and other public projects. This led to a broader responsibility for the military in nation building.

With its emphasis on counterinsurgency, the new professionalism was a product of the Cold War and may have been more in keeping with the Latin American political culture than the old professionalism was. Military skills were no longer viewed as separate or different from civilian skills such as management, administration, and nation building. The military was to acquire the ability to help solve those national problems that might lead to insurgency—which was, in its very essence, a political rather than an apolitical task. The new professionalism implied that, besides combating active guerrilla factions, the military would take care that social and economic reforms necessary to prevent insurgency were adopted if the civilian leadership proved incapable of doing so. Although the new professionalism was also seen in the developed Western world and in other parts of the Third World, it was particularly prevalent in Latin America, where it led to more military intervention in politics, not less.

The end result of this process is called "bureaucratic authoritarianism":[4] long-term rule by the military institution. Seen especially in Argentina, Brazil, Chile, Peru, and Uruguay, this new form of military government was controlled by the institution as a whole—not by an individual general—

and was based on the idea that the military could govern better than civilians. The bureaucratic-authoritarian military often governed repressively and violated human rights. This period lasted from the mid-1960s through the late 1970s, when the military in many countries was replaced by elected civilian governments.

Generally speaking, Latin American militaries have not been monolithic. For example, in Chile the officer corps has been made up of people from a variety of backgrounds and social groups. It has been said that Chile has a British navy, a U.S. air force, and a Prussian army, the navy having an aristocratic tradition while the army and air force draws many of their officers from the upper middle class. Members of the national police in Latin American countries often come from lower-middle-class backgrounds. The difference during the bureaucratic-authoritarian years was that the entire military establishment agreed to govern together. But that did not mean an end to the tensions among the branches of the military. In Chile, for example, there was tension over Pinochet's dominance and even disagreement over the advisability of his candidacy in 1988. The general, however, was able to use his control of the army to maintain a facade of unity and support.

In the last decade and a half of the twentieth century, the Latin American militaries initiated transitions to constitutionalism, becoming more subservient to civilian control and more supportive of democratically elected presidents. In some countries the transition is near complete. In Argentina, for example, the military's horrible human rights record during its dictatorship of the 1970s and its equally awful mismanagement of the economy left it without friends in any quarter. Public opinion is still hostile toward it, and in the 1990s President Carlos Menem had no difficulty in reducing its budget and its size.

In Honduras, to take a different case, the military was the most powerful actor in politics from the 1960s until the mid-1990s. Since then, its political influence has declined precipitously. Although General Osvaldo López Arellano championed land reform during the 1970s and General Gustavo Alvarez Martínez launched an anti-communist crusade in the 1980s, most Honduran military officers have been motivated by simple greed and lust for power. The armed forces have long been factionalized by personal and generational divisions. The military's loss of resources in the 1990s appears to have exacerbated these splits. President Carlos Flores's dismissal of a number of top officers in July 1999 was intended not only to strengthen civilian control over the military but also to reduce internal factional squabbling between the classes graduating from the military academy. Although it no longer enjoys great political power, the military in Honduras still controls the Military Pension Institute, which is reputed to be the fifth largest financial group in the country. However, President Flores has demonstrated his desire to further reduce the institutional autonomy of the armed forces by ordering that the institute accept the civilian defense minister as a permanent member of its governing board.

Militaries in many other Latin American countries still have great influence, as shown by the Superior War College (ESG) in Brazil. Founded in 1949, the ESG has been a center for training military and civilian elites. Somewhat similar to a think tank except that it is sponsored and subsidized by the government, it has trained several presidents, including Humberto Castelo Branco and Ernest Geisel, and the outstanding presidential adviser Golbery do Couto e Silva. The ESG's slogan, "Security and Development," became a banner for anti-communism during the military regimes, but the organization's scope goes far beyond anti-communism. It has been at the forefront of a great deal of sophisticated economic and strategic planning, and because it stresses its aim to educate and inspire leaders, whether military or civilian, it is likely to remain a formidable institution. Its extensive network of alumni serves as a recruiting source for both government and private enterprise, where many male and female ESG alumni are in key positions.

The transformation to civilian democracy has had its difficulties: The Brazilian military still holds institutional power; the Peruvian military supported a president who dismissed Congress and the courts; the Guatemalan military played a key role in overthrowing a president who attempted the same maneuver; the Venezuelan military put down coups d'état against chief executives but later became disillusioned and supported a new regime; the Ecuadoran military itself carried out such coups; and the Colombian military has failed to act even when key elements of public opinion and the United States ambassador apparently favored getting rid of the elected president. In general the Latin American militaries are now in the process of learning a new role, that of "democratic sustainment," or support for civilian democracy, something that the U.S. Army is trying to help them learn. The U.S. role in this transition is considered in Chapter 9.

It has always been difficult to compare the Latin American militaries cross-nationally. Trying to distinguish civilian regimes from military regimes can also be a meaningless task, or at best a difficult one: Often military personnel have temporarily resigned their commissions to take leadership positions in civilian bureaucracies or as government ministers, or they have held military and civilian positions at the same time. In some cases, an officer resigned his commission, was elected president, and then governed with strong military backing. In almost all instances, coups d'état have not been just simple military affairs; they have often been supported by groups of civilians as well, and it is not unheard of for civilians to take a significant part in the ensuing governments. Sometimes civilians have actually drawn the military into a larger political role. In short, Latin American governments have often been coalitions made between certain factions of the military and certain civilian groups in an attempt to control the pinnacles of power in the system.

Several dimensions of military involvement in politics are seen in the different Latin American countries. The first is the frequency with which the military still forcefully removes chief executives, an activity that in the new millennium seems to be becoming a thing of the past. Second is the extent to which the military leaders have a say in nonmilitary matters. In the past, generals have thus protected their large-landowner friends and relatives, but that phenomenon might also be passing. The final question is, to what extent does the moderating power of the military still obligate it to step in and unseat an incompetent president or one who has violated the rules of the game?

## The Roman Catholic Church

All Latin American countries were historically at least nominally Catholic, although the form of that religion varied from country to country. The Spanish and Portuguese came to Christianize "the heathen" as well as to seek precious metals. In areas of large Amerindian concentrations, religion became a mixture of pre-Columbian and Roman Catholic beliefs. To a lesser degree, Catholicism later blended with African religions, which also existed on their own in certain areas, especially in Brazil and Cuba. In contrast, religion in the large cities of Latin America modernized over time and became similar to that in the urban centers of the United States and western Europe. But in the more isolated small towns, Roman Catholicism is still of fifteenth-century vintage.

The power of the Church hierarchy in politics also varies, both between countries and across time. Traditionally the Church was one of the main sectors of Spanish and Portuguese corporate society undergirding social and political life, with rights and responsibilities in such areas as care for orphans, education, and public morals. During the nineteenth century, the Church was one of the three major groups in politics, along with the military and the landed interests. Yet during the same century, some lay people wanted to strip the Church of all its temporal power, including its ownership of land. Generally speaking, this conflict over the role of the Church had ended in most countries by the first part of the twentieth century.

Historically, the Roman Catholic Church in Colombia was one of the strongest politically in Latin America, in part because of the religious fervor of the people, and in part because of the Church's vast landholdings in the nineteenth century and its continuing alliances with upper-class groups. Until the beginning of the National Front (1958), there was a close relationship between the Church and the Conservative Party. During the early part of the civil war of 1946–1966, for example, bishops threatened to excommunicate anyone who voted for Liberal candidates, and some parish priests refused the sacraments, including burial, to Liberals. This attitude was best exemplified by the 1949 statement of certain bishops forbidding Catholics to vote for Liberal candidates because they might "wish to implant civil marriage, divorce, and coeducation, which would open the doors to immorality and Communism."[5] (All of these things did eventually come to Colombia, divorce arriving last with the Constitution of 1991.)

With the urbanization and secularization of Colombian life, the Church has lost power, and the Church hierarchy is no longer unified in support of the status quo (if, indeed, it ever was). Although growing numbers of priests come from the middle sectors, the upper level of the hierarchy is still dominated by sons of the upper classes. Even these upper- and middle-class priests differ, often not along strict class lines, and there have been priests who were anything but supportive of the status quo. The most dramatic case is that of Camilo Torres, son of a Bogotá upper-middle-class family, a sociologist as well as a priest, who concluded that to be Christian in Colombia was to be a revolutionary. After his failure to change society, either as a priest or as a member of the government's agrarian reform program, Torres left the clergy and went to the guerrilla wars, where he was killed in 1966.

As the new millennium arrived, the Church was changing—especially if by "Church" we mean the top levels of the hierarchy that control the religious and political fortunes of the institution. These transformations were occasioned by the new theologies of the past one hundred years, as expressed through various papal encyclicals, Vatican II, and the conferences of the Latin American bishops at Medellín, Colombia, in 1968 and Puebla, Mexico, in 1979. Significant numbers of bishops and many more parish priests and members of the various orders have subscribed to what is commonly called liberation theology. This theology professes that the Church is of and for this world and should take stands against repression and violence, including the "institutionalized violence"—the life-demeaning and life-threatening violence experienced by the poor of the area. Liberation theology also emphasizes the equality of all believers—laypeople as well as clerics and bishops—as opposed to the traditional stress on hierarchy. In some parts of Latin American, the end result has been new popular-level

People's Churches, with lay leadership and only minimal involvement of priests.

It would be a mistake, however, to assume that all, or even most, members of the Latin American clergy ever subscribed to liberation theology. Many believe that the new social doctrine has involved the Church too deeply in politics. Some are concerned with the loss of traditional authority that the erosion of hierarchy has caused. The various countries of Latin America differ substantially in the degree of Church authority and adherence of the bishops to liberation theology.

The result of these changes is a clergy that is no longer uniformly conservative—a clergy whose members hold a variety of opinions about the Church's role in socioeconomic reform and about the nature of hierarchical relations within the Church. At one extreme of this conflict is the traditional Church elite, usually with social origins in or aspirations to the upper class, still very conservative, and with close connections to other supporters of the status quo. At the other end of this intraclergy conflict are those priests, of various social backgrounds, who see the major objective of the Church as assisting the masses to obtain social justice. Some of these priests are openly revolutionary, fighting in guerrilla wars and participating in revolutionary governments. Other priests fall between these two extremes of political ideology, and still others favor a relaxation of the rigid hierarchy, giving more discretion to local parish priests.

The Church still participates in politics to defend its interests, although in most cases its wealth is no longer in land. Certain Church interests are still traditional, such as providing religious instruction in schools and running parochial high schools and universities, the cost of which has traditionally made higher education possible only for people of middle income or higher, and occasionally attempting to prevent divorce legislation or lobbying to make purely civil marriage difficult. At times, the Church has been a major proponent of human rights, especially when military governments deny or abuse them. A touchier issue is that of birth control, and in most cases the Latin American hierarchies have fought artificial methods. However, in the face of the population explosion, many Church officials have assisted in family-planning clinics, turning their heads when governments have promoted artificial methods of birth control and occasionally even supporting those governmental efforts.

Some analysts feel the Roman Catholic Church in Latin America is no longer a major power contender. They argue that on certain issues its sway is still considerable, but that the Church is no longer as influential politically as the army, the wealthy elites, or the U.S. embassies. They point out that modernization, urbanization, and secularism have also taken their toll on

Church attendance and the political power of the Church. Other analysts, pointing to the People's Churches inspired by liberation theology, argue that the Church or individual clerics are *more* powerful than ever before.

Yet just as the Church had different effects in the colonies in the sixteenth and seventeenth centuries, the Church in each Latin American country at the beginning of the twenty-first century is different. For example, in Venezuela the political role of the Roman Catholic Church continues to be influenced by the trauma of its loss of status in the wake of civil war during the 1860s. No significant recovery of clerical influence occurred until the 1920s, when General Juan Vicente Gómez restored the Church to its central position in education, and from then until the 1958 revolution, the ecclesiastical hierarchy supported opponents of mass political mobilization. However, the second government of Rómulo Betancourt (1959–1964) approached the Church on two of its greatest concerns. President Betancourt assured the hierarchy that governments of his Acción Democrática, or Democratic Action Party (AD), would continue state subsidies to the Church, and he communicated his vision of an educational system in which Catholic schools played an important role. These promises provided resources that allowed the historically weak Venezuelan Church to reach out into civil society. They also transformed the ecclesiastical hierarchy into supporters of democracy.

In the decades since, the ecclesiastical hierarchy in Venezuela has made peace with AD, and public statements by Venezuela's Catholic bishops have emphasized the Church's acceptance by all groups. However, the bishop's enthusiasm for post-1958 democracy was tempered by his acknowledgment of national problems, including corruption, decay in the judiciary, unemployment, inequality, and moral deterioration. A Jesuit think tank leveled especially biting criticism at the two main parties, AD and COPEI, the Social Christian Party. On the other hand, clerical leaders did support the government when it arrested and deported Father Francis Wuytack, a Belgian priest who had organized popular demonstrations against the shocking state of public services in the Caracas barrio of La Vega. As this decision illustrates, the Church hierarchy remained relatively passive until the final year of democratic government, continuing to reject the notion that it had authoritative political solutions or guidance to offer.

Even after the urban riots of February 1989 and two unsuccessful coups in 1992, public statements from the Venezuelan Bishops' Conference continued in this vein—deploring violence, calling for moral renovation, reaffirming support for democracy, and urging a more equitable sharing of the burdens occasioned by the economic crisis. Church leaders gave strong backing to the second government of Rafael Caldera and maneuvered behind the scenes to effect a reconciliation of the president and the COPEI. The bishops viewed the rise of current president Hugo Chávez with alarm, especially his reliance on advice from militant leftists whose antagonism toward the Church was strong. Still, the ecclesiastical hierarchy took no official position in the referendum that approved the 1999 Constitution, although some influential clerics saw its ratification as a first step in depriving the Church of the cultural influence it had enjoyed during the 1958–1999 years.

In Brazil, Vatican II did not mean a radical departure because a number of lay and Catholic groups had already become active among students, workers, and even explicitly political organizations, especially in the 1940s and 1950s. Vatican II did give a new impetus to this change of focus in the Church, however, and it gave Brazilian theologians the opportunity to advocate liberation theology and greater attention to the poor. In the early 1960s this refocusing coincided with President João Goulart's call for populist measures such as agrarian reform and expansion of the welfare system.

At the time of the 1964 military coup in Brazil, the Church was deeply divided, with some members of the clergy supporting Goulart and others seeking to undermine him. Some supported his populism, but others saw it simply as a demagogic appeal. Many people feared that the Church's growing political involvement would entangle it in matters that were not crucial to it as a religious institution. Large parades in the major cities often had the tacit approval and support of the Church, with parishioners calling for moral renewal and decrying the chaos of everyday life. In the Northeast, priests were among those who helped landless peasants take over large and often unused tracts of land. The possibility of a divided Church did not help Goulart's cause.

This split continued after the advent of a military regime in 1964. At first many people continued to be wary of what they perceived as the politicization of the Church. Others, however, increasingly denounced government repression and accused the government of failing to conform to Brazilian tradition by refusing to return to the barracks and give power back to civilians. By the 1970s much of the Brazilian Church hierarchy was behind the effort to organize popular Catholic base communities in order to obtain greater social justice and respect for human rights, and the churches also provided sanctuary for striking workers who were being pursued by the military. With the democratic opening in the late 1980s, Church leaders and laypeople alike were involved in the formation of political parties and eventually in the drafting of the new constitution. Perhaps not by coincidence, the greater political involvement of the Catholic Church occurred simultaneously with a growing challenge to Catholicism by a variety of Protestant sects, especially the more charismatic and evangelical groups and those concentrating their proselytizing efforts on the poor, the illiterate, and the displaced in the urban areas.

In Chile, 76 percent of the populace claim to be Catholic (although the percentage of Chileans who actively practice that faith is much lower), and 12 percent identify themselves as Protestant. There are significant numbers of Lutherans descended from earlier German immigrants, and there is a small Jewish colony and a rapidly expanding number of evangelicals and fundamentalists. Although Church and state have been separated since 1925, the Catholic Church retains considerable national influence. Several of the elite private secondary schools are Church-related, and the Catholic universities in Santiago and Valparaiso are important educational institutions. Church publications are influential, and the declarations of the Chilean Bishops' Conference are given wide publicity by the media. The bishops repeatedly criticized the human rights abuses of the Pinochet government, and the Church-sponsored human rights group, the Vicariate of Solidarity, has actively assisted the victims of repression. In the past a progressive majority has dominated the Chilean Bishops' Conference, but recent Vatican appointments have increased conservative influence. Opus Dei, the conservative lay Catholic group, has become increasingly influential through its university and secondary schools and its support of Joaquín Lavin, the Conservative presidential candidate in the 1999–2000 elections.

Chile still prohibits divorce, but annulments are easy to obtain. The fraud associated with the annulment procedure has led leading Christian Democrats to propose a divorce law, but Church opposition so far has prevented its adoption. During the 1999–2000 campaign, abortion also became an issue as Socialist candidate Ricardo Lagos, an avowed agnostic, successively announced, first, that he favored therapeutic abortion, then, that he would not legislate on the subject, and finally, seeking Christian Democratic votes before the second round, that he favored the right to life from the moment of conception.

In Paraguay the Catholic Church and Church-related groups were a moral voice that challenged the Stroessner dictatorship in the face of unbending repression, calling attention to human rights abuses, corruption, and the extreme concentration of landholdings in the hands of regime elites. Following the 1989 coup, something of a modus vivendi occurred between government and the Church, with the latter remaining a persistent institution calling for social justice in the new democracy. The clergy also remain traditional defenders of Church prerogatives concerning abortion, education policy, and religious orthodoxy.

In Haiti, the Catholic church's influence has rivaled that of the government. After the 1860s the Church fulfilled an important educational mission and provided to isolated communities the rudiments of continuity with and linkage to the outside world. Not surprisingly, the spiritual and political worlds have occasionally overlapped. As recently as the 1960s, President François Duvalier pushed through a "Haitianization" of the clergy, also reviving age-old friction among those seeking appointments in the Church hierarchy. As elsewhere in the region, the clergy in Haiti is split between conservative and liberal contingents, with the liberal influence gaining ground; for example, the Catholic Church played a decisive role in the 1986 ouster of Jean-Claude Duvalier.

The Church in Haiti has become the conduit through which human rights and other sociopolitical concerns are exposed to the world community, sometimes with spectacular results. The grassroots "Ti Legliz" movement in the 1980s provided support for Jean-Bertrand Aristide's arrival to power in 1990 but in turn created deep splits within the Church hierarchy and more generally within Haitian society. The expanding involvement of evangelical and mainstream Protestant denominations at the community level is also changing the sociopolitical landscape historically dominated by the Roman Catholic Church.

One of the most interesting phenomena in Latin America in recent decades has been the explosive growth of Protestant religious groups. In some countries, Protestants number upwards of 25–35 percent of the population; in Guatemala, a Protestant general became president and dictator for a time. The fastest growing of these sects are the evangelical Christians, not the older, mainline churches. Protestantism is associated with the middle class, making it socially attractive, and it is also identified with a strong work ethic, as it encourages its members to work hard and save. However, until recently, the Protestant groups have generally not become politically active.

## Large Landowners

In all the countries of Latin America, save Costa Rica and Paraguay, the colonial period led to the establishment of a group of landowners who had received large tracts of lands, called *latifundios,* as royal grants. With the coming of independence, these *latifundistas* were more powerful than before and developed into one of the three major power groups of nineteenth-century politics. This was not to say that they operated monolithically; in some cases they were divided against each other.

In recent times, such rifts have still remained among the large landowners, usually developing around issues of crop production. They might disagree, for example, on a governmental policy favoring livestock raising to the detriment of crop planting. However, the major conflict has been between those who have large tracts of land and the many landless peasants. When faced with this conflict, the various groups of large landowners tend to coalesce. In some cases, there is an umbrella organization to bring all of the various producer organizations together formally; in other cases, the coalition is much more informal.

In the 1960s, the pressures for land reform were considerable, both from landless peasants and from foreign and domestic groups who saw this type of reform as a way to achieve social justice and to avoid Castro-like revolutions. In some countries, such as Mexico, land reform had previously come by revolution; in others, such as Venezuela, a good bit of land had been distributed by the government to the landless; in still others, the power of the landed, in coalition with other status quo groups, succeeded in blocking any but a semblance of real land reform.

In many Latin American countries, especially those in which the amount of arable land is limited and where the population explosion has led to higher person-to-land ratios, the issue of breaking up large estates will continue for the foreseeable future. Given the historic power of the landed elite, such change is likely to be slow in the absence of something approaching a social revolution. This was the case, for example, in El Salvador in the 1970s, when a military government tried to carry out a land reform that was then effectively blocked by the landowners' organization.

Since the 1960s, with Latin America rapidly urbanizing and in some areas even industrializing, rural issues have become less important. The traditional landowners still dominate in some countries, but in others, power has passed to newer commercial and industrial elites. And although land reform may still be necessary in some areas, with such large percentages of the population moving to the cities, many of the major social issues have become urban rather than rural.

## Other Major Interest Groups

### Commercial and Industrial Elites

Although not part of the traditional oligarchy, commercial elites have existed in Latin America since independence; one of the early political conflicts was between those who wanted free trade—the commercial elites and allied landed interests producing crops for export—and those who wanted protection of nascent industry—the industrial elites with allied landed groups not producing for export. In recent decades the strength of these commercial and industrial groups has steadily grown.

For example, in Colombia the National Association of [Large] Industrialists (ANDI), founded in 1944, is the leading advocate of free enterprise among the national organizations. More than five hundred of the largest industrial enterprises are affiliated with ANDI throughout the entire country, and its power in Colombian politics comes from the wealth and prestige of its members and the tendency of its interests to overlap with those of large agricultural producers. Furthermore, industrialization has been a goal of Colombian presidents for half a century, especially during the National Front period and since.

With the exception of Colombia, the real push for industrialization in Latin America did not come until the Great Depression and World War II, when Latin America was cut off from trade with the industrialized world. Before those crises, industrial goods from England and the United States were cheaper, even with transportation costs and import duties, than locally produced goods.

Then, between the mid-1930s and the mid-1980s, Latin American countries experienced import-substitution industrialization—that is, they began producing goods that formerly were imported from the industrialized countries. These include light consumer goods, some consumer durables including products assembled for North American and European automobiles, and some other heavy industrial products such as cement and steel. Because the need to import capital goods under ISI necessitated an increase in foreign trade, there no longer was much conflict between commercial and industrial elites, who agreed that expanded trade and industrialization go together.

Examples of this consensus abound: In Honduras the leading organized interest groups of the economic elite, such as the Coordinating Committee of Agricultural, Commercial, Industrial, and Financial Associations (CACIF), lobby in much the same way as any special interest group in the United States does, and they are very successful at working within the system to get their policy preferences enacted. They are well organized, legitimate in the eyes of most military and government leaders, and deeply involved in most national policy issues that arise. Likewise, Uruguay has well-organized economic interests, including national associations of ranchers and business enterprises.

Chilean industry and agriculture were fundamentally altered by the policies of the Pinochet government. Inefficient companies protected by high tariffs went bankrupt, while new export-oriented businesses in everything from kiwis to rose-hip tea flourished. Ownership became concentrated in a few financial-industrial groups after the sell-off of state enterprises following the coup. Some of the largest groups went bankrupt and were taken over by the government in 1982; along with many other state enterprises, their holdings have since been privatized, and new or restructured conglomerates have emerged. Chilean industry and business are formally organized into the Society for the Promotion of Manufacturing (SOFOFA) and the Confederation for Production and Commerce.

In agriculture, too, a process of restructuring has taken place in Chile. Seized lands were returned to their owners after the coup, and the land that had been legally distributed into cooperatives under the 1967 agrarian reform law was divided into individual holdings. Many of the small holdings were later sold to agribusiness entrepreneurs, resulting in a process of reconcentration—though often the new owners did not belong to the traditional landowner families. The landowners are organized into the National Agricultural Society (SNA), one of Chile's oldest interest groups. Other groups such as shopkeepers, truckers, and others are represented by organized occupational groups—as are lawyers, doctors, nurses, and architects. In keeping with the government's individualist philosophy, however, its legal right to set rules for the professions was withdrawn in the late 1970s, and state influence has diminished since the return to democracy.

Since the 1980s, neoliberal presidents and policies in Latin America have pushed for more foreign commerce, and for a world with lower trade barriers or none at all. In this globalization of the Latin American economies, foreign trade is of utmost importance. Hence, the commercial elites are equally important. As the Chilean experience shows, however, globalization is not without its price; economic groups are being restructured as previously protected businesses face the international environment.

Argentina during the Menem years of the 1990s illustrates some of the dynamics of these changes. In the past, pressure groups filled the political vacuum left by an unstable government that had been based on weak parties. The old populist system, with its protected "hothouse" economy, nurtured well-organized interests—the military, labor, and business—that had an important stake in government policy. Business bribed, labor struck, and the army rolled out the tanks. Now all that has changed. All of the traditional interest groups have undergone change. As discussed above, the military's human rights abuses under the dictatorship and its failure to manage the economy left it open to severe criticism. During the Menem years, public opinion was still hostile toward the military, and Menem had no difficulty in reducing its power. Labor was split between those who continued to vote Peronist and those who rejected Menem as a traitor to the movement. Moreover, changes in Argentina's leading capitalist enterprises, which are no longer labor intensive, reduced the size of the blue-collar workforce. Fewer workers were unionized and more were self-employed.

Unemployment and underemployment also kept wages depressed and discouraged labor militancy. Finally, downsizing the state and selling off its many companies undermined the position of those business owners who previously depended on government subsidies and contracts. Other entrepreneurs prospered in the new free market system, building huge conglomerates and squeezing out their smaller competitors. Like labor, businesses in a free market prosper or decline according to which sector of the economy they are in, and whether they can compete in an open economy.

One factor that complicates our consideration of the industrial elite is its relationship with the landed elite. In some countries, such as Argentina, the early industrialists were linked to the landed groups; later, individuals who began as industrialists invested in land. The result was two intertwined groups—a marriage of older landed wealth with newer moneyed wealth, with only vague boundaries separating them and with some families and individuals straddling the line. All these groups were opposed to agrarian reform.

In Colombia, development has depended not only on industrialization but also on exporting coffee to earn the foreign exchange needed to purchase capital and other goods. Therefore, it is not surprising that another important group is the National Federation of Coffee Growers (FEDECAFE). Founded in 1927, this private association is open to all people interested in developing the coffee industry, but the association tends to be dominated by the larger coffee producers and exporters. The relations between the coffee growers and the government are close.

Industrialists and commercial elites are highly organized in various chambers of commerce, industrial associations, and the like; they are strategically located in major cities of Latin America; generally they favor a status quo that benefits themselves; and they are often the driving forces in Latin American economic development. For these reasons and because they are frequently represented in high official circles, no matter what government is in control, they are very powerful. Neoliberalism and globalism have made these groups even more essential to the functioning of the economy, and hence also to the political system.

## The Middle Sectors

Although the Latin American countries began independence with what was basically a two-class system, there have always been individuals who fell into the middle ranges, neither very rich nor abjectly poor. During the nineteenth century these few individuals were primarily artisans and shopkeepers and, later, doctors and lawyers. The emergence of a larger middle sector was a twentieth-century phenomenon, associated with urbanization, technological advances, industrialization, and the expansion of public education and the role of the government.

All of these changes necessitated a large increase in the number of white-collar, managerial workers. New teachers and government bureaucrats constituted part of this sector, as did office workers in private businesses. In addition, small businesses grew, particularly in the service sector of the economy. Many of these new nonmanual professions have been organized into teachers' associations, small-business associations, lawyers' associations, organizations of governmental bureaucrats, and so forth. Military officers, university students, political party officials, even union and peasant group leaders are also usually considered middle class.

The people who filled the new middle-sector jobs were the product of social mobility, some coming from the lower class and others "fallen aristocrats" from the upper classes. Thus, they lacked a prolonged, common historical experience. Their varied backgrounds, together with their numerous and heterogeneous occupations, temporarily impeded the formation of a sense of common identity as members of a middle class. Indeed, in some of the countries of Latin America, this identification has yet to emerge, partly because the middle-class ideal is still to be a part of "society," preferably high society.

In those Latin American countries in which a large middle-sector group has emerged, certain generalizations about its political behavior can be made. In the early stages of political activism, middle sectors tended to form coalitions with groups from the lower classes against the more traditional and oligarchic groups in power. Major goals included expanded suffrage, the promotion of urban growth and economic development, a greater role for public education, increased industrialization, and more social-welfare programs.

In the later stages of middle-sector political evolution, the tendency has been to side with the established order against rising mass or populist movements. In some cases the middle-class movements have allied with landowners, industrialists, and the Church against their working-class partners of earlier years; in other cases, when the more numerous lower class seemed ready to take power on its own, the middle sectors were instrumental in fomenting a middle-class military coup, to prevent "premature democratization,"[6] that is, a democratic system that the middle sectors could not control. Over the years, then, the politics of middle-class movements have changed dramatically.

Since the status of the middle class varies greatly in Latin America, a number of factors should be considered as we examine this group in the individual countries. These factors include the size of the middle-income group, its cohesion and its relationships with political parties, and the degree of self-identification as members of a "middle class." Only time will tell whether the behavior of the middle sectors will change because of the years of bureaucratic authoritarianism, whether the middle sectors will serve as a new, invigorated social base for democracy, or whether they will continue to ape and imitate the upper class and thus perpetuate an essentially two-class and polarized social structure. Currently the middle class favors stability at all costs and sees democracy as the best way of achieving and continuing stability, but one can easily imagine circumstances, such as economic or political crises, under which this stance could change.

## Labor Unions

From its inception, organized labor in Latin America has been highly political. Virtually all the important trade unions in the area have been closely associated with a government or a political party or a strong leader. Some labor unions have grown independently until they are co-opted or repressed. In other cases, labor unions can trace their origins directly to the efforts of a party, leader, or government.

Several characteristics of the Latin American economies have favored partisan unionism: Unions appeared relatively early in the economic development of the region, in some cases earlier than in the United States and western Europe. Latin American unionism was influenced by ideological currents that came from southern Europe, including anarchist and Marxist orientations. The labor pool of employables has been much larger than the number who can get the relatively well-paid jobs in industry. An employer in that situation can almost always find people to replace striking workers unless the strikers are protected by a party or by the government. Finally, inflation has been a problem in Latin America in recent decades, making it important for unions to win the support of other political groups in the continual renegotiation of contracts to obtain higher salaries, which often need governmental approval.

The Latin American legal tradition required that unions be officially recognized by the government before they could collectively bargain. If a group could not obtain or retain this legal standing, it had little power. Labor legislation varied greatly, including codes that made it mandatory that labor organizers be employed full time by the industry that they were organizing, limiting the power of those unions that lacked leaders who were paid full salary to spend part of the working day in union activities. This was only one of the many governmental restrictions placed on labor unions. In general, there is now a movement away from corporate or state control of unions toward greater freedom of association, often accompanied by conflict between the state and the free unions.

Some union organizations have been co-opted by the state; others remain outside the system. Key issues that still remain include the extent to which workers are organized, how the labor code is used to prevent or facilitate worker organization, the nature of the relationships between labor and the political parties or between labor and the government, and the extent to which unions have been co-opted or repressed.

The history of labor in several Latin American countries illustrates all of these issues, beginning with Argentina during the Perón years, when organized labor had great political power. What really distinguished Perón from the other military officers and politicians was his ability to speak the language of the masses. He quickly perceived that the great number of uprooted, impoverished urban slum dwellers were looking for a protector. In 1943 he also took over the hitherto neglected Department of Labor and made it his political vehicle; backed by the power of a military dictatorship, he began vigorously applying labor legislation that had long lain dormant on the books. Old-age pensions, accident and health insurance, annual paid vacations, factory safety codes, minimum wage and maximum hour legislation—all were expanded and enforced. Employers who had fought the creation of labor unions were now forced to accept them. All of this made Perón enormously popular with the working classes.

Some of Perón's fellow officers began to get alarmed, however, and at the beginning of October 1945, they moved to oust him from all his government posts and put him under arrest. To their astonishment, the masses rallied to Perón. Crowds of people marched in from the working-class barrios to fill the great square in front of the presidential palace, where they demanded Perón's return. Unwilling to fire upon the women and children in the crowd, the military finally gave in and brought Perón to the balcony. From then on—for the next thirty years—he was to be the dominant figure of Argentine politics.

In Colombia, two dominant labor federations emerged, each one affiliated with one of the traditional political parties. The Confederation of Colombian Workers (CTC) was founded in 1935 during the first presidency of Alfonso López Pumarejo, and it flourished during the rest of the Liberal hegemony (1930–1946). The Union of Colombian Workers (UTC) was founded in 1946, during the Conservative presidency of Mariano Ospina Pérez, and by the late 1950s it had become the largest labor federation in the country. By the 1980s this distinction went to the Syndical Confederation of Workers of Colombia (CSTC), which at times caused more difficulties for the government than either the CTC or the UTC. Although the latter two owe much to their respective parties, neither is formally a part of its party, as such membership is prohibited by law. Further, not all of the local labor unions in Colombia are organized into one of these national federations; more locals remain unaffiliated with any national federation than there are in any of the three major groups.

In Colombia, labor legislation has generally been unrestrictive. Labor leaders are required to be full-time workers in their industries, a requirement that if enforced would militate against unionization. Colombian political leaders accept active unions but do not hesitate to enforce the law more rigorously against unions with communist ties or those that take actions that the government has prohibited. In 1985, for example, the CSTC lost its right to exist for six months for participating in a general strike previously declared illegal by the government of Belisario Betancur.

In Chile organized labor changed dramatically with the Pinochet coup of 1973. The Marxist-dominated Unitary Labor Central (CUT) was dissolved, and its leaders were persecuted. The Christian Democratic labor leaders were treated less severely. In the late 1970s union activity was renewed, and in the early 1980s a National Labor Command (CNT) was organized, later renaming itself the Unitary Labor Central (CUT). With the return of democracy, new legislation expanded the rights of labor, but it is much weaker than before 1973; only 16 percent of wage earners are unionized, and industry-wide bargaining is still prohibited, although this may be changed by the government of Ricardo Lagos.

In Venezuela, labor and peasant groups crystallized in the late 1930s and 1940s. Reformist party leaders organized labor and peasant organizations as part of their mobilization strategy to win political power. Labor and peasant leaders, as well as professionals, were subject to party discipline through the period from 1958 to 1999. Failure to comply with instructions from the leaders of one's political party risked sanctions, and possibly expulsion from the party. Because most members of these interest groups also belong to disciplined, mass-based parties, a leader's expulsion from the party usually entailed loss of leadership within the interest group. Building on these connections, the two main parties, AD and COPEI, extended power sharing into worker, peasant, and professional organizations. Following approval of the 1999 Constitution, however, organized labor opened negotiations with the government and offered to eliminate the influence of the traditional political parties in the unions in return for recognition by the national government. President Chávez appears to have accepted this arrangement.

## Peasants

The term "peasants" refers to many different kinds of people in Latin America. Some prefer the Spanish term *campesinos* (people who work in the *campo*, the countryside) rather than the English term with its European-based connotations. The major groups of campesinos, who vary in influence from country to country, include indigenous groups who speak only their native language or who are bilingual in that language and Spanish or Portuguese; workers on the traditional hacienda who till the fields in return for wages or part of the crops, with the owner as a *patrón* to care for the campesinos or, more frequently, a manager-patron who represents the absentee owner; workers on modern plantations, receiving wages but remaining outside the older patron-client relationship; persons with a legally held small landholding, or *minifundio*, large enough to provide a bare existence; persons who cultivate small plots, with no legal claim, perhaps moving every few years after the slash-and-burn method and the lack of crop rotation deplete the soil; and persons who are given a small plot of land to work by a landowner in exchange for work on a large estate.

What all of these campesinos have in common, in the context of the extremely inequitable distribution of arable lands in Latin America, is a marginal existence due to their small amount of land or income and a high degree of insecurity due to their uncertain claims to the lands they cultivate. It was estimated in 1961 that over 5 million very small farms (below 30 acres or 12 hectares) occupied only 3.7 percent of the land, while, at the other extreme, 100,000 large holdings (more than 1,500 acres or 607 hectares) took up some 65 percent of the land. Three decades later, the situation had changed little. At least 80 million people still lived on small landholdings with insufficient land to earn a minimum subsistence, or they worked as agricultural laborers with no land at all.

For many of these rural masses, the only real chance of breaking out of this circle of poverty is to move to an urban area, where they face another—in some ways even worse—culture of poverty. For those who remain on the land, unless there is a dramatic restructuring of ownership, the present subhuman existence is likely to continue. Moreover, as commercial agriculture for export has increased in many countries, more campesinos have been shoved off the fertile lands into the sterile hillsides, where their ability to subsist has become even more precarious.

Rural peasant elements have long been active in politics, but only recently have they been mobilized as independent, organized interest groups. The traditional political structure of the countryside was one in which participation in national politics meant taking part in the patronage system. The local patrons, besides expecting work on the estate from the campesino, expected certain political behavior. In some countries, this meant that the campesino belonged to the same political party as the *patrón*, voted for the *patrón's* party on election day, and, if necessary, served as cannon fodder in its civil wars. In other countries, the national party organizations never reached the rural levels, and restrictive suffrage laws prevented the peasants from participating in elections. In either pattern, for the peasants there was no such thing as national politics—only local politics, which might or might not have national party labels attached to the local person or groups in power.

This traditional system still exists in many areas of Latin America. But since the 1950s, signs of agrarian unrest and political mobilization have been more and more evident. In many cases, major agrarian movements were organized by urban interests—mainly political parties and especially those of the Marxist Left. Some of these peasant movements have been openly revolutionary, seeking to reform and improve the land tenure system and to reform significantly the entire power structure of the nation. Their strategies include the illegal seizure of land, the elimination of landowners, and armed defense of the gains thus achieved. We could call these revolutionary-agrarian movements. Less radical were the movements that sought to reform the social order partially, eliminating a few of the most oppressive effects of the existing power structure that weighs on the peasant subculture, but without threatening the power structure as such.

Though the peasants are numerically the largest group in Latin America, they remain politically weak, a characteristic that is likely to continue as their numbers dwindle through urbanization. Their weakness is due to their lack of organization. Because land and labor patterns vary widely, peasant populations are dispersed throughout the countryside, and illiteracy rates are high, it is difficult to mobilize a strong peasant movement. Their distance from the urban centers of power also makes it hard for peasants to effect change. Meanwhile, millions of peasants are leaving the land, migrating to cities or the United States, and thus weakening the peasant movements still more.

## The United States

Another important power element in Latin American politics is the United States. This influence can be examined in terms of three interrelated interest groups: U.S. governmental representatives, U.S.-based private business, and U.S.-dominated international agencies. At times these groups work in harmony, and at times they operate at cross-purposes.

*U.S. Government.* The U.S. government has been interested in the area since Latin America's independence. Its first concern, that the new nations not fall under the control of European powers, led to the Monroe Doctrine in 1823. Originally a defensive statement, the doctrine was later changed through various corollaries to adopt a more aggressive tone, telling the Latin Americans that they could not sell strategically located lands to governments or businesses outside the hemisphere, and that the United States would intervene to collect debts that Latin American countries owed to powers outside the hemisphere (the Roosevelt Corollary).

At various times, the U.S. government has set standards that must be met before full diplomatic recognition is accorded to a Latin American nation. This de jure recognition policy, most memorable in the Wilson, early Kennedy, and Carter administrations, has favored elected democratic governments, exclusion of the military from government, and a vision of human rights that should be applied in Latin America. At other times the United States has pursued a de facto recognition policy, according full diplomatic standing to any government with effective control of its nation's territory.

Whatever recognition policy is followed, the U.S. ambassador to a Latin American country usually has had impressive powers. One ambassador to pre-Castro Cuba testified that he was the most influential individual in the country, second only to the president. This ambassadorial power has typically been used to support or defeat governments, to guide governmental policy of the Latin American countries in certain directions, and often to assist U.S.-based corporations in the various countries. In Central America during the 1980s a number of U.S. ambassadors played this strong proconsular role, as did the ambassador to Colombia during the government of Ernesto Samper (1994–1998) because of the president's suspected ties to drug groups.

With the end of the Cold War, U.S. interests in Latin America changed. The United States spent less diplomatic effort in the region, and its primary diplomatic priority changed from prevention of communism to support for democracy. For example, the interest of the United States government in Honduras declined dramatically after the end of the Central American civil wars. Nevertheless, the U.S. embassy has remained a major political actor there, with the U.S. ambassador playing a key role in promoting the rise of the antimilitary movement in the early 1990s. In addition, U.S. economic leverage has helped international financial institutions force Honduran presidents to adopt unpopular neoliberal economic programs throughout the last decade. The U.S. government also continues to be an important source of resources. It contributed substantial funds to the international rebuilding effort that began after Hurricane Mitch and sought to influence the national reconstruction plan.

*U.S. Business.* Since their early beginnings, particularly in agribusinesses such as sugar and banana production, U.S.-based corporations in Latin America have grown dramatically. In addition to agribusiness, U.S. corporations later entered the extractive field (petroleum, copper, coal, iron ore), retailing, the service industry (accounting firms, computer outfits), and communications (telephones, telegraphs, computers). The most recent kind of U.S. corporation introduced into Latin America has been the export-platform company, which takes advantage of the low wages in Latin America to produce manufactured goods, such as pocket calculators in Mexico or baseballs in Haiti, mainly for export to the industrialized world.

U.S. corporations in Latin America often enter into the politics of their host countries. Some of the interventions have been flagrant: bribing public officials to keep taxes low or threatening to cut off the import of a country's products if certain policies were or were not approved by its government. But most political activities of U.S. corporations are now much less dramatic. Latin Americans in the host countries almost always buy stock in the U.S. corporations and hold high managerial positions in them. In many cases, U.S. businesses purchase Latin American corporations, the leaders of which then work for the new owners. The result is that the U.S. corporation develops contacts, obligations, and political influence similar to those possessed by domestic interest groups.

In the 1980s there were some indications that the era of large U.S. corporate holdings and hence influence in Latin America might be in decline. Many U.S. corporations, as a result of the recession and the debt crisis in Latin America, pulled up stakes, withdrew their capital, and moved on to more profitable and stable areas. Yet by the end of the 1980s the business climate improved: Latin American governments rescinded restrictions on maximum profits and repatriation. In the 1990s, as Latin American economies recovered, massive U.S. capital flowed back into the area.

*International Agencies.* Most foreign-aid and international lending organizations have been dominated historically by the United States. These agencies, especially active during the 1960s when large amounts of aid began to flow to Latin America, have included the U.S. Agency for International Development (USAID), which administers most U.S. foreign aid, the World Bank, the IMF, the Inter-American Development Bank (IADB), and a variety of others. The World Bank and the IMF are international agencies, the products of post–World War II agreements between the countries of the West. However, the United States donates significant amounts to the agencies and so has a powerful representation on their governing boards, and the interests of the agencies closely converge with those of the U.S. government, so in effect the IMF and the World Bank can be considered U.S.-oriented groups, as can the IADB. Although the IADB was established at the request of Latin American leaders who wanted a lending agency less dominated by the United States, in effect the IADB cannot lend to countries if the U.S. government does not want it to. Because economic development has been a central goal of the Latin American states since the 1980s, because loans for that development have come predominantly from the USAID, the World Bank, and the IADB, and because those loans are contingent many times on the adoption of a monetary policy judged healthy by the IMF, the officials of these four groups have much influence in the day-to-day policies of the governments of the area.

This power of the lending agencies was probably greatest during the 1960s, and then again during the debt crisis of the 1980s. The USAID had the most leverage or "conditionality" during the Alliance for Progress. This foreign-aid program, initiated by the Kennedy administration, attempted to change Latin America dramatically in a decade. Even though it failed, it did lead to large loans from the U.S. government, substantial progress in some fields, and much influence for the local USAID representatives in the domestic politics of some Latin American countries. Some USAID representatives sat in on cabinet meetings and wrote speeches for and gave advice to the local officials with whom they worked, and others largely ran the agencies or even ministries of the host government to which they were assigned.

The Alliance for Progress was terminated by the Nixon administration. Further, the power of the World Bank waned in the wake of the energy crisis among the industrialized economies of the West, brought on by the Arab oil embargo of 1973–1974 and the growing power of OPEC. At this time, it was the private banks, recycling petrodollars, that provided loans to the Latin American countries. However, with the debt crisis of the 1980s, the IMF and its Bretton Woods partner, the World Bank, regained much of their lost power.

In the 1990s, the economies of Latin America were facing crisis, and in the importing nations, protectionist measures were implemented. The Latin American nations were clamoring for access to U.S. markets, and they were likely to be partially successful in that quest. The U.S. government also initiated a new massive assistance program for Central America and the Caribbean designed to restore solvency and preserve stability.

More recently through NAFTA, protectionism started to end tariff barriers in Mexico, and the Initiative of the Americas promised a free trade area for the whole hemisphere. This promise was slowed down when the U.S. Congress ended "fast track" legislation supported by the Clinton administration.

Foreign aid has dwindled with the end of the Cold War. However, in June 2000 the U.S. Congress approved aid of US$1.3 billion over two years for Colombia in an effort to stop the production of cocaine and heroine in that country. With passage of this aid package, Colombia became the largest recipient of U.S. foreign aid in the world, passing Israel and Egypt.

The influence of groups directed and oriented by the United States—including diplomatic, business, and foreign assistance groups—is considerable in Latin America. This does not mean that their power has been equal in all the Latin American countries. When a Latin American country is important strategically to the United States and when U.S. private investors have established a large investment in the national economy (as in Cuba before Castro), U.S. elements are extremely powerful in domestic Latin politics. This does not mean that the United States cannot have considerable influence in domestic politics in distant countries with relatively little private investment by U.S. corporations, as the example of Allende's Chile showed. But with the end of the Cold War, U.S. foreign policy interest in Latin America, with the exception of a few countries, has certainly waned; private transactions are now more important than official ones.

## New Interest Groups

Many new interest groups have appeared in Latin America in recent decades. In many countries they are collectively called "civil society," with the clear implication that anyone who wants to form a group can—without the permission of the government. This is in clear contrast to the earlier system of corporatism, in which the state regulated all interest groups. As we have seen in the case of Honduras, civil society has become stronger in recent years as many new types of interest groups have become active. Human rights groups such as the Committee for the Defense of Human Rights in Honduras (CODEH) have joined traditional actors like the Roman Catholic Church to entreat government officials to respect civil and political liberties. In addition, the Church has backed the economic demands of newly organized urban slum dwellers and indigenous communities. Student groups and women's organizations also have become more active in the last two decades. In the late 1990s, unions, peasant organizations, slum dwellers, and indigenous groups have increasingly resorted to direct actions such as road blockages and marches on the capital to press their demands for governmental assistance and cooperation.

Looking at Latin America as a whole, we see three kinds of new groups that seem of particular importance: indigenous groups, women's groups, and NGOs.

*Indigenous Groups*

Indigenous peoples constitute 10 percent of the total population of Latin America, or an estimated 40 million people. In some four hundred distinct groups, they are concentrated in southern Mexico, Central America, and the central Andes of South America.[7] In these regions, they comprise between 10 and 70 percent of the population. Some individual language groups have more than 1 million members. A dozen groups have more than a quarter million members each, making up some 73 percent of the total indigenous population of the region. Finally, two hundred groups have fewer than one thousand members each.

In the 1970s, Amerindian populations in Latin America began an unprecedented political mobilization to protect their lands and cultures from the increasing influence of multinational companies, colonists, the state, and other intruders. In the 1980s, they placed a greater emphasis on the recuperation of ethnic identities and the construction of a pan-indigenous cultural identity. Although local approaches and objectives vary throughout the region, Latin American indigenous peoples share the common goal of ending ethnic discrimination and revoking the assimilationist policies of Latin American governments.

An example of the conflict between native and mainstream interests occurred in April 2000, when celebrations marking Brazil's 500th anniversary were marred by violence as police clashed with thousands of Indians and their supporters, who were protesting what they called Portugal's "invasion." Police used clubs and tear gas to break up the protests, and there were unofficial reports that fifteen Indians were injured. More than one hundred forty people were detained and charged with disturbing public order, said Gustavo Rios, the local public security chief. "We came to march in peace," said Nailton Pataxo, a demonstration leader. "It is the government that is meeting us with violence. This is the true face of Brazil, 500 years later."[8]

Contemporary Latin American indigenous organizations seek equal and legitimate status for their cultures, their forms of social organization, and their laws and the means to facilitate and control their own economic development. Their ultimate goal is the transformation of what they view to be a discriminatory, homogeneous state into a "plurinational state," one whose institutions reflect the cultural diversity of Latin American society. In the 1990s, seven Latin American states—Bolivia, Colombia, Ecuador, Mexico, Nicaragua, Peru, and Paraguay—recognized a milder version of this claim, declaring their societies "pluricultural and multiethnic." At the same time many individuals of indigenous background continue to follow the traditional assimilationist strategy for integrating themselves into Hispanic culture: professing Catholic faith, speaking Spanish or Portuguese, and adopting Western clothes and manners.

The main component of rising indigenous nationalism is the struggle for territorial, political, economic, and cultural autonomy. Until 1987, only the Kuna of Panama enjoyed what could be described as territorial and political autonomy. In 1987 the Nicaraguan government established two multiethnic autonomous regions to accommodate claims of the Miskito and other smaller indigenous groups, who had joined the anti-Sandinista counterrevolutionary guerrilla movement supported by the United States. Although the autonomous regions were largely a failure in terms of indigenous peoples' aspirations, their establishment inspired indigenous organizations throughout Latin America to make similar claims.

At this point only Colombia's indigenous population has achieved politico-territorial autonomy. The 1991 Colombian Constitution elevated indigenous reserves *(resguardos)* to the status of municipal governments, recognized traditional indigenous leaders as public authorities, accepted indigenous customary law as public and binding, with some restrictions, and provided guaranteed indigenous representation in the national Senate. Following constitutional reforms or peace agreements with armed groups concluded in the 1990s, the governments of Bolivia, Ecuador, Guatemala, and Mexico are currently negotiating some type of politico-territorial autonomy arrangements with indigenous groups.

The most notable case of an Amerindian leader in national politics was in Bolivia. In 1993 Víctor Hugo Cárdenas, an Aymara linguist who had been in the Bolivian Congress between 1985 and 1989, was elected vice president. Although that victory was noteworthy, as was the participation of two indigenous members in the Colombian constituent assembly in 1991, in neither country have these indigenous leaders continued in high positions in government. Also important was the candidacy of Alejandro Toledo in the 2000 presidential campaign in Peru. Although he withdrew his candidacy before the final vote, alleging that a fair election was not possible given the shady actions of President Fujimori, the important thing is the viability of an indigenous candidate, who grew up shining shoes in the port city of Chimbote, one of sixteen brothers and sisters whose father was a bricklayer and whose mother sold fish in a street market.[9]

## Women's Groups

There is little doubt that women in Latin America are making progress in their efforts to ascend to leadership positions in government, politics, and civil society. One recent study shows that women have greater representation in Latin American national congresses (15 percent) than they do in the U.S. Congress (12 percent), and although women's representation in national cabinets in Latin America is lower (11 percent) than in the United States (21 percent), their numbers overall are second only to the Nordic countries of Europe, where women fill 36 percent of congressional positions and 35 percent of cabinet positions.[10]

Politicized women's groups grew in number in the 1970s and 1980s, playing a prominent role in the struggles against authoritarian rule and raising hopes that the return to democracy would generate greater opportunities for women in the region. The consolidation of democracy was expected to promote greater participation of women in the formulation and execution of laws governing their lives. Although a decade later the number of women in leadership positions remains low, their situation does appear to be improving. In the 1990s, women's presence in the public spheres of politics, the economy, and society has grown. Such growth is a reflection of social changes such as women's entry into the labor force, rising educational levels, and changing attitudes about the role of women. Most notably, two women have been elected president in their countries—Violeta Barrios de Chamorro in Nicaragua in 1990 and Mireya Moscoso de Gruber in Panama in 1999.

Figures on women's representation in politics show that their opportunities to exercise leadership are greater outside the main centers of power—in the lower levels of organizational hierarchy, outside the capital city area, and in less powerful governmental agencies. For example, in the judicial branch of government, women make up 45 percent of the trial judges but only 20 percent at the appellate court level, and virtually zero at the supreme court level.

One important consequence of women's organizing has been the adoption of quota laws, intended to increase women's representation in political office. After pressure from organized women's groups, Argentina, Bolivia, Brazil, Costa Rica, the Dominican Republic, Ecuador, Panama, and Peru have passed national laws requiring political parties to reserve 20 to 40 percent of candidacies for women. Of course, that women are nominated does not necessarily mean that they are elected.

Despite the growth of women's representation, the women's movement has appeared to some observers to be increasingly fragmented and to have lost its visibility and capacity for political intervention. One reason for this is the weakening of cross-class links between middle-class feminist groups and working-class women's groups. In an important sense, this is a consequence of democracy: As the access of middle-class women to power has increased with the expansion of democracy, their connections with the lower classes seem to have grown weaker. Another split is between more traditional, social service–oriented women's groups and their often more militant, younger, feminist sisters.

In El Salvador, in preparation for the 1994 elections, a broad coalition of women's organizations hammered out an agenda called "Mujeres '94," which it asked every party to adopt as part of its platform. Only the National Liberation Front of Farabundo Martí (FMLN) agreed, thanks to the pressure of its women members. The FMLN also adopted a rule that one-third of all its candidates for office be women. This was a compromise; the women had pushed for 50 percent. By the mid-1990s, women's organizations had formulated legislative bills to guarantee workers' rights in the U.S.-owned assembly plants, or *maquiladoras*; to make rape a public crime; to make it possible to press rape charges without a witness (other than the victim); to put the burden of proof in paternity suits on men; and to ensure that articles protecting women are placed in the new penal code. None of these issues had been on the national agenda five years earlier. Further, a new education law guaranteed equal access for girls, barred discrimination based on gender, and proscribed sexist stereotypes in textbooks. Another new issue, which had been absent from the national agenda at the end of the war, was violence against women. Before the end of the decade the issue was receiving attention in the major newspapers.

In Ecuador in the last decade of the twentieth century, dozens of organizations were established to deal with women's issues. Yet progress toward sexual equality in politics, the workplace, and at home has been painfully slow, which is ironic, given the fact that Ecuador was the first South American country to give women the right to vote.

The obstacles to women's full participation in Latin American democracies and economies stem from women's weaker social position, from the traditional gender roles, cultural expectations, and stereotypes that were built around these roles, and from blatant sex discrimination. Few Latin American countries have made efforts to make motherhood and work compatible. No Latin American country has a comprehensive child care policy. Although most countries have laws that require businesses that employ twenty or more women to have on-site day care facilities, these laws are rarely enforced. Pregnancy discrimination is widespread in the region: some companies require a pregnancy test or a sterilization certificate as a condition of employment, and some employers fire women once they become pregnant. Although both actions are against the law, once again, the laws are seldom enforced. Cultural changes resulting from improvements in women's lives will help erode such discriminatory barriers, but this is likely to happen only in the very long run.

*Non-Governmental Organizations*

Another newer group of organizations are the non-governmental organizations (NGOs), which are increasingly important actors in Latin American politics.[11] While some are specific to individual countries, others are dedicated to a general theme (e.g., the environment, human rights, family planning, education, democratic elections) and have offices in many Latin American countries. Some NGOs are transnational, with headquarters in one country and activities in many countries. Amnesty International, the Environmental Defense Fund, and the International Red Cross are transnational NGOs that have influenced recent events in Latin America. Local NGOs are shaping contemporary politics, too. For example, NGOs are providing community services in Mexico, raising racial consciousness in Brazil, extending credit to poor people in Colombia, defending indigenous peoples in Bolivia, and asserting women's rights in Argentina. Unlike interest groups, NGOs do not focus their activities exclusively on governments. They also work to change the policies of international institutions such as the World Bank, the practices of private businesses and entire industries, and the behavior of individuals and society as a whole.

*Other Groups*

There are many other kinds of organized groups in Latin America. Colombian society, for example, is replete with groups at the upper- and middle-income levels—merchants, large landowners, teachers at all levels, doctors, and so forth. It is no exaggeration to say that any Colombian of middle or upper income fits into an occupational group that is organized, has a license allowing it to operate (a requirement that is presumably becoming less important as the region liberalizes), and has at least some power in the political process. The National Association of Land Users (ANUC) includes about half a million small farmers who use government services, and the National Agrarian Association, an affiliate of the UTC, claims to represent one hundred thousand campesinos. But these organizations are incomplete, established by members of the elite, and divided along traditional party lines. Moreover, the great majority of the Colombian people—especially campesinos and the urban poor—is not well organized.

Civil society groups have proliferated in Colombia during the last decade, but their impact on politics is weaker compared to those in other Latin American countries. Moreover, most Colombian NGOs tend to represent the interests of professionals rather than the huge portion of Colombians who are marginalized socially, economically, and politically.

In Brazil, besides the churches, the unions, the military, the business sector, and the political parties, a number of other organizations act as pressure groups, with varying degrees of success. Thus during the military regimes, the Brazilian Order of Lawyers actively sought the restoration and enforcement of legal protections. The Brazilian Press Association opposed censorship and publicized the plight of persecuted Brazilian journalists, bringing their cause to international attention. A number of women's organizations emerged, particularly after the International Women's Year in 1975. The National Student Union, abolished at the time of the 1964 coup, continued to operate underground and sometimes even fairly openly. Race-based groups, a novelty in Brazil, also emerged and began to demand real versus theoretical equality for all. More focused and militant African-Brazilian groups have also coalesced in more recent years. Benedita da Silva Sampaio, a former Workers' Party (PT) federal senator and vice governor of Rio de Janeiro, is probably the best known voice for these groups. With the *abertura* (the "opening") and the holding of elections, literally hundreds of groups organized around issues, policies, and candidates and began to compete, though most of them have been transitory.

But not all groups in Latin American countries are peaceful organizations that follow the law. The Shining Path guerrillas still exist in Peru, albeit in weakened form, and the Zapatista Front of National Liberation (FZLN) is occasionally somewhat active in the Chiapas area of Mexico. However, in the new millennium, it is Colombia that is most affected by outlaw groups.

Three major new groups challenge the traditional Colombian system: the guerrillas, the drug dealers, and the paramilitary groups. The guerrillas desire a new system with more power and benefits for the common people; the drug dealers seek to carry out their illicit trade with impunity; and the paramilitary groups seek a country that is free of guerrillas and poor people making demands. All three groups use violence in seeking their goals; all three are willing to kill the "innocent" rather than let the "guilty" live.

## Conclusions and Implications

The preceding discussion has focused on the diversity of politically relevant groups in Latin America and their use of various means to secure and retain political power. Yet we should introduce at least two other themes, which tend to complicate the picture.

First, it should be noted that the urban poor, or lumpen proletariat, who fall outside the labor unions, have not been included in the discussion. Their absence reveals one of the biases of the system. Traditionally, a necessary first step in attaining political relevance is becoming organized. This means that *potential* groups, especially poorly educated and geographically dispersed ones like the peasants and the urban poor, face difficulties in becoming politically relevant, since they have difficulties in organizing themselves or in being organized from the outside. These tend to be the weakest groups in politics, although often they are numerically the largest.

Second, not all politically relevant groups fall into the neat categories of this chapter. Anthony Leeds's research in Brazil has shown that (at least in small towns, probably larger cities, and even perhaps the whole nation) a politically more relevant series of groups is the patronage- and family-based *panelinhas* ("little saucepans").[12] The same kind of informal family-based networks exist in other countries as well. These groups are composed of individuals of common interest but different occupations—say, a doctor, a large landowner, surely a lawyer, and a governmental official. The *panelinha* at the local level endeavors to establish and control contacts with the *panelinha* at the state level, which might have contacts with a national *panelinha*. Of course, at the local level there are rival *panelinhas*, with contacts with like-minded groups at the state level and with participants in the national patronage system as well. As is generally the case with such patrimonial relations, all interactions (except those within the *panelinhas* themselves) are vertical, and one level of *panelinha* must take care to ally itself with the winning *panelinha* at the next higher level if it wants to have political power.

Similar research in other countries has revealed a parallel pattern of informal, elitist, familial, patronage politics. Whether called the *panelinha* system in Brazil or the *camarilla* system in Mexico, the process and dynamics remain the same. The aspiring politician connects himself or herself with an aspiring politician at a higher level, who has connections with an aspiring politician at an even higher level, and so forth on up to an aspiring candidate for the presidency. If the person in question becomes president, the various levels of camarillas prosper; if he remains powerful without becoming president, the camarillas continue to function in hopes of success at the next presidential election. But if the aspiring top-level candidate is disgraced, dismissed from the official party, or dies, the whole system of various levels of camarillas connected with him disintegrates. The camarilla system operates outside the formal structure of interest groups and parties described here, even while overlapping with them.

This discussion of *panelinhas* and camarillas raises again the question of whether U.S.-style interest groups and political parties are operating and are important in Latin America. The answer is, They are and they aren't. In the larger and better-institutionalized systems, the parties and interest groups are often important and function not unlike their North American or European counterparts. But in the less institutionalized, personalistic countries of Central America, and even behind the scenes in the larger countries, it is frequently family groups, cliques, clan alliances, and patronage networks that are more important—often disguised behind the appearance of partisan or ideological dispute. One must be careful therefore not to minimize the importance of functional, operational party and interest-group systems in some countries, while recognizing that in others, politics is often carried out via the less formal networks—or a complex combination of the two: party and interest group politics on the one hand and informal, familial, and patronage-based politics on the other.

## Notes

1. Raymond Vernon, *The Dilemma of Mexico's Development* (Cambridge, Mass.: Harvard University Press, 1963).

2. Charles Anderson, *Politics and Economic Change in Latin America: The Governing of Restless Nations* (Princeton: Van Nostrand, 1967), especially chapter 4.

3. Ibid.

4. See David Collier, ed., *The New Authoritarianism in Latin America* (Princeton: Princeton University Press, 1979).

5. Quoted in John D. Martz, *Colombia: A Contemporary Political Survey* (Chapel Hill: University of North Carolina Press, 1962), p. 84.

6. José Nun, "The Middle Class Military Coup," in *The Politics of Conformity in Latin America*, ed. Claudio Véliz (London: Oxford University Press, 1967), pp. 66–118.

7. Much of this section is based on the article written by Donna Lee Van Cott for the *Encyclopedia of Nationalism*, volume 2, to be published in 2000.

8. "Brazil 500th Anniversary Protested," Associated Press, April 22, 2000.

9. *New York Times*, April 5, 2000.

10. Mala N. Htun, "Women's Political Participation, Representation and Leadership in Latin America." November 1998. Issue Brief from Women's Leadership Conference of the Americas Web site. Online. Available at: *www.thedialogue.org/htunpol.html*. October 15, 2000. Much of the analysis that follows is based on this source.

11. This section is based on suggestions from Vanessa Gray, a recent graduate of the doctoral program in political science at the University of Miami.

12. Anthony Leeds, "Brazilian Careers and Social Structure: A Case History and Model," *American Anthropologist* 66 (1964):1321–1347.

# 6

# Political Parties

In a democracy such as the United States or the countries of western Europe, the chief executive is usually elected as the candidate of a political party. In contrast, Latin American political parties have traditionally been only one of the groups involved in choosing the chief executive—probably no more (and perhaps less) important than the army or the economic oligarchy. Elections have not been the only legitimated route to power in the region, nor have the parties themselves been particularly strong or well organized. They have been important actors in the political process in some of the more or less democratic countries, representing the chief means to gain high office. But in other countries, the parties have frequently been peripheral to the main focal points of power, and the electoral arena has been considered only one arena among several. Many Latin Americans have viewed political parties as divisive elements and hence have not held them in high esteem.

Many of the groups described in the previous chapter have often joined together in political parties in their pursuit of governmental power. As a result there has been a myriad of political parties in the history of Latin America. Indeed, someone once quipped that to form a political party, all you needed was a president, a vice president, a secretary-treasurer, and a rubber stamp. (If times were bad, you could do without the vice president and the secretary-treasurer!)

Nevertheless, if democracy is really coming to Latin America, political parties are likely to be important. In this chapter we review the parties in the various nations, describing the past when necessary but focusing most of our attention on conditions in the first years of the twenty-first century.

## The Liberal and Conservative Parties

The first political parties were generally founded by elite groups in competition with other factions of the elite. Mass demands played only a small role, although campesinos were sometimes mobilized by the party leaders, often to vote as they were instructed or to serve as cannon fodder. In many cases, the first cleavage to inspire the establishment of parties was that between individuals in favor of free trade, federalism, and anticlericalism—the Liberals—and those who favored protectionism for nascent industry, centralism, and clericalism—the Conservatives. This cleavage existed in many countries (Colombia, Mexico, and Chile, for example), although in most these original party divisions have long since disappeared, replaced by others.

In many countries, the Liberal-Conservative cleavage resulted in frequent civil wars between the two parties. When religion became involved, the intensity of those wars increased. This was true in the case of Mexico, where in the 1850s President Benito Juárez and his Liberal followers attacked the institutions of Spanish origin that were bound to authoritarianism—Roman Catholicism and corporatism. These reformers promulgated the 1857 Constitution, which stressed individual rights and laissez-faire economics over corporatism, separated church and state, called for secular schools, strengthened the legislative branch at the expense of the executive, terminated the exemptions from civil jurisdictions enjoyed by soldiers and clerics, and attempted to dismantle most of the corporatist aspects of Mexican life arising from the colonial era. These changes sparked a bloody three-year "War of Reform" that ended with a Liberal victory in 1861. At this point, Napoleon III of France answered the pleas of local Conservatives and imposed Maximilian of Austria as emperor of Mexico.

## Colombia

Colombia is the only Latin American country where the initial Liberal-Conservative cleavage has been maintained, albeit with some changes in the 1990s. Founded in the 1840s, the two parties have garnered strong emotional support but have not been very well organized. The parties never approached the "mass party" model, nor indeed did they need such a structure to mobilize votes. Rather the frequent civil wars between the parties (six in the nineteenth century and two in the twentieth) resulted in intense political socialization in the countryside, where members of families in one party were robbed, raped, and killed by the other party, creating martyrs. Finally in 1957 the leaders of the two parties agreed to put conflict behind them and to establish a coalition government; only then did the intensity of party ties begin to diminish. The coalition, called the National Front, was based on a system whereby the presidency would alternate between the two parties and all legislative and appointive positions would be divided equally between them. This arrangement lasted for sixteen years.

One key fact of Colombian partisan life in the past thirty years has been the dominance of the Liberal Party. All public opinion polls have indicated that a majority of the electorate identifies with this party. Throughout the National Front period, more people voted for Liberals for Congress than for Conservatives. Colombians did elect Conservative presidents in 1982 and 1998; however, even in elections that they lost, Liberals had more votes than Conservatives. In 1982 the Liberals presented two candidates, Alfonso López Michelsen and Luis Carlos Galán, and this division allowed Conservative Belisario Betancur to win with 46.6 percent. Betancur thus became the first Conservative elected in a competitive election since 1946, but his election also exemplified the historical tradition of victory for a minority party when the majority party is split between two candidates.

By 1991 a new constitution, requiring an absolute majority, was adopted. Under this constitution Conservative Andrés Pastrana won election in 1998, no doubt in large part because of reaction to the drug-related presidency of Liberal Ernesto Samper. The Liberals, however, won the majority of seats in the Congress. Furthermore, in both 1986 and 1990, Liberal candidates had won the presidency by overwhelming margins—Virgilio Barco in 1986 and César Gaviria in 1990. In the first election requiring a majority, in 1994, Liberal Ernesto Samper won, although it took him two rounds to do so.

## Honduras

Since the 1980 Constituent Assembly elections restored electoral politics, Honduras has held five consecutive general elections. With the exception of 1985, all of these contests have taken place without serious irregularities. The Liberal Party won control of the presidency and National Congress in every election except that of 1989, when charismatic Rafael Leonardo Callejas led the National Party to victory.

The traditional Honduran Liberal Party (PLH) and the Honduran National Party (PNH) are both nonprogrammatic patron-client political machines primarily organized to capture state jobs and resources. Each party is divided into several personalist factions. Competing faction leaders are key national actors who wield great influence over candidate selection and patronage distribution. Both parties choose their presidential candidate by means of a national primary election that pits factional contenders against one another.

Both the Nationals and the Liberals are centrist, multiclass parties that benefit from widespread hereditary party affiliation. The party identification balance currently favors the Liberals. Voter support for the Liberals usually is strongest in urban areas such as San Pedro Sula and in the more developed north coast departments, although the PLH also has some traditional rural strongholds. The PNH finds its greatest electoral strength in the more rural, less developed parts of the country, but it also has built a sizable urban following and frequently does well in Tegucigalpa. There are other political parties in Honduras as well, but they are smaller and less influential; in the most recent national elections in 1997, three minor parties won only 4.5 percent of the presidential vote and 9 percent of the legislative vote.

*Uruguay*

Uruguay began its history of party politics with a similar two-part division: like Liberals and Conservatives elsewhere, Colorados and Blancos fought numerous civil wars in the nineteenth century. Then in the twentieth century, Colorado José Batlle y Ordóñez, elected president both in 1903 and in 1911, established the framework for modern Uruguayan politics and government. After defeating the Blancos in the last of the civil wars, he established a political compromise with them, based on the concepts of parity and coparticipation. That parity recognized the "legitimate" interests of the Blancos in the rural departments where they were strong, and Batlle all but ceded these departments to their control. He also accepted their participation in the national government, proportional to their share of the national vote, and allowed them a share of government patronage and revenues.

The Blanco party won only three subsequent national elections, in 1958, 1962, and 1989, and it became a virtually permanent minority. Batlle's Colorado Party consistently attracted more voters nationally than did the Blancos, but it was willing to share with the Blancos the exercise and benefits of power. The 1952 Constitution went so far as to formalize coparticipation by awarding two of five positions on the boards of all state enterprises to the minority party.

The electoral system that Battle designed incorporated parity and coparticipation both within and between the nation's political parties. It regulated parties, elections, and the distribution of legislative seats, and it established *lemas* and sub-*lemas*, which were equivalent to parties and party factions. Anyone could form a sub-*lema*, acquire formal identification within a *lema*, and in effect create a personal political organization with its own separate identity. The electoral strength of a sub-*lema* and its leader added to the total vote of a *lema,* which in turn determined both *lema* and sub-*lema* legislative representation. Ambitious political leaders were thereby permitted into the political system and could exercise political influence proportional to their ability to attract votes. Their organizations were integrated into the larger *lema,* or party coalition, and they had a vested interest in the success of other sub-*lemas,* which they nonetheless campaigned against since their representation was determined by their share of the cumulative vote for the *lema.* Presidential elections under this system in effect combined a primary election with a general election. But the winner was the candidate of the sub-*lema* with the most votes within the *lema* with the most votes—meaning that someone could be elected president even if someone else had more votes.

Over the years, the Blanco-Colorado monopoly ended, and the constitution was changed to end the system of *lemas* and sub-*lemas* (see Chapter 8).

## The Emergence of New Parties in the Twentieth Century

With the disappearance of intense partisan socialization and the acceleration of social and economic change in most countries of Latin America, the emergence of new social strata in the 1920s and 1930s led to the founding of new political parties. Some of these attracted the growing middle sectors, who were quite reformist in the early years but later changed to a more conservative and even right-wing position as they became part of the system. In other cases, new parties included elements of the working classes and had a more radical agenda, calling for a basic restructuring of society. Some of these originally radical parties were of international inspiration; most Latin American countries have had communist and socialist parties, which have varied in their effectiveness and legality. Other radical parties were primarily national in origin, albeit with ideological inspiration traceable to Marxism.

### *Chile*

This general pattern is perhaps clearest in the case of Chile. Before the military coup d'état of 1973, the political spectrum was split roughly into thirds between Right, Center, and Left. The Right was dominated by the National Party, which had been formed in 1966 by a fusion of the old Liberal and Conservative Parties, broadly representative of large landowners and large businesses. By ending the separation of the old Liberal and Conservative labels, the National Party showed that the issues of the nineteenth century were no longer salient enough to keep apart people who agreed on most socioeconomic issues.

The most significant centrist party was the Christian Democratic Party. The government party in the 1960s and the largest party before the 1973 coup, it maintained its internal structure and its youth, student, labor, and women's branches during the period of military rule. Drawing its political philosophy from Catholic social thought, the party supported the protection of human rights and the development of a welfare state with a mixed economy. The Christian Democratic Party was supported by the Chilean middle class, but it had an important labor component as well as support in the urban shantytowns. Another centrist group was the Radical Party, which before 1964 had been the fulcrum of the Chilean center. It was seriously weakened by frequent splits on the Left and Right, but it survives even today, with small numbers of supporters in the provincial towns and rural areas.

The Left was dominated by the Socialist and Communist Parties, which were allied in the Popular Action Front (FRAP) between 1957 and 1970 and formed the core of President Salvador Allende's Popular Unity coalition between 1970 and 1973. In the late 1960s the Socialists adopted an increasingly radical position, so that during the Allende period they represented the most "revolutionary" party in Allende's coalition, often taking positions to the left of Allende himself. The Communist Party was outlawed after the coup, and many of its leaders were persecuted and murdered, but it continued to be active among workers and in the shantytowns. Although between 1957 and 1973 it endorsed the *via pacifica,* the peaceful road to power, its support has largely been lost. As discussed further in Chapter 8, matters changed greatly after the end of the Pinochet dictatorship, with the election of Socialist Ricardo Lagos as president in 2000.

*Peru*

Another initially radical party was the American Popular Revolutionary Alliance (APRA). Founded in Mexico in 1923 by exiled Peruvian student leader Víctor Raúl Haya de la Torre, who hoped to have similar party organizations throughout Latin America, APRA soon became a genuinely mass-based political party in Peru, with a fully articulated, if not completely coherent, ideology. APRA was strong enough to determine the outcome of all open elections held in Peru after 1931, although until the 1980s, the military ensured that the party would never rule directly.

Although APRA has had a strong populist appeal through the years, the party's importance for Peruvian politics rests on its reformist ideology and its organizational capacity. Between the 1920s and the 1950s, APRA absorbed most of the newly emerging social forces outside of Lima in the more integrated parts of the country, especially labor, students, and the more marginal middle sectors of the north coast. The party's appeal thus helped prevent the emergence of a more radical alternative. Furthermore, even though APRA was an outsider for most of the period from its founding to 1956, it never overthrew the system. In a policy typical of the Latin American system of co-optation and repression, at key junctures the party leadership sought accommodation and compromise in order to gain entry to the system, even while it continued to resort to assassinations and abortive putsches in trying to impress political insiders with its power.

Between 1956 and 1982 APRA became a centrist-conservative party willing to make almost any compromise to gain greater formal political power. In 1956 APRA supported the conservative Manuel Prado in his successful bid for a second term as president and worked with him throughout his administration. When APRA won open elections in 1962 but was just shy of the constitutionally required one-third of the votes, the party agreed to share governing power with its former archenemy, the dictator Manual A. Odría.

At this point the military intervened and ran the country for a year before facilitating elections, which were won by its favored candidate, Fernando Belaúnde Terry of Popular Action (AP). During the Belaúnde administration (1963–1968), APRA formed an alliance with Odría forces in Congress to attain a majority and block or water down many of AP's reforms. Although such actions discredited APRA in the eyes of many people, the party remained Peru's best-organized and most unified political force.

At the beginning of the new millennium, party politics in Peru are quite fragmented. Furthermore, the party system is dominated by personalism across the entire ideological spectrum. AP was split into pro- and anti-Belaúnde factions; although it came back together with the Belaúnde victory in 1980, it was divided again after 1985. APRA became divided after the death of Haya de la Torre in 1979, but the progressive faction regained control after the election of Haya's protégé, Alán García, as party head in 1982 and president in 1985. The García government's problems after 1987 contributed to new divisions within APRA.

The small but influential Christian Democratic Party (DC) was also divided: Between 1988 and 1992, a tiny leftist faction was allied with the United Left Party (IU), while a larger conservative group, the Popular Christian Party (PPC), formed part of the Democratic Front (Fredemo). The PPC reclaimed its independent status after the alliance with Fredemo collapsed.

The Marxist political movement in Peru was founded by José Carlos Mariátegui, a leading Peruvian intellectual of the 1920s who started what became the Communist Party of Peru (PCP). The party retained its Moscow-oriented core but fragmented almost endlessly into Maoist, Castroist, and Trotskyite splinter groups. All shared pieces of equally divided urban and rural union movements, though the PCP controlled the largest portion (about 75 percent). With economic crises and economic liberalization initiatives, union membership has declined from about 30 percent of the formal work force in the early 1980s to less than 10 percent in the late 1990s, and membership in these parties has likewise declined.

The public prominence of the leftist movement Shining Path after 1980 and its recourse to guerrilla tactics evoked an almost universally negative response from Peru's Marxist Left; most of the Communist movement is not inclined to pursue its goals through violence. During the 1980s, when the majority of its members were joined, however loosely, in the IU, the Communists were the second largest political force in terms of electoral support, peaking in the 1986 municipal elections at 31 percent of the total vote. This rise of an organized Left operating within rather than outside the political system was one of the positive legacies of the ten-year military rule, or *docenio*, but IU's breakup in 1989 sharply reduced the role of the Left in national party politics after 1990.

Throughout the 1990s Peru's parties have become even more divided and numerous. In part this is because several parties exercised power carelessly in the 1980s, thus discrediting them in the public view. Another reason is that party leadership has continued to place personal over institutional concerns. The decline of independent parties is also the result of the adroit manipulation of new political rules and procedures by the governments of Alberto Fujimori, thereby encouraging weak new political groups rather than strong parties. In 1995, fourteen groups contended for the presidency and twenty for Congress, with traditional parties capturing less than 15 percent of the valid vote. The 1998 municipal elections consisted largely of "flash" parties that appear only for the vote itself, with eighty-nine of ninety-four Lima districts and department capitals won by candidates from these groups. This dispersal of politics toward personalities rather than organizations favors the most visible political personality, President Fujimori himself. In 2000 he won a disputed election and later announced his early resignation, as discussed in Chapter 8.

*Venezuela*

Inspired by Haya de la Torre's APRA, several young Latin Americans founded similar national parties, the most successful of which was Democratic Action (AD) in Venezuela. Many of AD's programs have been advocated by numerous other parties of this type, including the Party of National Liberation (PLN) in Costa Rica and the National Revolutionary Movement (MNR) in Bolivia, as well as parties in Paraguay, the Dominican Republic, Guatemala, Honduras, and Argentina. APRA came to power in Peru in 1986, although founder Haya was no longer living.

In most cases in Latin America, the Aprista parties were led by members of the middle sectors, and they received much of their electoral support from middle- and lower-class ranks. Only in Venezuela, the Dominican Republic, and Costa Rica did the Aprista parties come to more than temporary power, and then in a much less radical form. They favored liberal democracy, rapid reform, and economic growth.

AD and COPEI made up the core of Venezuelan democracy between 1959 and 1999. Both had strong indigenous roots, although AD kept ties to the European Social Democrats, and COPEI to the Christian Democrats. For many years AD and COPEI efficiently performed the functions most often associated with modern political parties: mobilizing supporters, recruiting individuals to fill government positions, mediating the demands of competing interests, and creating symbols that strengthened support for the political regime. But at the beginning of 2000, voter identification with the AD barely topped 10 percent and COPEI teetered on the brink of extinction. They were shells of the organizations that had institutionalized and dominated Venezuela's competitive, centrist party system. Meanwhile, a populist leader, Hugo Chávez, governed on the basis of charisma and personality, almost entirely independent of political parties.

*Costa Rica*

In Costa Rica in 1947 José "Pepe" Figueres began to build the National Liberation Party to compete in the 1953 elections, which he won handily. From that moment through 1998, the presidency has oscillated between control by the PLN and control by a coalition of opposition forces.

**Other Parties**

Other parties in Latin America have been based on the leadership of one or few persons or the military. Quite often the traditional "man on horseback" has been more important than the program of a party. This tradition of the caudillo was present in the case of Brazil, where Getúlio Vargas founded not one but two official political parties; in Ecuador, where personalistic parties have been strong contenders for the presidency; in revolutionary Nicaragua, where collegial leadership during the insurrection and the early years of power gave way to a clear leader, Daniel Ortega; and in Communist Cuba, where in the 1960s the party was more Castroist than Communist. In other countries, such as El Salvador, the military played an active role, at times even setting up its own political party, which always won.

## El Salvador

Political parties did not emerge in El Salvador until the 1920s; until that time, the presidency was passed around among members of the upper class. The first modern party was the El Salvadoran Communist Party (PCS), which was founded during a period of political liberalization in the late 1920s by Augustín Farabundo Martí, the educated son of a mestizo landowner. The party participated in the January 1932 municipal and Assembly elections, although the government was unwilling to recognize PCS victories at the local level. Another left-leaning party, the Salvadoran Labor Party, had won the 1931 presidential election, but its candidate, Arturo Araujo, a progressive oligarch, was toppled in a coup d'état a month before the local elections. The coup and the uprising brought Araujo's vice president, General Maximiliano Hernández Martínez, to power.

The PCS was banned after the uprising, and for the next thirteen years, the Pro-Fatherland National Party, a personalist party created by Hernández Martínez, became the only official political party allowed. Hernández Martínez's excesses led to his overthrow in 1944, the first of five coups that would be attempted by dissident elements in the army over the next thirty-five years. The official party changed names several times, finally becoming the National Conciliation Party (PCN) in 1961, and it dominated elections until 1982. This ensured that its candidate, always an army colonel or general, was always elected president.

A political opening in the early 1960s led to the creation of several opposition parties, most notably the Christian Democratic Party (PDC), a social democratic party, the National Revolutionary Movement (MNR), and the Nationalist Democratic Union (UDN), which was the legal front for the PCS. The Christian Democrats won increasing numbers of seats in the Assembly during the 1960s, then the mayoralties of the three largest cities, including San Salvador, in 1968. These gains, together with smaller gains by other opposition parties, presented a growing challenge to the PCN. Success also suggested to the members of opposition parties that if they managed to win a national majority, they would be allowed to win the chief prize—the presidency. That was not to be, as was borne out by the 1972 presidential elections, in which a civilian coalition comprised of the PDC, MNR, and UDN was denied electoral victory by the army.

This event led many Salvadorans to conclude that electoral politics would get them nowhere, and they opted for a revolutionary alternative that included both political and military dimensions. During the 1970s five revolutionary organizations—which had their roots in peasant uprisings of the previous century, in labor organizations of the 1920s, and in the PCS—began working among urban laborers and peasants. Divided over ideology and strategy for a decade, the five came together in the FMLN in October 1980. In January 1981 the FMLN initiated military operations that would plunge El Salvador into eleven years of civil war.

In the 1984 presidential elections, the man who had been denied his victory in 1972, José Napoleón Duarte, defeated Roberto D'Aubuisson, a former member of the military with ties to death squads. This and subsequent elections in the next decade, for the Legislative Assembly in 1985, 1988, and 1991 and for president in 1989, provided a "democratic government" that rarely exhibited the conditions of a functioning democracy: freedom of speech, the media, and party organization; freedom for interest groups; the absence of state-sponsored terror; the absence of fear and coercion among the population; and subordination of the military to civilian rule. Indeed, the armed forces, formally removed from power, continued to wield effective political control of the country. Duarte, elected on a platform of economic reforms and peace negotiations with the FMLN, delivered neither while presiding over one of the most corrupt governments in Salvadoran history. The PDC, rent by internal squabbles, split again in 1988 and lost the 1989 presidential election to a center-right Nationalist Republican Alliance (ARENA) candidate, Alfredo Cristiani, who successfully negotiated an end to the civil war.

## Brazil

The largest country of Latin America, Brazil, really had no competitive elections before 1946. Long controlled by the strong states of Minas Gerais and São Paulo and by a dictator, Getúlio Vargas, the citizens were untrained for democracy, especially one with dozens of political parties and thousands of candidates organized through a proportional representation system. Between 1946 and the military takeover in 1964, there were three principal political parties. Two of these were founded by Vargas: the Brazilian Labor Party (PTB) and the Social Democratic Party (PSD). The latter attracted the middle-income supporters of the former dictator, while the former contained his supporters from organized labor. The third major party was the Nationalist Democratic Union (UDN), much like the PSD with the important difference that its members were middle-income individuals who were anti-Vargas.

Vargas was elected president in 1950, but he committed suicide when it appeared that the military was planning to overthrow him again. One of his protégés, João Goulart, was elected vice president in 1960 and became president when President Jânio da Silva Quadros resigned. On April 1, 1964, the military carried out a coup against Goulart, beginning fifteen years of bureaucratic authoritarian rule.

At first the military regime allowed no political parties. Eventually, however, it saw the need to promote a more "popular" image and decreed that there would be two political organizations, the progovernment National Renovating Alliance (ARENA) and the opposition Brazilian Democratic Movement (MDB). These were coalitions of parties and ideological factions rather than U.S.-style political parties.

In 1973, under an administration-sponsored bill, Congress abolished the two-party system and implemented a multiparty system. Five parties were recognized under the party reorganization law; two of them were actual continuations of those allowed previously. The opposition MDB became the Brazilian Democratic Movement Party (PMDB), based in part on the old PTB and a few smaller political groupings, including whatever remained of the more progressive elements of President Eurico Gaspar Dutra's PSD. In its new incarnation, the PMDB counted among its supporters the expanding urban middle class, intellectuals, and workers. Its program called for greater control of the economy, income redistribution in order to help the disadvantaged, full political democracy, and direct elections.

The former government party, ARENA, went back to being the old UDN, which in turn had been the main opposition to Vargas in the 1940s and early 1950s and had backed Quadros's successful presidential campaign in 1960. Most of ARENA's members had supported the 1964 coup, and many of its leaders had served in the cabinet during the military administration. In its new guise, ARENA became the Democratic Social Party (PDS). It tried to appeal to the expanding urban middle class, but its greatest strength continued to be in the rural areas.

The pre-1964 PTB suffered much infighting in its attempt to regain its preeminence, and out of the struggle emerged the Democratic Workers' Party (PDT). The PDT was most active in the state of Rio de Janeiro, where it was led by Governor Leonel Brizola. The governor, closely associated by family, state, and political ties with the deposed Goulart, sought to model the party on the European social democratic parties, but most observers saw the PDT as a personalistic vehicle for the ambitious governor rather than an independent party based on ideology. Another party in search of the labor vote was the Workers' Party (PT), which competed primarily with the PMDB and the PDT for the votes of industrial workers and for the ideological backing of urban intellectuals.

The Liberal Front Party (PFL) was led by former Vice President Aureliano Chaves of Minas Gerais, who split from the PDS in the 1984 presidential campaign to support the PMDB and fellow *mineiro* presidential candidate Tancredo Neves. In fact, most of the PFL, which in 1985 became a junior partner in President José Sarney's democratic alliance, was composed of politicians who had been elected in 1982 on the PSD ticket but who had subsequently broken away from that party in order to support Neves. The PFL had capable young leaders, but it nonetheless fared poorly in the 1986 election, giving rise to the joke that it was a party of great leaders and a tiny following. Its modest strength lay in small and rural enclaves, and this support worked to its disadvantage in a country increasingly urban and urban-oriented.

## Nicaragua

Until the end of the dictatorship, Nicaragua was dominated by the Liberal Party (of which Anastasio Somoza was a member), and after the revolution, it was dominated by the FSLN. Since 1990 the political scene has been dominated by the Liberal Alliance and the FSLN. The Liberal Alliance, headed by President José Arnoldo Alemán, merges three elements of Nicaragua's traditional Liberal Party. Since this party was long the vehicle of the Somoza dynasty, it is frequently accused of having ties with elements of that regime. The party has strong support among Nicaragua's upper and middle classes. It is probusiness, generally supportive of the United States in international affairs, and has traditionally been strongly anti-Sandinista.

Modifying its Marxist rhetoric, the FSLN now portrays itself as more of a social democratic party. It has strong support within the labor movement and in other mass popular organizations. It advocates increased government control over the economy, expanded social welfare policies, and an independent foreign policy. Its support has been damaged by a reputation for corruption derived from the massive looting of state resources at the end of its period in power, by deep internal divisions that resulted in the defection of some of the leadership before the 1996 elections, and by personal scandals revolving around the party's leader and the former president of Nicaragua, Daniel Ortega. At the start of 2000, four members of the FSLN's legislative bloc had openly broken with the party leadership, risking expulsion.

## Panama

The cycles of elitist democracy and authoritarian populism in Panama have been reflected in the types of political parties established there and in the general nature of the country's party system. During periods of civilian elite domination, political parties have tended to reflect divisions along personalist lines within the urban commercial class. There have generally been few real differences between the policy agendas of these parties, and their extreme fragmentation is reflected in the large number of parties and in the fact that few party structures survive any given election.

While Panama's political party system has historically been fragmented and elitist, the sporadic emergence of both civilian and military authoritarian populist movements has on occasion led to efforts by populist leaders to create dominant parties through outright elimination or manipulation of the competition. The power of the urban commercial elite has resided primarily in its financial assets, while the power of the populists has resided in their control of the government apparatus itself. Thus, when populist leaders such as Arnulfo Arias and Omar Torrijos came to power, they attempted to create dominant political parties largely based on their support in the government bureaucracies.

During the period of elitist democracy that immediately preceded the military coup of 1968, approximately twenty personalist political parties vied for power. These parties were banned when General Torrijos assumed dictatorial control in the name of popular reform. However, deteriorating economic conditions in the mid-1970s led Torrijos to reassess the costs and benefits of direct military rule, and in 1978 he formed the Democratic Revolutionary Party (PRD) to incorporate the various groups that supported his military regime.

Responding to internal and external pressures, the military allowed multiparty elections to be held after 1976, but the political system clearly remained dominated by the PRD and its allies. Formation of the PRD suggested that the military wished to give permanent institutional form to its reformist ideals through the establishment of a new political party that would regularly win elections with military backing. When presidential elections were held in 1984 and 1989, the military had to resort to fraud to ensure a victory for the PRD's candidate.

The restoration of elitist democracy following the U.S. military invasion in 1989 led to the return of highly fragmented and personalistic party politics. The coalition of political parties that attempted to govern Panama in the wake of General Manuel Noriega's removal quickly collapsed when leaders found that they had little in common beyond opposition to military government. Although the elections of 1994 and 1999 were generally democratic, they also took place within the context of a multiparty system that remained unstable and highly polarized. In sum, the historical tendency toward extreme party fragmentation associated with elitist or externally imposed democracy has persisted into the 1990s.

Although Panamanian politics retains many of the features it exhibited prior to twenty years of military rule, there have been a number of significant changes. One of the most important of these has been the growing gap between the traditional parties and the newly emerging sectors and interest groups. The party leadership is aging and is increasingly out of touch with the realities faced by a new generation of Panamanians, whose aspirations the party leaders have not been able to fully ascertain. Continued movement of rural dwellers to Panama City has created a new electorate that is largely detached from the patterns of self-interest and coercion that assured votes for the traditional parties in the past. In an effort to deal with this growing gap between political parties and the electorate, both the PRD and the Panamenistas (a populist party rooted in popular disenchantment with the civilian elitist democracy ruling Panama during the 1960s) selected candidates for the 1999 election that would appeal to young voters and to women.

*Paraguay*

The historic Colorado Party supported dictator Alfredo Stroessner for thirty-four years, splintering in the end only over the succession issue. Since Stroessner's fall, the Colorado Party's unity has eroded further, with infighting among the various factions and subfactions clustering around political bosses. Nonetheless, as the party in power for over fifty years, the Colorados still hold vast financial and organizational advantages over all other parties.

The Liberal Party has been out of power since the end of the Chaco War, and it was illegal from 1942 to 1967. Despite their claim to "democratic" ideals, during their years in power (1904–1936) the Liberals showed themselves to be the same kind of elitist, exclusionary group as the Colorados. Further, the traditional Liberal Party, the only party with a mass base sufficient to challenge Stroessner and the Colorados, put up only a token or "kept" opposition during the dictatorship in exchange for recognition. Best known for its charismatic leader, Domingo Laíno, the Authentic Liberal Radical Party (PLRA) was promised the vice presidency in the new coalition government of President Luis González Macchi.

The Febrerista Party, begun in 1936 by disillusioned military veterans of the Chaco War against Bolivia, adheres to the ideals of European social democracy. Contemporary Febreristas assert that they were the true opposition to the Stroessner regime in that, unlike the PLRA, the Febrerista Party boycotted all regime-controlled elections from 1968 to 1988. Confined largely to Asunción, Febreristas advocate agrarian and social reform.

Perhaps a more important challenge to the two traditional political parties in Paraguay is the rise of independent movements and candidates, challenging the myth of unshakable family partisan support of either the Colorados or Liberals. Carlos Filizzola's election as mayor of Asunción under his Asunción for All movement (APT) is the most notable example of electoral victory independent of the two traditional parties. The National Encounter Party (EN)—inspired by Filizzola's APT victory and headed by prominent businessman Guillermo Caballero Vargas—emerged as another challenger to the traditional parties, contesting the presidential elections in 1993 and 1998. A social democratic movement, the EN has important support among intellectuals, youth, and other Paraguayans disenchanted with the Colorado or Liberal Parties.

*Ecuador*

Ecuador's parties began with the familiar Liberal-Conservative division, but their history since has been quite different from that in neighboring Colombia. The original division broke down, in part, because of one caudillo, José María Velasco Ibarra, who was elected president five times but completed only one of his terms. Military intervention has been common in the country's history, a characteristic still apparent even as the new millennium begins.

By the 1970s the Conservative Party and the Radical Liberal Party had faded into the background, and the oft-resuscitated *velasquista* movement faded away after the collapse of Velasco Ibarra's fifth and final administration in 1972. What gradually emerged were new, more programmatically oriented organizations, accompanied by modernizing movements consistent with well-established populist traditions. Thus, the elections of 1978–1979, the first since 1970, reflected the political changes then in progress. Traditionalistic forces were fragmented: The Democratic Left (ID)—originally formed by dissident Liberal reformers—was joined by the Christian Democratic Popular Democracy (DP), which had a distinguishable ideological foundation. The Marxist Left was split into several splinter groups, but it also shared in the emergence of a new generation of leaders. Ecuadorean populism was epitomized by the Concentration of Popular Forces (CFP), a Guayaquil-based party long controlled by Assad Bucaram, a charismatic if controversial figure who rose from an impoverished background to become the nation's single most popular mass leader since the venerable Velasco.

*Mexico*

Unlike most Latin American countries, Mexico had two dramatic watersheds of party politics. The first was the civil wars in the nineteenth century, culminating in the victory of the Liberals; the second came from the Mexican Revolution (1910–1920), an uprising so violent that perhaps as many as 1 million people lost their lives. After the revolutionary forces won, the question became, Which of the leaders should be president? The answer came only in 1929, when Plutarco Elías Calles called a meeting of "notables," including military strongmen, civilian chieftains, and some agrarian and labor leaders. This conclave gave birth to a "revolutionary party" that was dominated by military chiefs who treated their localities as fiefdoms and who allied themselves with grassroots peasant and worker groups. From the beginning, these leaders downplayed ideology in favor of channeling popular support into an effective power apparatus that would maximize their freedom of action in their own geographic zones. Federal employees were required to join the new national organization and contribute one week's pay in the form of annual dues, thus funding a professional staff and forging links to the bureaucracy that would become a hallmark of the official party. Through innovative governance and forceful leadership, Calles provided a brilliant entrée for his successor, General Lázaro Cárdenas.

Calles, trying to recruit a puppet attractive to the left wing, selected Cárdenas to carry the official party's banner in the 1934 presidential contest. Much to Calles's shock, the youthful general from Michoacán set about establishing a power base independent of the supreme chief. Even though he faced only token opposition, Cárdenas barnstormed the country as if the outcome of the contest hinged on every vote. His crusade enabled him to imprint his face and name on the psyches of millions of Mexicans, to learn the problems of the diverse nation, and to recruit fresh talent for his administration.

Once in power, Cárdenas showed a genius for crafting a durable party edifice, which he constructed on four major pillars: the peasant, labor, popular, and military sectors. Each corporatist collectivity exerted influence through a mass-membership organization with smaller constituent parts. These included the National Peasant Confederation (CNC), the CTM, and in 1943 the National Confederation of Popular Organizations (CNOP) for teachers, bureaucrats, clerks, professionals, shopkeepers, and other middle-class citizens. These occupationally based entities were linked only through the party's central apparatus—the National Executive Committee.

Cárdenas's radical recasting of the revolutionary party displayed corporatist tenets, but in a manner that would divide social groups and fortify presidential authority. Although the president regarded Mexico's workers and peasants—long reviled by elites as faceless masses—as the most important components of society, he assigned them to separate sectors. Moreover, he separated government employees—concentrated in the Federation of State Workers' Unions (FSTSE)—from their blue-collar CTM brethren. He also applied the "no reelection mandate" only selectively. Nothing was more sacred to leaders of the Mexican revolution than the no reelection mandate, which was salient because dictator Porfirio Díaz had promised when he was elected in 1876 to keep power only until 1910. While President Cárdenas required FSTSE leaders to adhere to the mandate, no such restriction applied to secretaries-general of unions in the labor sector.

Cárdenas changed the name of the party, and it was changed once again in the ensuing years, but the candidate of the oxymoronic PRI in the 2000 campaign represents a political party that remained in power for seventy-four years. In Chapter 8 we will discuss the watershed election of 2000, in which the candidate of the opposition National Action Party (PAN), Vicente Fox, defeated the PRI candidate.

## Conclusion

The discussion above makes it clear that, with a few notable exceptions, the Latin American political parties defy neat classification. At a very general level one might categorize the region's political parties into broad groups: traditional parties, Aprista parties, social democratic parties, Christian democratic parties, Marxist parties, personalist parties, military parties, and revolutionary parties.

However, the system of co-optation further complicates any attempt at classification. How is one to classify a political party that is traditional in origin and includes, at the same time, large landowners and the peasants tied to them as well as trade-union members organized by the party with the assistance of parts of the clergy? How does one classify a party such as the PRI, which until the mid-1990s made a conscious effort to co-opt and include all politically relevant sectors of the society?

The number of popularly elected governments in Latin America increased in the 1990s and beyond, and political parties have generally become more important than before. Democracy only exists if there is real competition between candidates, and throughout the world, political parties have been the organizations that have presented such rival candidates. However, in some Latin American countries (Peru and Venezuela, for example) political parties are held in such low esteem that some leaders have attempted to create democracy without parties. In other countries, parties still function, but the public tends to ignore or repudiate them.

So in addition to the traditional questions posed about parties in Latin America—focusing on the number of major parties, their programs and policies, the nature of electoral laws, and the relationships between parties and the military—we need to ask questions posed in democracies all over the world. How are parties funded? Do they come up with programs, articulate them to the public, and follow them after the elections? Are voters well informed by the mass media about political party activities? Are countries that are trying to have democracy without parties having any success? Are parties in decline in Latin America, as they seem to be in the United States and western Europe? Can democracy exist without parties? And if so, what groups or institutions would take their place?

# 7

# Government Machinery, the Role of the State, and Public Policy

Neither the classic Marxian categories nor the theory of liberalism give more than secondary importance to the role of the state. In the Marxian paradigm the state or governmental system is viewed as part of the superstructure that is shaped, if not determined, by the underlying structure of class relations. In the liberal model the state is generally conceived as a referee, umpiring the competition among the interest groups but not itself participating in the game; the liberal state acts as a kind of "black box": Into the box flow the "inputs" of the system—the competing interests and pressures—and out from the box flow the "outputs"—the public policies. Neither of these two classic models have adequately explained the Latin American political systems.

In Latin America, the state has historically been more important than that envisioned in the classic models. The traditional state was viewed as a powerful and independent agency in its own right, above and frequently autonomous from the class and interest-group struggle. Whether in socialist regimes such as Cuba's or capitalist systems like Brazil's, it was the state and its central leadership that largely determined the shape of the system and its developmental directions. In this sense the Latin American state is closer to the French or Continental European tradition than to that of the United States and Great Britain.

The traditional state did not merely *reflect* the class structure but, through its control of economic and political resources, also *shaped* the class system. The state was viewed as the prime regulator, coordinator, and pacesetter of the entire national system, the apex of the Latin American pyramid from which patronage, wealth, power, and programs flowed. The state played the role of patron, responsible for the general welfare of its citizens. The critical importance of the state in the Latin American nations helps explain why the competition for control of the state was so intense and sometimes violent.

One way to understand the role of the state in Latin America is to compare Latin Americans' view of government with the view of North Americans. In North America, government has usually been considered something of a necessary evil requiring elaborate checks and balances. Political theory in Iberia and Latin America, in contrast, has viewed government as good, natural, and necessary for the welfare of society. If government is good, there is little reason to limit or put checks and balances on it. Hence, before we fall into the trap of condemning Latin America for its powerful autocratic executives, subservient parliaments, and weak local government, we must remember the different assumptions on which the Latin American systems are based.

With the neoliberal changes of the 1990s, there has been a change in the procedures by which much of Latin American politics takes place. The fundamental issues still involve those who control the state apparatus and the immense power, patronage, and funds at its disposal, and the historically constant efforts of the state or strong presidents to expand their power. But now the issues also include questions, such as, How much of the old corporatist structure will be retained, if any? How neoliberal will the political and economic systems be? And how can the historically powerful role of the state be harmonized with the new demands for limited government, privatization, and democracy?

## The Theory of the State: Constitutions and Legal Systems

After achieving independence early in the nineteenth century, the Latin American nations faced a severe legitimacy crisis. Monarchy was a possibility and some nations did consider or experiment briefly with monarchical rule, but Latin America had just struggled through years of independence wars to rid itself of the Spanish imperial yoke, and monarchy had been discredited. Liberalism and republicanism were attractive and seemed the wave of the future, but Latin America had no prior experience with liberal or republican rule.

The solution was ingenious, though it has often been woefully misunderstood. The new nations of Latin America moved to adopt liberal and democratic forms, while at the same time preserving many of the organic, elitist, and authoritarian principles of the colonial tradition. The liberal and democratic forms provided goals and aspirations toward which society could strive; they also helped present a progressive picture to the outside world. But the liberal and republican principles were circumscribed by a series of measures, authoritarian in content, that were truer to the realities and history of the area and to its existing oligarchic power relationships.

Virtually all the Latin American constitutions have provided for the historical, three-part division of powers among the executive, the legislature, and the judiciary. But in fact the three powers are not coequal in the Latin American system, nor were they intended to be. The executive is constitutionally given extensive powers to bypass the legislature, and judicial review until recently has been largely outside the Latin American legal tradition. And similar apparent contradictions exist in other areas. Although one part of a constitution may be devoted to civilian institutions and the traditional three branches of government, another may give the armed forces a higher-order role to protect the nation, preserve internal order, and prevent internal disruption. Now, however, the legislative branch is becoming increasingly powerful in many countries.

The same emphasis is apparent when we look at human rights. Even though all the Latin American constitutions contain long lists of human and political rights, these same constitutions also give to the executive the power to declare a state of siege or emergency, to suspend human rights, and to rule by decree. The same applies to privilege: while one section of the constitution may proclaim democratic and egalitarian principles, other parts may give special privileges to the Church, the army, or the landed elites. While representative and republican precepts are enshrined in one quarter, authoritarian and elitist assumptions are legitimated in another. Increasingly, however, human rights and democratic precepts are being incorporated into basic law in Latin America.

None of this is meant to imply approval of human rights violations or to condone the overthrow of democratic governments, but only to point out how such events have often been perceived differently in Latin America. Hence, the real questions may concern the *degree* of military intervention or the *scope* of limits on legislative authority, and how and why these actions are taken. Such actions have not simply been a matter of the military usurping the constitution, since it was often the constitution itself that gave the military the right, even the obligation, to intervene in the political process under certain circumstances.

Similarly, when human rights violations are reported, we must understand them within the Latin American constitutional and legal tradition as well as from our own perspective. Human rights have not been conceived as constitutional absolutes in the Latin American tradition, and frequently there is a constitutional provision for their suspension. Recently, however, human rights as well as democracy in Latin America are being viewed more and more according to universal standards.

The most important issues of Latin American politics center on the dynamics of change and process from the Latin American as well as a global perspective. We cannot understand the area if we look only at the liberal and republican side of the Latin American tradition while ignoring the rest; nor should we simply condemn some action from the point of view of the North American constitutional tradition without seeing it in the Latin American context. If the civil and military spheres in Latin America are not as strictly segregated as in the U.S. tradition, then what are their dynamic relations and what are the causes of military intervention? If strict separation of powers is not seen in the same light in Latin America and if the branches are not equal, how then are their respective powers and interrelations defined? If hierarchy, authority, and special privilege have long been legitimated along with democratic and egalitarian principles, then how is either set of principles reconciled, glossed over, or challenged, and why? And how are these relations all changing as Latin America enters a more democratic era?

The Latin American constitutions are also misunderstood because of their sheer numbers. The number of constitutions (thirty or more in some countries) points to the fact that in most of the countries a new constitution is generally promulgated whenever a new amendment is added or when a major new interpretation requires official legitimation. Keep these two facts in mind: First, the Latin American constitutional tradition has been far more stable than the number of constitutions implies, and second, in most countries of the area there are only two main constitutional traditions, the one more centralized and even authoritarian, and the other liberal and democratic, with the trend now increasing toward the democratic side. The many constitutions, then, signify the repeated alternations between these two basic traditions, with variations.

These perspectives on the constitutional tradition also provide hints about the distinct legal tradition of Latin America. Whereas in the United States, laws and the Constitution are based upon a history and practice derived from British common law, the laws and constitutions of Latin America derive from a code-law tradition. This difference has several implications. The U.S. legal system is founded on precedent and reinterpretation, while the Latin American codes are complete bodies of law allowing little room for precedent or judicial reinterpretation. The codes are fixed and absolute and embody a comprehensive framework of operating principles; unlike the common-law tradition with its inductive reasoning based upon cases, the codes are enforced through a process of deductive reasoning. One begins not with facts or cases but with general truth (the codes or constitution) and deduces rules or applications for specific circumstances from this.

Although one should not overstress the point and although mixed forms exist throughout Latin America, an understanding of the code-law system and its philosophical underpinnings carries us a considerable distance toward understanding Latin American political behavior. The truths embodied in the codes and constitutions and the deductive methods of interpreting them have their origins in the Roman, medieval, and Catholic-scholastic tradition. The authoritarian, absolutist nature of the codes also reflects and helps reinforce a historically absolutist and authoritarian political culture. The effort to cover all contingencies with one code or to engage in almost constant constitutional engineering to obtain a "perfect" document tends to rule out the logrolling, the compromise, the informal understandings, and the unwritten rules that lie at the heart of U.S. or British political culture. And because courts and judges are applicators and enforcers rather than creative interpreters of the law, they tend to be seen as bureaucrats and bureaucratic agencies and do not enjoy the respect their counterparts do in the United States. This makes judicial review and even an independent judiciary difficult at best. Now these precepts and practices are changing as Latin America becomes more democratic and as U.S. legal precepts are incorporated into Latin America law.

### Executive-Legislative-Judicial Relations

Power in the Latin American systems has historically been concentrated in the executive branch, specifically the presidency. Terms like *continuismo* (prolonging one's term of office beyond its constitutional limits) and *personalismo* (an emphasis on the person of the presidency rather than on the office), to say nothing of *machismo* (strong, manly authority), are all now so familiar that they form part of our political lexicon. The present-day Latin American executive is heir to an imperial and autocratic tradition stemming from the absolute, virtually unlimited authority of the Spanish and Portuguese crowns. Of course, modern authoritarianism has multiple origins and forms: It can be seen as a reaction against earlier mass mobilization by populist and leftist leaders, as the result of stresses generated by modernization, or as the strategy of civilian and military elites for accelerating development; it can appear in caudillistic or in more institutionalized arrangements. In any case, the Latin American presidency has long been imperial in ways that no president of the United States ever conceived.

The formal authority of Latin American executives is extensive. It derives from a president's powers as chief executive, commander in chief, and head of state, and from the broad emergency powers to declare a state of siege or emergency, suspend constitutional guarantees, and rule by decree. The Latin American presidency has been a chief beneficiary of many twentieth-century changes; among them—the use of radio and television, the concentration of war-making powers, and a broadening responsibility for the economy. In addition, many Latin American chief executives serve simultaneously as heads of state and presidents of their party machines. If the potential leader's route to power is the army, the president also has the enormous weight of armed might for use against foreign enemies and domestic foes. Considerable wealth, often generated because the lines between private and public wealth are not so sharply drawn as in North American political society, may also become an effective instrument of rule.

Perhaps the main difference lies in the fact that the Latin American systems, by tradition and history, are more centralized, more oriented to the executive than in the United States. National life swirls around the presidency. The president is responsible not only for governance but also for the well-being of society as a whole; the president is the symbol of national society in ways that a U.S. president is not. Not only are politics concentrated in the office and person of the president, but it is through presidential favors and patronage that contracts are determined, different clientele are served, and wealth, privilege, and social position are parceled out. The president is *the* national *patrón*, replacing the local landowners and men on horseback of the past. With both broad appointive powers and wide latitude to favor friends and others who show loyalty, the Latin American president is truly the hub of the national system. Hence, when a good, able executive is in power, the system works exceedingly well; when this is not the case, the whole system tends to break down.

Various gimmicks have been used to try to limit executive authority. Few have worked well. These range from the disastrous Uruguayan experiment with a plural executive, which consisted of a nine-person government by committee, to the varied unsuccessful efforts at parliamentary or semiparliamentary rule in Chile, Brazil, Cuba, and Costa Rica. Constitutional gimmickry has not worked in limiting executive rule because an area-wide tradition and cultural pattern is in effect, not just some legal article. Now, however, the spread of democracy in Latin America is forcing most presidents to work within a different constitutional framework.

## The Legislative Branch

The role of the congress in the traditional Latin American system has not been to initiate or veto laws, much less to serve as a separate and coequal branch of government. Legislative functions in the region can be understood if we begin not with the image of an independent branch of government but with the image of an agency that has historically been subservient to the presidency and was, along with the executive, a part of an organic, integrated state system. The congress's role was thus to give advice and consent, but not much dissent, to presidential acts, to serve as a sounding board for new programs, to represent the varied interests of the nation, and to modify laws in some particulars (but not usually to nullify them). The legislature was also the place where some new faces were brought into government, where old-timers were pensioned off, where political friends and cronies were rewarded, and where the opposition was ensured a voice while guaranteeing that it remained a minority. In recent years, however, the congress in several Latin American countries has acquired newfound power and autonomy. By examining the legislatures of several individual countries, we can see how traditional state organization remains in tension with impulses toward greater legislative power.

The traditional separation of powers in Latin America is exemplified in the case of Panama. Under the terms of the 1972 Constitution, political power continues to be concentrated in the executive branch and, more specifically, in the office of the president. The president governs with the help of a Cabinet Council comprised of the various ministers of state. The Legislative Assembly is limited in its general powers and has little control over the national budget. Although a Supreme Court does exist, it has historically demonstrated minimal independence from the executive branch, and various presidents, including Ernesto Pérez Balladares (1994–1999), have attempted to pack it with their followers.

The Honduran governmental system also is highly centralized, with power concentrated in the presidency. The president introduces most legislation, directs the activities of executive branch agencies, and appoints all departmental governors. If the president heads a majority coalition of party factions in the National Congress, his policy initiatives usually become law, often with little modification. However, public policymaking is seldom the president's highest priority. The chief executives in Honduras have spent much of their time protecting their personal power base by distributing patronage and other material payoffs to supporters in their own and allied party factions and by countering the political moves of their enemies.

The National Congress traditionally has not played a significant policymaking role; congressional seats generally have been viewed as rewards for factional loyalty rather than as opportunities for public service. However, in recent years the National Congress has become somewhat more involved in policymaking and executive oversight. This has been especially true when the National Congress has been controlled by party factions not affiliated with the president or when the president of the National Congress has ambitions to become chief executive. Factions in the minority party become most influential in the National Congress when the president proposes constitutional reforms that require a two-thirds majority in two consecutive legislative sessions.

In Ecuador, the 1978 Constitution gave the country a unicameral system. The National Chamber of Representatives (CNR) has sometimes been as irresponsible and destructive as the Congress was in earlier times; in the early 1980s there was still occasional reliance on side arms, and galleries were packed by either pro- or anti-government mobs. Even so, the expanding vistas promised by democratic government have contributed to greater congressional authority. If presidents have tilted angrily with the CNR, they have also sought to deal with it as a legitimate arm of constitutional government.

In some countries (Chile, Colombia, Costa Rica, Venezuela) the congress has long enjoyed considerable independence and strength. A few congresses have gone so far as to defy the executive—and have gotten away with it. In 1992–1993, congresses in both Brazil and Venezuela removed the president from office for fiscal improprieties. The congress may also serve as a forum that allows the opposition to embarrass or undermine the government, as a means of gauging who is rising and who is falling in official favor, or as a way of weighing the relative strength of the various factions within the regime.

In Brazil, the 1988 Constitution gave greater powers to the Congress and denied the presidency the wide decree powers it had held before. It was no longer possible for a strong or a dictatorial president to dismiss the legislature, as had been done several times in the past. However, the realities of the entrenched system have remained far more powerful than any constitutional provisions. The presidency was weakened when President Fernando Collor de Mello was impeached for malfeasance; old-timers recalled that his father had, with impunity, killed a fellow senator in chambers. Congress was discredited when it too saw so many of its members tarnished by grand larceny, rampant favoritism, and even the crude elimination of estranged wives and inconvenient enemies.

In the same way the 1991 Colombian Constitution gave more power to the Congress, and less to the president. By the end of the century, however, it was apparent that the Congress was not using these powers; to make matters worse, congressional leaders were becoming millionaires through rampant corruption. In early 2000, President Andrés Pastrana considered offering the people a chance to vote on a referendum that would end the terms of all members of Congress, followed by new elections. This idea was dropped, however, when members of Congress suggested that the president's term also be ended, with new elections for that post also.

Venezuelan state organization will be in flux well into 2001, as political elites implement the 1999 Constitution. This constitution prescribes a presidential system with five separate branches of government: the executive, the legislative, the judicial, the electoral, and the people's power. Twenty-three states and a capital district interact in a polity whose leaders have yet to agree on the balance of power between the central, regional, and municipal governments. Under the 1961 Constitution the polity had grown more decentralized in practice, and the 1999 Constitution establishes the Federal Council of Government to oversee de jure decentralization. Nevertheless, for reasons peculiar to the unitary, centralist tensions in Hispanic and Roman Catholic constitutional development, Venezuela's local and regional politics have remained closely connected with patterns set in Caracas. This seems unlikely to change under President Hugo Chávez's new democracy. The national executive remains by far the most important branch of government.

The 1999 Constitution of Venezuela also replaced the bicameral Congress, which under the 1961 Constitution was the font of all lawmaking, with a unicameral National Assembly. This National Assembly has less autonomy and fewer prerogatives in relation to the national executive than did its predecessor, which reflects the disrepute into which Congress had fallen at the end of the 1990s. Most importantly, the president can now dissolve a recalcitrant National Assembly and call for new elections. In addition, legislation can be introduced into the National Assembly from seven sources: the national executive, the Delegative Commission of the National Assembly, any three members (deputies) of the National Assembly, the Supreme Tribunal, the Electoral Power, the Citizen's Power, and a petition bearing the signature of 0.1 percent of registered voters.

*The Judiciary*

Although many of the general comments offered above with regard to the congress also apply to the courts and the court system, describing several other characteristics of the traditional Latin American court system will help us understand it better. First, the court system has not historically been a separate and coequal branch—nor was it intended or generally expected to be. Many Latin American supreme courts would declare a law unconstitutional or defy a determined executive only at the risk of embarrassment and danger to itself, something they have assiduously avoided. Second, within their limits, the Latin American court systems have often functioned fairly well. Third, the courts, through such devices as popular action, the writ of *amparo* in Mexico and Argentina, the *tutela* in Colombia, and *segurança* in Brazil, have played an increasingly important role in controlling and overseeing governmental action, protecting civil liberties, and restricting executive authority even under dictatorial regimes.

The court system has its origins in the Iberian tradition. The chief influences historically were Roman law, Christianity and the Thomistic hierarchy of laws, and the traditional Iberian legal concepts, most notably the Siete Partidas of Alfonso the Wise. The influence of the French Napoleonic Code has been pronounced in Latin American codes, lists of human rights, and hierarchies of courts. And the U.S. inspiration is clear in provisions that at least theoretically allow a supreme court to pass judgment on the constitutionality of executive or legislative acts. Now the courts in various countries are gaining power and beginning to assert themselves. But they often face problems of incompetence, corruption, and lack of adequate training.

Both federal and state courts exist in Brazil, and the federal Supreme Court there has usually enjoyed a reputation for judicial wisdom and impartiality. The federal system is made up of the Supreme Court, the court of appeals, and the specialized military, electoral, administrative, and labor courts. The size of the Supreme Court has varied, with different presidents adding members in an effort to obtain more favorable judgments.

During the period that ended in 1999, Venezuelans viewed the judicial branch of government as even more corrupt than the Congress. This assessment was driven home in 1997, when television cameras recorded one eminent judge emptying a briefcase filled with cash from the balcony of her fifteenth-floor apartment as the police entered on the ground floor to arrest her for accepting bribes. Indeed, since at least the 1950s, judges had often done the bidding of others. When democratic governments were fighting for their survival in the 1960s, Presidents Rómulo Betancourt (1959–1964) and Raúl Leoni (1964–1969) overrode legal protections in order to remove leftist judges that they viewed as favorable to the guerrilla insurgency. The new judges were AD loyalists, and although COPEI did receive its quota of judicial appointments, AD dominated the judiciary until the 1990s. The record of the judges on matters of human rights represented a significant improvement over that of the Marcus Pérez Jiménez dictatorship, but on balance it was mixed.

The 1999 Constitution places the Supreme Judicial Tribunal at the apex of judicial power. The Supreme Judicial Tribunal meets in several kinds of sessions: plenary, political-administrative, and electoral sessions and sessions that deal with civil, penal, and social matters. Justices of the Supreme Tribunal are to be elected for terms of twelve years and cannot run for reelection. During their term in office they are forbidden to engage in partisan political activity; indeed, the 1999 Constitution goes to great length to shield the entire judiciary from the influence of political parties. For example, entry into the judicial career and promotion is by competitive examination only. The development of procedures for institutionalizing the judiciary awaits action by the first National Assembly. Finally, like its predecessor, the Constitution of 1999 establishes separate courts for the military. Going back to the Castillian tradition of the military *fuero* (right or privilege), this system protects members of the armed forces from being tried by civilian courts.

The Colombian Constitution of 1991 attempted to reform the judicial system in order to make punishment more likely for crimes, including insurrection and narcotrafficking. To that end, a National Prosecutor's Office (Fiscalía) was set up, along the lines of the Attorney General's Office in the United States. The national prosecutor, or *fiscal*, is charged with coordinating the entire system of justice. Early evidence suggested that this new system is more efficient in prosecuting criminals, although progress has been very slow due to lack of trained personnel.

It should be remembered, however, that what has made the Latin American political system work in most countries is not so much the legislature or the judiciary but the executive. The U.S.-style checks and balances that formally institutionalize limits on executive power are still not implemented extensively and even when they are, can frequently be bypassed. A more significant key to success has been the informal balance of power within the system and the set of generally agreed upon understandings and rules of the game; even the strongest of Latin American presidents goes beyond these only at severe risk to his regime's survival. Nevertheless, the growing importance of congress and the courts in many countries is a subject for further study.

## Local Government and Federalism

Federalism in Latin America emerged from a situation that was the exact reverse of that in the United States. In the United States in 1789, a national government was reluctantly accepted by thirteen self-governing colonies that had never had a central administration. In Latin America, by contrast, including Argentina, Venezuela, Mexico, and Brazil, a federal structure was adopted in some countries that had always been centrally administered.

## Federalism in Latin America: The Four Cases

Although these four nations were federal in principle, in each the central government reserved the right to "intervene" in the states. As the authority of the central government grew during the 1920s and 1930s, its inclination to intervene also increased, thereby often negating the federal principle. Over a long period, these large countries were progressively centralized, with virtually all power concentrated in the national capital. Nevertheless, the dynamics of relations and tensions between the central government and its component states and regions, who still have some independent autonomy, make for one of the most interesting of all political arenas. Recently there have been pressures to decentralize, but in all countries it is the central state that remains dominant.

Mexico has traditionally been a federal system on paper, but in fact it is centralized by the power of the president. The country's official name, the United States of Mexico, implies a federal system of government, and Mexico's thirty-one states approximate their neighbors to the north in terms of formal organization, institutions, and rights vis-à-vis the national government. In addition, Mexico's capital—known as the Distrito Federal (D.F.)—exists as a quasi-independent enclave and seat of national power like the District of Columbia.

However, the predominant role of the president came from unofficial powers that rivaled those granted by the constitution. Before Ernesto Zedillo began to share authority with other political actors, presidents not only chose candidates, but also arbitrarily intervened in state affairs, removed governors and other officials at will, rewarded allies with generous government contracts, treated lawmakers like lackeys, manipulated leaders of peasant and labor organizations, named their favorites to key PRI and bureaucratic positions, and spent millions of dollars in discretionary funds as they saw fit.

Brazil, under its constitution, is a federal republic composed of twenty-six states and a federal district where the capital of the country, Brasília, is located. Each state has its own government; the states' structures mirror the federal structures, and they have powers that are not reserved for the federal government or assigned to municipal councils. The governor is elected by direct popular vote and the state legislatures are unicameral. Likewise, the state judiciary mirrors the federal model, and its jurisdiction is defined to avoid conflicts with federal courts. Brazil also has some forty-four hundred municipal councils that handle local affairs. Clearly the president of Brazil lacks the impressive power that the president of Mexico has, and indeed many of the policies desired by Brazilian president Fernando Enrique Cardoso have been blocked by the governors of powerful states.

Like Mexico, Argentina's federal system also is a great deal more centralized than a formal reading of the country's Constitution would indicate. The federal government has specific, enumerated powers, leaving the provinces with unspecified "reserve" powers, which in practice are quite narrow. Provinces are referred to in the Constitution as "the natural agents of the Federal Government, to see that the laws of the land are obeyed." Federal law and treaties always trump provincial law.

The real sources of provincial weakness, however, are the provinces' financial dependence on the capital and the federal government's right to intervene in the provinces to maintain order. Concerning finances, the provinces have only a restricted ability to levy taxes. By contrast, the federal government enjoys the revenues derived from the port of Buenos Aires and other (mostly indirect) taxes. Even those are hardly sufficient to cover its responsibilities, given the widespread practice of tax evasion, so there is little left over for revenue sharing with the provinces. As for the federal government's power of intervention, this is a power that frequently has been abused. Citing electoral fraud or financial mismanagement, past presidents have often used their own handpicked intervenors to replace provincial governors or legislators who belonged to the opposition party. Venezuela conforms to this pattern: a federal system in law and constitution but centralization in fact.

## Unitary Systems

Most Latin American countries are not federalist but are structured after the French system of local government, with virtually all power concentrated in the central government and its ministries and with authority flowing from the top down. Local government is ordinarily administered through the ministry of the interior, which is also responsible for the national police. In these "unitary systems," almost all local officials are appointed by the central government and serve as its agents at the local level.

Local governments in these systems have almost no power to tax or to run local social programs. These activities are generally administered by the central government according to a national plan. This system of centralized rule is also a means of concentrating power in oftentimes weak and uninstitutionalized nations. The Colombian Constitution of 1991 gave many powers to departmental and municipal governments, including that of education, for example. However, recognizing the absence of taxation powers at those two levels of government, the Constitution also came up with a formula for the national government to share revenue with local and regional bodies.

And yet, even though the constitutions of these countries suggest, at least in theory, that they are fully centralized states, the reality in many countries has always been somewhat different. The Spanish and Portuguese crowns had difficulty enforcing their authority in the American interior, which was far away from the centers of power and virtually autonomous. With the withdrawal of the Crown early in the nineteenth century, centrifugal tendencies were accelerated. Power drained into the hands of local landowners or regional "men on horseback," or caudillos, who competed for control of the national palace. With a weak central state and powerful centrifugal tendencies, a strong de facto system of local rule did emerge in Latin America, often contrary to what the laws or constitutions proclaimed.

Thereafter, nation building in Latin America often consisted of two major tendencies: populating and thus "civilizing" the vast empty interior, and extending the central government's authority over the national territory. Toward the end of the nineteenth century, national armies and bureaucracies were created to replace the unprofessional armed bands under the local caudillos; national police agencies enforced the central government's authority at the local level; and the collection of customs duties was centralized. Authority became concentrated in the central state, the regional isolation of the *patria chica* broke down as roads and communications grids were developed, and the economy was similarly centralized under the direction of the state.

In most of Latin America the process of centralization, begun in the 1870s and 1880s, is still going forward. Indeed, that is how "development" is often defined throughout the area. A developed political system is one in which the central agencies of the state exercise control over the disparate and centrifugal forces that make up the system. In many countries, this process is still incomplete, so that in the vast interior, in the highlands, in diverse Indian communities, and among groups such as landowners, large industrialists, the military, and big multinationals, the authority of the central state is still tenuous. Even today, isolated areas, especially those in the rugged mountains or tropical jungles, often have little governmental presence. Local strongmen—sometimes guerrillas or drug traffickers—may be more powerful than the national government's representatives. Indeed, the efforts of the central government to extend its sway over the entire nation constitutes one of the main challenges of Latin American politics. Conversely, the local units—be they regions, towns, parishes, or Indian communities—still attempt to maintain some degree of autonomy. Thus, centralization and decentralization are often going forward at the same time.

## A Fourth Branch of Government: The Autonomous State Agencies

One of the primary tools in the struggle to centralize power in Latin America from the 1930s to the 1980s was the autonomous agency. The growth of these agencies, in many ways parallel to that of the "alphabet agencies" in the United States, gave the central government a way to extend its control into new areas. These agencies became so large and so pervasive that they could be termed a separate branch of government, and indeed, some Latin American constitutions recognized them as such.

In some countries these agencies soon numbered in the hundreds. Many were regulatory agencies, often with far broader powers than their North American counterparts, with the authority to set or regulate prices, wages, and production quotas. Others administered vast government corporations; among them—steel, mining, electricity, sugar, coffee, tobacco, railroads, utilities, and petrochemicals. Still others were involved in social programs—education, social security, housing, relief activities, and the like. Many more participated in the administration of new services that the state had been called upon to perform, such as national planning, agrarian reform, water supplies, and family planning.

These agencies were established for a wide variety of purposes. Some, such as the agrarian reform or family planning agencies, were established as much to please the U.S. government and to qualify a country for U.S. and World Bank loans as to carry out agrarian reform or family planning. Others were created to bring under government control and direction a recalcitrant or rebellious economic sector, such as labor or the business community. Some were used to stimulate economic growth and development, to increase government efficiency and hence its legitimacy, or to create a capitalist structure and an officially sanctioned entrepreneurial class where none had existed before. They also added more job seekers to the public payroll.

The common feature of all these myriad agencies was that they tended to serve as agents of centralization in that historic quest to "civilize" and bring order to what was, in the past even more than now, a vast, often unruly, near empty territory with strong centrifugal propensities. The growth of these agencies, specifically the government corporations, meant that the degree of central state control and even ownership of the means of production increased significantly as well. As a result, it has been a fundamental mistake to think of the Latin American economies as systems dominated by private enterprise. It is not only Cuba that has had a large public sector; in fact, all the Latin American economies have been heavily influenced by the state.

This phenomenon has had important implications. It has raised the stakes in the struggles for control of the central government, with its vast resources. It has also implied that very rapid structural change was readily possible. In countries where between 40 and 60 percent of the GNP (gross national product) was generated by the public sector (a far higher percentage than in the United States) and where so much power was concentrated in the central state, the transformation from a state-capitalist to a state-socialist system was relatively easy and could happen almost overnight, as in Cuba, or Peru for a time. A leftist or socialist element had only to capture the pinnacles of these highly centralized systems. Now this process is being reversed, as many Latin America countries move toward privatization.

The growth of all these centralized state agencies has had another implication deserving mention. Though established as autonomous and self-governing bodies, the state corporations in fact became heavily political agencies. They have provided an abundance of sinecures, a means to put nearly everyone on the public payroll. They became giant patronage agencies by which the leadership rewarded friends and cronies and found places for the opposition, hence guaranteeing their loyalty or at least their neutrality. Depending on the country, anywhere from 30 to 50 percent of the gainfully employed labor force has worked for the government at one time or another. Many of the agencies have been woefully inefficient, and the immense funds involved have provided nearly endless opportunities for private enrichment from the great public trough. In performing these patronage and spoils functions, the state agencies have preserved the status quo, since large numbers of people, indeed virtually the entire middle class, were dependent upon them for their livelihood and opportunities for advancement. It is not surprising that a significant part of the debt problem faced by many Latin American countries has resulted from foreign loans, not to the national governments, but to state agencies.

Today the Latin American countries are trying to solve the problems of corruption, inefficiency, and overcentralization. With the neoliberal reforms of the 1990s, governments have reduced the number and diminished the role of centralized government agencies. Many that were in productive activities have been privatized. In the process, the benefit to poorer people has often been reduced, as has the number of jobs to be passed out to political supporters.

## Public Policy and the Policy Process

By "public policy" we mean the actions taken by groups and leaders in authority to implement their decisions in the public sphere. No political system is completely successful in accomplishing what it wishes, and this is especially the case in those societies that are underdeveloped politically and economically like the Latin American countries. Further, there are certain uniquely Latin American traits, over and above the area's underdeveloped character, that militate against effective public policies.

## Major Issues of Public Policy

Most of the historic issues of the nineteenth century—the role of the Church, centralism or federalism, free trade or protectionism—have been resolved or at least placed on the back burner in post–World War II Latin America. Although from time to time these old issues reemerge in some countries, in the past three decades the newer issues of economic development, agrarian reform, urban reform, population growth, narcotics, and law enforcement have largely replaced them.

*Economic Development.* One goal of almost all sectors in the Latin American political process is economic development, although policymakers still sometimes disagree on its definition and the best way to obtain it. For some, economic development means no more than growth in the national economy, resulting in a larger gross domestic product. In this conception, the nature and structure of the developed economy would not necessarily change at all—only the size. The kinds of products would remain the same, and although trade relations with the outside world would be expanded, they would change only slightly in character.

Other Latin Americans define economic development as the industrialization and diversification of their economies. Traditionally, Latin American countries have produced agricultural or other primary goods, often concentrating on a single product. These products are then traded for industrial goods with the more developed countries of the North. Although they might have had comparative advantage in those primary products, the national economies suffered when there was a glut in the global supply, and they were also vulnerable to crop failures and to quotas fixed by the industrial nations.

From independence until the Great Depression of the 1930s most Latin American countries produced primary goods that gave them comparative advantage—sugar in Cuba, coffee in Colombia and Brazil, petroleum in Venezuela, tin in Bolivia, copper in Chile, wheat and beef in Argentina. In so doing, they were following the advice of Adam Smith to allow an "invisible hand" to lead different economies in different directions. Perhaps this was best stated by Colombian Treasury Secretary Florentino González:

> In a country rich in mines and agricultural products, which can sustain a considerable and beneficial export trade, the latter [country] should not attempt to encourage industries that distract the inhabitants from agricultural and

mining occupations.... Europe, with an intelligent population, and with the possession of steam power and its applications, educated in the art of manufacturing, is fulfilling its mission in the industrial world by giving various forms to raw materials. We too should fulfill our mission, and there is no doubt as to what it is.... We should offer Europe raw materials and open our doors to her manufactures.[1]

Most Latin American countries followed this advice until the Great Depression, when suddenly no industrial country had either manufactured goods to export or money with which to buy primary goods. As a result many countries implemented ISI policies in an attempt to maintain the standard of living to which their citizens were accustomed. Yet they soon discovered that to import machinery for industrialization, they would still have to export goods, mainly primary products.

Economists recommended that the countries of Latin America discover an export that would be "price inelastic," that is, people would buy it, no matter how expensive it was, and that also had "value added," that is, it had been changed in some way to give it more value than the original product. The idea was that the Latin American economies would be more stable if they could predict the volume of products that they could sell and if the job market was employing people with a fairly good guarantee that employment would continue. Unfortunately, no Latin American country could find such a product, at least until the 1980s when Colombia started exporting cocaine. Needless to say, the economists had envisioned a product that was not illicit.

By the early 1960s, it became evident that there was a general decline in the relative value for all primary goods exported from the region. The long-term trend was for industrial goods to go up in price more rapidly than primary goods. Although economies could still enjoy comparative advantage in their primary product, by the 1960s this advantage was generally outweighed by other factors; a frost in Brazil might still mean a short-term increase in the price of Guatemalan coffee, but a tractor imported to Guatemala from the United States might cost more bags of coffee beans than it had twenty years before. Although this was not the case with Venezuelan oil between 1973 and 1982, almost all other Latin American countries lost income from the declining terms of trade.

The middle position on economic development, then, would call for two major economic policies: industrialization and diversification. The former would be for the purpose of import substitution; rather than importing industrial goods, the Latin American country imports capital goods and technology, which it then uses to produce the goods that formerly were imported. Further, in order to lessen the dependence on a single crop, a government makes tax and credit decisions that will encourage the production of additional goods for export. This vision of the new, economically developed society is one in which more goods of greater variety are produced for export, while fewer manufactured goods are imported. Increased trade is an important facet of this policy, since hard currency is needed for the purchase of these capital goods.

A notable attempt at implementing this policy came in revolutionary Cuba. In the 1960s, after all foreign multinational companies had been nationalized, Fidel Castro decided that industrialization and diversification were called for. To diversify, producing sugarcane fields were dug up and other crops were planted. To industrialize, foreign machinery was purchased from Eastern Europe, using foreign aid from the Soviet Union.

The result was a complete failure. The new agricultural crops were even less profitable than sugar. Industrial products produced in Cuba were more expensive than those that could have been imported. For example, Cuba built a factory to produce cooking oil, only to discover that it cost more to produce oil in Cuba than to import oil. The visible hand of Nikita Khrushchev entered at that point; the Soviet leader told Castro that Cuba should go back to doing what it could do best, growing and exporting sugar, and use the money from sugar sales to import other things from eastern Europe.

Elsewhere it was obvious by the 1970s that ISI was not working. Although there may have been success with some new export products such as foodstuffs and other light industrial goods, it did not seem likely that the economies would continue to produce heavier industrial goods. It was in light of that failure that in the late 1980s a new, neoliberal policy emerged in most Latin American countries. To a certain extent it was like the traditional policy, in that it encouraged the production of goods that promised a comparative advantage. But it also included the privatization of government-owned enterprises and the adoption of pricing schemes based on the international market rather than on local living standards, in effect ending subsidies for the poor. In the short run, at the least, these new policies led to more unemployment and greater disparity of income. The neoliberal leaders urged patience, but some politicians paid more attention to the cries of large numbers of suffering people. Hence in the 1990s, there was a new conflict, in some ways much like the struggle of the 1930s: that between the neoliberals and the supporters of the government-controlled economy.

Economic policy is often more complex than the preceding discussion indicates. Policy questions often arise from current market conditions and shifts in the global economy. For example, for many years Latin America has faced the question, What should be done about inflation? For at least three decades, Latin American countries experienced "stagflation," the combination of a stagnant economy and high inflation, which reached its most acute form in the first half of the 1980s. Are the neoliberals right in saying that this problem is to be solved by monetary measures such as printing less money, balancing budgets, and maintaining a balance of trade between imports and exports? Or is the real cause for inflation a structural problem, based on the declining terms of trade and the concentration of economic power in the hands of a small group at the top in most of the Latin American countries? If the reason is structural, more dramatic public policies are needed.

Before the 1980s another key question was, Who is to develop industry? The supporters of a strong role for the government suggested that national enterprise do it, while neoliberals encouraged the involvement of foreign investment and multinational corporations. How will the generally negative balances of payment be redressed? What kinds of laws, if any, are needed to encourage the importation of capital goods and infrastructure materials while discouraging the purchase of consumer goods from foreign countries? If national industry is to be developed, how is capital to be generated? Is this to be done by stopping capital flight, by reducing consumption by the lower and middle classes through forced savings, or by some combination of techniques?

After October 1973 there was a new economic issue: the value of petroleum. For the oil-exporting countries of Venezuela, Mexico, and Ecuador, the question became, How do we best use the new wealth while keeping inflationary pressures at a minimum and protecting national industry? For the petroleum importers, the question was, How do we keep economic growth going during this time when we have to spend more of the scarce hard-currency export earnings and reserves to purchase needed oil? Later, when oil prices declined, the oil-producing economies also went into a tailspin.

Whether these policy issues were successfully resolved or not, in the early 1980s the question changed again: Could the debt crisis be resolved? This crisis was caused by the energy crisis in two ways. First, by the late 1970s all Latin American countries found that private banks were recycling petrodollars invested by OPEC members and were willing to lend money at *real* interest rates (corrected for inflation) that were near or even below zero. Huge debts were incurred throughout the region. The debts were impossible to repay, however, because as a result of recession in the industrial world in the early 1980s, fewer Latin American exports were being bought.

Second, the oil-exporting countries, especially Mexico and Venezuela, contracted debts under the assumption that the price of petroleum would continue to increase. By 1982, however, the oil glut led to much lower prices for their exports and they were left with large debts and less oil revenue.

By the late 1980s, the new economic agenda revolved around the neoliberal proposals to open markets, free trade, and decrease protectionism. As in the struggle between the traditional and democratic models of government, the economic contest was held between individuals and groups who had benefited from the old mercantilist system and those who thought that they would benefit more from a neoliberal one. At this writing it is not clear that where there is democracy, the majority of the people will consistently chose neoliberal leaders.

More recently the issue has become globalization. With the end of the Cold War and the decline in foreign aid, the Latin American economies are on their own more than ever before. They must compete in global markets because no one is there to give them aid or bail them out any more. Inefficiency, corruption, and patronage politics must all be tamed because they are costly and make Latin America noncompetitive. Hence it is not only the United States or the international lending agencies that are pushing Latin American countries to modernize and streamline; often their own business sectors and educated citizens are also calling for change. Latin America *must* become a part of the global, competitive economy because it no longer has any choice in the matter.

Globalization has not come easily to Latin America. One of the first countries to attempt the transformation was Chile during the Pinochet dictatorship. At first the economy suffered a drastic contraction as a result of the "shock treatment" of price and wage controls. Then the "Chilean economic miracle" occurred from 1977 until 1981, with the economy expanding from 6 to 8 percent a year. With tariff rates down to 10 percent from an average of 100 percent during the Allende period, cheap foreign imports flooded the country. The exchange rate was fixed at thirty-nine pesos to the dollar, and nontraditional exports such as fruit, lumber, and seafood reduced the share of copper in earning foreign exchange from 80 percent to less than 40 percent. It was possible to take out dollar loans at the overvalued exchange rate, and Japanese cars and Scotch whiskey could be purchased more cheaply in Chile than in their countries of origin.

In Argentina after the election of President Carlos Saúl Menem in 1989, the old system came under a similar full-scale attack by neoliberal reformists. In January 1991 Domingo Cavallo, Menem's economics minister, announced a radical package of neoliberal economic reforms that effectively opened the country to foreign competition and investment, forced the government to cut back on its spending, and began a rapid process of divesting the state of its enterprises. The impact was devastating for Argentina's urban middle- and working classes. Stripped of protection and subsidies, many small businesses disappeared, gobbled up by larger foreign and domestic companies. Within a few years the "shopkeeper society" was transformed into one dominated by large private conglomerates. Because these were capital-intensive rather than labor-intensive enterprises, unemployment rose among the working classes as well, especially among women and youth. Although with the underground economy it is hard to pinpoint the exact level of joblessness, official figures put it at around 18 percent. In some provinces, however, it is acknowledged to be over 40 percent. Beyond that, there is an equally large number of people who are underemployed, working at marginal jobs well below their skill level. All of that adds up to a potentially volatile political situation. It may well explode unless the world economy picks up soon and gives Argentina a chance to grow out of its present troubles.

If Argentina is one of the wealthier countries of Latin America, then Guatemala is one of the poorer ones. Here liberalized trade regulations increased opportunities for the *maquila* (assembly) industries, major mainstays of Guatemala's growth. Ironically, as social problems, including labor strife, threatened to increase, neoliberal pressures generally reduced the role of the state in solving these problems. Hence globalization produced economic growth that benefited economic elites and some sectors of the middle classes, but it did not generate enough wealth to trickle down and resolve major social problems. Simultaneously, the Guatemalan state seems less capable of dealing with these issues because its role in society is diminishing as the economy shifts more toward the laissez-faire end of the continuum.

*Agrarian Reform.* A second public policy issue in Latin America is that of the ownership of land, which is very inequitably distributed, with a small number of very large landholders and a great number of very small landholders and landless, illegal squatters. Only in a few countries are there substantial numbers of middle-class farmers. During the 1960s, in large part because of the influence of the United States and the fear of an agrarian revolution (such as the Cuban Revolution was perceived to have been), many Latin American countries set up agencies to deal with the problems of land. Yet only in Venezuela and Mexico were there significant land reforms—and even there advances were very limited.

Even though land reform was not the issue by the turn of the century that it had been in the 1960s, the problem still exists: Land ownership is very unevenly distributed, and over 80 million Latin Americans live in the countryside under subhuman conditions. Guerrilla movements took root in many Latin American countries because of the land problem; the agrarian problem was one of the reasons for the victory of the Sandinistas in Nicaragua in July 1979. Since then, some Latin American governments—often supported by the USAID—have continued to advocate land reform as a way to prevent revolutions.

A key factor in the failure of dramatic land reform is the power of the large landowners, who have been adept at preventing what they see as an attack on their property. In some countries, however, the landowners have used the co-optation strategy—giving up a little land to avoid giving up a lot. Another reason for the failure of land reform is the lack of good technical information about who owns what land and what it is being used for. If the land were divided among peasants, would production go up or down? What would the best crops be? Which kinds of seeds and fertilizers would be best? What would the peasants need in addition to land?

Further, there are economic reasons for not breaking up the large tracts of land. The latifundios vary greatly in use and economic output. If a sizable estate is not used or is used very inefficiently, then granting the land to campesinos would lead to increased agricultural production for either national consumption or export. However, if the estate is effectively utilized by the large landowner, the goals of land reform are, at least for the short run, in conflict with the goals of increased agricultural production. Moreover, there are certain agricultural products that have economies of scale—that is, they cannot be successfully grown on a family-sized farm. In this case, agrarian reform means lower production in the long term unless the landholdings are held collectively. There are both Spanish and Amerindian traditions of collective ownership of lands, and in Peru such traditions are being used through communal ownership. The Cuban case shows that another alternative, although so far not a successful one, is state farms—those owned by the government with campesinos receiving wages for work.

There are still immense social, economic, and political inequalities and inefficiencies in the Latin American countryside that need to be addressed. The continuing need for land reform is illustrated by the Brazilian Landless Movement. The appearance of the Zapatista National Liberation Army (EZLN) in Chiapas, Mexico, in the mid-1990s also demonstrates that there are still areas within Latin American countries where the land issue has major importance.

Nonetheless, the agrarian issue has faded in importance. The fact is that Latin America is now more urban than rural, a reversal of the situation forty to fifty years ago, when land reform was first offered as a solution. With more and more people moving to the cities, the land problem is not as important as it was, and it is unlikely that any new agrarian revolutions will succeed in seizing national power. There are too few peasants, and most of those who remain in the countryside are too unorganized to form a strong political movement. Many of the peasants who would presumably stand to benefit from agrarian reform are themselves "thinking with their feet" by moving to the cities—or abroad.

*Urban Reform.* With few jobs or little future in the rural areas, many people have left the countryside to seek a better life in the cities. Both push factors and pull factors account for this internal migration. Some campesinos are pushed off the land, either because there are more children than the land can support or because the large landowners have mechanized production. Others are pulled to the cities by the better life that they believe will be found there. The movement has been dramatic: It is estimated that every year from 1970 to 1985 a population of some 8.75 million persons was incorporated into the cities of Latin America, and in the 1985–2000 period this increased to between 11 and 12 million people every year. This urban growth has dramatic effects on the major cities, many of which have doubled or tripled in size over the past decade.

Cities in Latin America were not prepared for such rapid growth; the same was true of U.S. cities during similar growth periods at the end of the nineteenth century and the beginning of the twentieth. But there are important differences. Unlike urban growth in the United States and western Europe, Latin American urbanization was not accompanied by a surge of industrial growth. Few of the new urbanites receive jobs in industry, and those who do not settle for hand-labor or construction work or remain underemployed or unemployed. The political dimension is also different in Latin America, given the greater centralization of the state. Policies to meet the new problems of the cities are more likely to come from national governments than from city governments.

The urban problems that the national governments face are numerous and difficult. One is housing. Although some of the urban migrants rent rooms in large old houses where certain public utilities already exist, even more build makeshift homes in the open areas in and around the cities. Most of these new slums are built illegally on private or state-owned land and are completely devoid of such urban services as water, sewerage facilities, electricity, roads, and effective police and fire protection. Some studies have shown that the life expectancy is lower among dwellers in these shantytowns than among campesinos. Other problems also abound: Cities such as Mexico City, Rio de Janeiro, and São Paulo, among the very largest in the world, suffer from extreme pollution, rampant lawlessness, and other characteristics that make them unlivable for many residents.

Urban reform has been no more a success than agrarian reform was. One key reason is that the urban dwellers have not organized into effective political movements. The following explanations for this lack of organization have been mentioned in the literature:

1. The new urban poor are too busy in the day-to-day struggle to make enough money to feed themselves and their children to have time for political activities;
2. People often develop a sense of community in the shantytowns that seems to provide considerable security;
3. Additional security is received from the extended family and from the ceremonial kinship relationship, in which people slightly higher in the social structure are godparents of a person's children;
4. Close contact is maintained between the urban poor and the rural areas from which they came, making it possible to return if things get extremely bad economically;
5. A high percentage of the urban poor are engaged in service work and petty commercial activities such as street vending; the labor force is thus atomized and workers lack association with others like themselves;
6. Many who do obtain factory jobs work in very small factories, often of the cottage variety, with the owner filling the traditional *patrón* function;
7. Business people, industrialists, and governments participate in strategic activities designed to give the urban poor a portion of what they want;
8. These same elite groups can sanction the urban poor for political involvement, most easily by taking away their jobs, since their labor can be easily replaced by the unemployed; and
9. Even though their life expectancies tend to be lower than that of campesinos, the new urban poor perceive themselves to be better off—or at least to hope that their children will be better off—than they were in the countryside.

Whatever the precise reasons for lack of political influence of these lower class urban residents, the flow of people into the cities has continued unabated.

*Population Policy.* Another issue to be dealt with by Latin American public policy is population growth. During the last quarter of the twentieth century, Latin America had the highest growth rate in the world. Although the birthrate is higher in certain parts of Asia and Africa, death rates are lower in Latin America, and the result is a regional population growth rate of roughly 3 percent per year. This of course varies from country to country: Argentina and Uruguay both increase in population at about 1.0 percent a year, roughly comparable to the United States. But other countries, such as Brazil and Mexico, grow between 2 and 3 percent a year, which means that the population doubles every twenty-four to thirty-six years.

Population growth is related to another issue previously discussed—economic growth. Economic growth must be at least equal to population growth if a country is to avoid declines in per capita income. If an increase in per capita income is a target, then economic growth must be greater than population growth. The Alliance for Progress of the 1960s led to impressive growth in the GDPs (gross domestic products) of many Latin American nations, but the GDP per capita gained only slightly in the face of population growth. Later, in the 1980s, population growth had slowed down, but this was the "Lost Decade," when Latin American economies were in crisis. Again, per capita income growth did not increase much, but now the stagnant economies were the cause.

Two of the key reasons for population growth in the region are the increase in life expectancy and the decrease in infant mortality rates, both of which have changed dramatically since World War II. These improved rates are the result of better health care and education, more doctors, better sanitary conditions, and the eradication of some diseases, such as smallpox and malaria, through public health programs. In many places the birthrate did not decrease dramatically while life expectancy kept rising. The way to slow this growth, therefore, has to be through some control of the high birthrate.

Some countries, including strongly Catholic Colombia, have developed family planning programs. Further, it has become evident that even in those countries that lack effective programs, the birthrate has begun to fall. This decline seems related to increased urbanization and better education about ways to limit family size, and is not necessarily the product of organized family planning programs. After all, it may make some sense for a rural peasant to have lots of children, both to put to work in the fields and to take care of the parents in their old age, especially in nations that have few effective social security programs. But for the urban poor, the argument for fewer rather than more children makes more sense, and it is precisely in the urban areas that the population growth rate has begun to fall.

*Narcotics.* Although illicit narcotics have long been sent from Latin America to the United States, it has only been since the 1980s that policymakers have been seriously concerned about the drug traffic—especially of cocaine and more recently heroine. Nearly every country in Latin America is involved in narcotrafficking in some way, either as a producer of drugs or as a transit point between the producing countries and the United States and Europe. The cocaine producing countries are primarily Colombia, Peru, and Bolivia, while the transit countries include nearly every other Latin American country, even including those that are not on direct routes between the producers and the consumers.

Colombia is more identified with narcotics than any other country. There have been three major competing groups of Colombian drug dealers: the Medellín cartel, the Cali cartel, and the Atlantic Coast cartel. Although the first two had disappeared by the late 1990s, many other smaller groups soon emerged, ready to make enormous profits. There are numerous documented cases of the diversion of drug earnings into legitimate business (including a professional soccer team), politics, and the military and police forces. Drug leaders have orchestrated the assassinations of ministers of justice, attorneys general, and newspaper editors who openly oppose their activities. Through bribes and intimidation, the *narcos* have been able to corrupt individual Colombians of every rank.

On August 18, 1989, drug dealers assassinated Colombian Senator Luis Carlos Galán, an exceptionally bright and dynamic reformer and the leader in the preference polls for the 1990 presidential election. Galán was articulate and outspoken in favor of stronger action against the *narcos*. The next day, President Barco called for an all-out war against the *narcos*, which received strong backing from U.S. president George Bush. Actions taken by the Colombian government included confiscation of the possessions of suspected drug leaders and the extradition to the United States of those indicted there. The drug dealers responded with a massive bombing campaign, especially in Bogotá and Medellín. By the end of 1989 several middle-level *narcos* had been extradited, and one of the leaders of the Medellín cartel, José Gonzalo Rodríguez Gacha, had been killed during a battle with government troops.

President César Gaviria (1990–1994) initiated a kind of plea bargaining with drug dealers that had little precedent in Colombian history. Drug dealers who surrendered and confessed to at least one crime were promised reduced sentences (a Constituent Assembly had made extradition unconstitutional). Notable successes of this policy included the surrender of the three Ochoa brothers of the Medellín group and its leader Pablo Escobar. However, after a bit more than thirteen months in prison, Escobar escaped on July 22, 1992, and for fifteen months the government was unable to capture him. His death in a shoot-out with government troops on December 2, 1993, did not end the problem of drugs in Colombia.

During the presidency of Ernesto Samper (1994–1998), the leaders of the Cali drug group, the Rodríguez Orejuela brothers, either surrendered or were captured by the police. Although the trial process led to short sentences for the leaders, at least in theory their criminal organization had been ended. Yet Colombian cocaine exports did not decline; other leaders and alternative, smaller groups soon replaced the earlier ones. It is estimated that the illicit trade has produced six billionaires and some one hundred sixty millionaires. With so much money to be made, there will always be someone to take the place of any drug chieftain captured by the government.

In Peru it is estimated that up to three hundred thousand peasant families live off the coca and cocaine-paste industry, which in the 1980s and early 1990s was concentrated in the Huallaga Valley, two hundred fifty miles northeast of Lima. Peru was until 1997 the world's largest producer of coca leaf, the raw material for cocaine, providing 60–65 percent of the global supply. After the capture of Shining Path leaders in the early 1990s, the protective relationship between the guerrillas and the coca growers declined, leading to a reduction of coca production. Nevertheless, although recently supplanted by Colombia, Peru still produces about one-third of the world's coca leaf.

By the mid-1980s Bolivia had become the world's second-most-important source of coca leaf and the third largest producer of cocaine hydrochloride. The United States has made action on the drug issue a higher priority than issues of much greater concern to Bolivians, such as reactivating the stagnant economy and reducing poverty. Since cocaine is Bolivia's chief source of income, bringing more than half a billion dollars into the economy annually, drug interdiction tends to conflict with economic aspirations. The narcotics issue also is sensitive because of the imposing presence of the U.S. drug enforcement complex in Bolivia and the legitimacy problems this has caused since 1985 for Bolivian governments, all of whom have been heavily dependent on U.S. economic assistance that is tied to U.S. drug-interdiction targets.

The suppression of coca growing is complicated by the traditional consumption and spiritual use of coca leaf within indigenous cultures, which enables coca growers to defend as a cultural right their production of coca leaf in export-growing zones like the Chaparé River region. Coca growers forcibly resist the government's eradication policies, provoking repeated violent confrontations that have led to credible charges of human rights violations. The coca growers have launched several disruptive national demonstrations, taking advantage of growing public support for indigenous rights. In the 1995 municipal elections, the growers' newly formed political party, the Sovereign Assembly of the People, swept municipalities in the Chaparé region and won a total of ten mayoralties and forty-nine councilorships in Cochabamba and five councilorships in other highland departments. The four congressional seats the party won in 1997 provided a national platform for its anti-eradication agenda.

Meeting U.S. coca eradication targets is among Bolivian President Hugo Banzer's highest priorities, since it was under his military government in the late 1970s that the expansion of export coca production occurred. He has pledged to rid Bolivia of the cocaine trade before his term ends in 2002. The Banzer government's focus on the coca issue and the decline of other sectors of the indigenous movement have left the coca growers as the principal political players interacting with the government.

Although space does not allow a consideration of all the transit countries, Mexico should be discussed as the principal example. The increased demand for cocaine, heroin, and marijuana in the U.S. market encouraged Mexican drug traffickers, who originally furnished transport for Colombian producers, to distribute narcotics north of the Rio Grande. By the late 1990s, U.S. officials identified five major cartels and a score of minor drug bands in Mexico. Narcocriminals proved especially adept at corrupting Mexico's judges, prosecutors, state authorities, and the Federal Judicial Police (PFJ).

Originally, the Mexican Attorney General's Office, which directs the PFJ, spearheaded Mexico's drug war. In October 1995, following a visit from U.S. Secretary of Defense William J. Perry, President Zedillo assigned the lead role to the less corrupt Mexican Army, which received training and equipment from the U.S. Department of Defense and the Central Intelligence Agency. Mexico dispatched several hundred young men to study antidrug tactics at U.S. bases, and the CIA quietly complemented this initiative by providing instruction, resources, and operational support for a Mexican Army intelligence unit, the Center for Anti-Narcotics Investigations (CIAN). Although CIAN claimed some initial successes against two of the cartels, the majority of Mexico's military brass deeply resented the dominant antidrug role thrust upon them because of its corrosive effect on their once extremely popular institution. Far from stopping the northward export of narcotics, changing the lead agency only magnified corruption within Mexico's armed forces, as evidenced by the three dozen officers publicly charged with drug-related crimes.

The most embarrassing moment in United States–Mexican relations concerning narcotics came in February 1997, when the Mexican Defense Ministry announced that Brigadier General Jesús Gutiérrez Rebollo, Mexico's top military drug war point man, had been arrested on charges of receiving payoffs from Juarez cartel kingpin Amado Carrillo Fuentes. Only weeks earlier, U.S. drug czar General Barry McCaffrey had called General

Gutiérrez "a guy of absolute unquestioned integrity." The Clinton administration admitted that General Gutiérrez, as head of the National Institute to Combat Drugs, had received high-level intelligence briefings in the United States.

*Law Enforcement.* Related to the increase in illicit drug trafficking in Latin America is the increase in crime. According to one report, between 1987 and 1992 Latin American countries led the world in homicide rates, headed up by Colombia with an annual average of 77.5 per 100,000 people, followed by Brazil (24.6), Panama (22.9), Mexico (20.6), Nicaragua (16.7), and Venezuela (16.4). The United States averaged 8.0 homicides per 100,000 people during this six-year period.[2]

Yet homicides were not the only crimes rampant in Latin America. Colombia also led the world in per capita kidnapping rates. The most important policy issue in that country today is the restoration of public order, given that the Colombian state by no means has a monopoly of force in its territory. The 1992 escape of drug kingpin Pablo Escobar showed that military officers could be bribed, and the same has proved true of members of the national police. Although no one knows the exact proportions, substantial parts of the national territory are controlled by guerrilla groups, drug bands, and death squads. Cocaine money has made these groups very wealthy and well armed. Laws passed by the Colombian government can at best be enforced in the major cities but not in the hinterlands. When we asked a high-level official of the Office of the President, a specialist in the death-squad problem, how much money it would take to create a national police force that was resistant to most bribes, he replied, "That's a good question, one I have thought about. I should have an answer, but I don't."[3]

Other Latin American countries suffer the same problems, albeit at a lower level than Colombia. In Paraguay, always an emporium for contraband, organized crime now intersects with Middle Eastern terrorism, with Hezbollah guerrillas taking refuge in Arab communities there, acquiring fake documents, and undertaking smuggling operations to finance terrorist operations, such as bombing attacks on Jewish buildings in Argentina. A legacy of the Stroessner dictatorship, the culture of corruption in Paraguay heightens U.S. fears of the "Colombianization" of Paraguay as a rising gangster-state.

In Nicaragua, courts are poorly staffed and overwhelmed by the rising crime rate. Conviction rates in criminal cases have run under 5 percent. One result is that prisoners are often incarcerated for prolonged periods before coming to trial. Prisons are badly overcrowded, and conditions fall well below minimal international standards. Violence by the police themselves has been reported in many countries, including Mexico and Brazil.

In the Dominican Republic, the police violence is especially important when one considers the occasional deportation of Haitians and Dominicans who "look" Haitian, as well as the rise in violent crime due, in part, to the increased use of the Dominican Republic for drug trafficking. The courts are seen to have a strong bias against poor citizens, and there has been little evidence to suggest the contrary.

Hence it seems clear that many Latin American countries lack court systems and police forces sufficient to enforce the laws and protect lives and property. It is also obvious that such governmental abilities are costly. These needs are likely to be issues in the new millennium.

## Constraints in Latin American Policymaking

In the previous section, some of the major issues of Latin American public policy were considered. The aim of this section is to outline some of the constraints to policymaking in the region—both the conditions that affect political decisions and those that impede effective transition from policy outputs to policy outcomes.

*Underdevelopment.* The key feature of economic underdevelopment is that even when a government wishes to change many things, it seldom has the revenue to do so. All allocative policies have money costs. If the governing coalition of a Latin American country decides that economic development through agrarian reform, urban reform, and birth control are desirable, there might not be enough money to fund all policies adequately. As the case of Honduras shows, effective policymaking is difficult.

Government resources in Honduras are scarce, the state bureaucracy is notoriously inefficient, and the political class is driven by spoils rather than policy goals. A few Honduran presidents, such as reformer Carlos Roberto Reina, have come into office with clear policy objectives; however, the enactment of public policies to address national problems usually is driven by external pressure or by an acute internal crisis. The fundamental changes in Honduran economic policy in the 1990s, for example, were forced by an international credit boycott orchestrated by international financial institutions and the U.S. government.

In some instances in Latin America, policymakers honestly cannot do all that they would like; in other cases, legislation creates programs that are simply never funded. Governmental policy in Latin America, therefore, should be analyzed not only by studying established law but by looking at the actual expenditures of governmental revenues.

Yet another feature of underdevelopment, more political than economic, is the lack of bureaucratic expertise. Government bureaucracies in Latin

America have had one very important purpose: to provide white-collar, nonmanual employment for the members of the middle sectors, especially those who, in the absence of such employment, would be likely to join the political opposition. Because of this co-optive and patronage purpose, the bureaucracies of the area many times are not efficient in the day-to-day running of governmental programs. They are staffed by people whose jobs are based not on merit or skill but on personal connections, people who do not have the necessary educational background, and people who hold several bureaucratic jobs at the same time and who might work only briefly or not at all in any one of them.

For this reason, some Latin American governments established decentralized agencies, insulated from the more corrupt regular bureaucracy, to implement specific policies. But in many countries even this has failed to produce an effective bureaucracy, as we saw above in the discussion of autonomous state agencies. Therefore, even in the case of a policy that is accepted by the ruling coalition and adequately funded, the policy consequence still might fall short of the intention.

The neoliberal reforms have called for smaller, more efficient, less corrupt bureaucracies. To a certain extent that reform has happened in many Latin American countries, albeit with considerable difficulties. Politicians do not want to cut their supporters out of the state bureaucracy; nor do most want to increase unemployment by laying off large numbers of bureaucrats. Such a reform is especially dangerous, since most bureaucrats are highly educated and fairly well paid and could contribute to the opposition with both money and technical expertise.

*The Dilemma of the Political System.*   The rules of the traditional Latin American political game were described in Chapter 2. Here they are in summary form: A new group entering into the accepted circle of power groups traditionally needed to demonstrate that it would not do anything to harm already existent groups. This meant that many public policy initiatives were blocked by the rules of the game. In most countries of Latin America, there were two possible ways to solve this dilemma. First, public policy could work in such a political system if the economy was expanding and governmental income was steadily increasing. In such a case, new revenues could be allocated to public policies in a *distributive* fashion—that is, by dividing up the growing pie. It was not surprising, for example, that before the fall in oil prices in the early 1980s, Venezuela had one of the most successful reformist governments in Latin America, made possible by governmental taxes on foreign oil producers (and after 1976 by profits made by the government oil enterprise). The country's reforms included one of the most successful agrarian reform programs in the region, using lands that the government already owned. Yet the Hugo Chávez phenomenon of

1999–2000 shows that even in such favorable conditions, the Venezuelans could not be successful—either because of corruption on the part of the politicians or because of constraints of the international political economy or a combination of the two.

Governments still had difficulties with distributive policies, since industrialists, for example, might prefer that the new revenue used for urban reform, which benefited them only indirectly, be employed instead for infrastructure improvements (roads, railroads), which helped them directly. However, the controversy over distributive policies was much milder than that over the second solution: *redistributive* policies—that is, policies that would take something away from one group and give it to another. This controversy is why land reform encountered so many difficulties. Yet not all the governments of Latin America had the luxury of participating in only distributive policies; many required redistributive policies as well.

Unfortunately, sometimes underdevelopment meant that neither distributive nor redistributive policies would work because there simply wasn't the money. If the economy was stagnant, and even worse if it was shrinking, there could hardly be any governmental programs at all. So another possibility was a case-by-case, eclectic policy strategy in which one group won on one policy issue, another group on another issue, and so forth. Although politically this was a good short-run strategy, the long-term result often had contradictory effects, with detrimental ramifications for the economy, the people, and even the political system. In the 1990s, Venezuela discovered that low petroleum prices forced the government, which had long used distributive policies, to shift to redistributive policies. The shift was accompanied by mass dissatisfaction, bloodshed, attempted military coups d'état, the end of the political parties who had successfully brought democracy to the country for the first time in its history, the election of a president who had led a military coup d'état, and the convening of a constituent assembly to repair the nation's weakened democracy.

This dilemma of policymaking in the Latin American context was most evident in countries where almost all individuals were organized into groups that had accepted the traditional rules of the game, leaving no room for change and no opposition to call for reform. This was certainly the case in Mexico.[4] Argentina presented at worst a situation of almost complete governmental stalemate and at best one of very eclectic and contradictory policies. Since all groups were politically relevant and involved, and since all groups had agreed not to harm the interests of others, practically no consensus on public policy was possible.

It remains to be seen whether the new movement to democracy in Latin America has changed this dilemma of policymaking. It might be that strong political parties will develop, resulting in majority rule that will in turn produce effective presidential-congressional collaboration on successful redistributive policies. On the other hand, democracy might lead to executive-legislative gridlock, as the United States has had in recent years. In the 1990s, the Menem government in Argentina seemed to have solved the problem to a considerable extent, while it is not clear what will happen in Mexico with increased democratization. During the last half of his government, President Ernesto Zedillo had to deal with a Congress that lacked a PRI majority in the lower house. Then Vicente Fox was elected—the first president to be elected from a party other than the PRI in more than seventy years (see Chapter 8). Clearly Mexico is no longer facing the dilemma referred to above, but it is not at all clear at this writing what the newly democratized political system will look like.

*The Dominance of the United States and the International Political Economy.* A third set of constraints on Latin American public policymaking relates to the position of these countries in the international political economy and in a hemisphere dominated politically and economically by the United States. Some of the resulting constraints on policymaking are so dramatic that they appear on the front pages of newspapers. For example, Guatemala in 1954 demonstrated that a Central American government could not enact a dramatic land reform that adversely affected U.S. business interests or launch a general social revolution backed and participated in by the local Communist Party without prompting a CIA-sponsored overthrow of the government. Eleven years later, the case of the Dominican Republic showed that the U.S. government might intervene militarily even if a coalition about to come to power only *appeared* dangerous from a U.S. security point of view (i.e., threatening "another Cuba"). Nicaragua during the Sandinista government (1979–1990) provides more examples of policy options constrained by U.S. intervention. Chile in the 1970s illustrated that no matter how geographically remote and economically unimportant a country might be to the United States, the "giant of the north" can intervene through both governmental and private business agencies.

The obvious exception to these generalizations is Cuba. There the government predicted U.S. opposition, and through planning and the clear leadership of Fidel Castro the revolution survived. In Peru and Venezuela as well, major U.S. properties were nationalized without provoking a Marine intervention. So far, however, these cases are the exceptions and not the rule.

As the twentieth century came to an end, intervention by the United States was designed to favor democracy. As shown in the cases of Paraguay and Ecuador in 1999 and 2000, respectively, at times U.S. intervention was decisive in the maintenance of democracy. The case of Peru in 2000, however, shows that even the U.S. government works under constraints: While tempted to impose sanctions on the Fujimori government because of its dubious handling of the second round of the presidential election, officials of the U.S. government realized that Fujimori's government had been an effective ally in the war against drug production in Peru. Hence there were no sanctions.

There are other, more subtle ways in which the United States manipulates Latin America. The USAID uses its leverage to push certain programs: land reform in the 1960s, birth control in the 1970s, private-sector initiatives in the 1980s and 1990s. Although USAID influence is much less now than it was thirty years ago, USAID officials continue to assist the Latin American governments in operational plans within these areas and others. Likewise, international agencies that are heavily influenced by the United States, such as the World Bank, the IMF, and the IADB, traditionally encourage the Latin American governments to implement austerity-based economic and fiscal policies. For example, the IMF might push a Latin American government to devalue its currency and tighten its belt. If the country refuses, World Bank and IADB loans become unlikely, USAID will be hesitant to offer credit to the country, and even the private banks of the United States and western Europe will be reluctant to extend credit.

During the 1970s and early 1980s, many Latin Americans accepted "dependency theory," which argued that they were underdeveloped because the United States had exploited their resources, concluding that they needed to break the hold of this dependency on the United States. Regardless of the arguments of the dependency theorists, however, most Latin American governments recognize pragmatically that they must deal realistically with the United States. For better or worse, the United States is the major political and economic power in the hemisphere. Latin America is stuck in a dependency position, but it also desperately needs U.S. and other capital if it is to develop.

Until the 1990s, the real question was not whether Latin America could dispense with the United States but whether the Latin American countries could reap some advantages from this relationship. The trick was to get the capital and help that they needed from the United States without losing their sovereignty. To try to achieve that goal, clever Latin American presidents adeptly manipulated the U.S. Embassy, even as the embassy manipulated the politics of the Latin American countries—particularly if they had commodities or strategic assets that the United States believed it must have.

As the new millennium began everyone in both the United States and in Latin America recognized that the region needed investment capital for economic growth. It was also recognized by all that in the Americas, that capital was most likely to come from the United States.

## Conclusions and Implications

In the previous pages, we have generalized about the issues and constraints of public policy in Latin America. Although there are great commonalties among the Latin American countries on these matters, there are also notable differences.

Latin American countries have changed dramatically in the past thirty years, and so has the world in which they and the United States operate. Latin American leaders primarily see the U.S. government as a positive force in the new century, and through democratization and globalization, the two parts of the New World have more in common than they had previously. Demographic changes in Latin America suggest that agrarian reform and population control are likely to be less important in the future than they were in the past. However, urbanization in Latin America means that the problems of cities—sanitation, infrastructure, schools, health care, crime—are likely to be around for many years. Almost all Latin American countries are either producers of illicit drugs or transit countries for their trade, and the consumption of narcotics in the region is also an increasing problem.

In all these problem areas, the issues of public policy in Latin America are more like the topics of governmental concern in the United States and the nations of western Europe. Perhaps the new century will see genuine cooperation in problem resolution.

## Notes

1. Quoted in Miguel Urrútia, *The Development of the Colombian Labor Movement* (New Haven: Yale University Press, 1969), pp. 6–7.

2. Armando Montenegro Trujillo, "Justicia y Desarrollo" (Bogotá, Colombia: Departamento Nacional de Planeación, April 20, 1994). The only other country in this ranking was the Bahamas, which had 22.7 homicides per 100,000 inhabitants.

3. Staff member of the Office of the Presidency, confidential interview by Harvey F. Kline, Bogotá, July 23, 1992.

4. Raymond Vernon, *The Dilemma of Mexico's Development* (Cambridge: Harvard University Press, 1963).

# 8
# The Struggle for Democracy in Latin America

While the Latin American countries have become increasingly diverse over time, the common currents that we have examined in this book remain equally interesting. These include the continued decline of the traditional semifeudal order in all countries, the emergence throughout the region of greater social and political pluralism, the continued weakness of modern institutions, including those necessary for democracy, and the ongoing power of elite groups. The balance of power within Latin American politics is changing as the Roman Catholic Church, the armed forces, and the landed oligarchy lose power relative to the expanded influence of commercial, banking, manufacturing, and political elites. Similar changes are occurring at the international level, with the United States being less interested in the domestic politics of Latin America but more interested in trade and commercial relations. While Latin America as a whole is undoubtedly more democratic than it was two or three decades ago, its democracy often remains limited, partial, and blended with authoritarian and corporatist features.

We must never forget that Latin America is made up of twenty nations that, despite their commonalties, have many differences. The nations vary in size, economic wealth, natural resources, climate, racial composition, importance to the European colonizer in the colonial period, and importance to the United States and Europe since independence. Below we rank those twenty countries into seven different groups, arranged on a scale from most democratic to least democratic. The groups range as follows: (1) the most democratic, (2) democratic but not fully consolidated, (3) democratic in the past but now threatened, (3) formally democratic but with weak institutions, (4) in transition from authoritarianism to democracy,

(5) some fragile democratic institutions but lacking a democratic base, (6) Marxist-Leninist, undemocratic. Although our classification of these countries seems justified in mid-2000, the countries of Latin America are so dynamic that no doubt there will be variations over the coming years.

**The Most Democratic**

Today Argentina, Chile, Costa Rica, and Uruguay are the most democratic of the twenty Latin American nations. While space does not allow us to go into great depth about each country, the following will provide an overview of these "democratic success stories."

*Argentina*

Argentina went through a radical reformation during the 1990s. The Menem administration pushed through a capitalist revolution that has, in turn, brought far-reaching changes in the society and political system. The corporatist system, built by Perón and maintained intact by all subsequent governments, was swept away as Menem sold off large state-owned corporations and downsized the government bureaucracy. His elimination of protectionism, subsidies, and bureaucratic regulations resulted in the disappearance of many small, inefficient manufacturers and the loss of thousands of jobs, transforming Argentina from an economy of mostly small-scale enterprises nursed by a paternalistic state into a highly competitive economy in which large conglomerates, many of them foreign, dominated the scene.

Such a radical change had a great impact on Argentina's social classes. Many urban workers and former middle-class entrepreneurs saw their living standards decline sharply. Many joined the growing numbers of "self-employed" workers in the informal economy. Former government employees, unskilled laborers, and rural workers faced real poverty. On the other hand, people with managerial or high-technology skills improved their economic position, as did investors in the more modern sectors of the economy. As the decade progressed, so did the gap between the rich and the poor.

The old political system, dominated by the twin poles of powerful Peronist trade unions and the military, also disappeared. Chastened, downsized, and professionalized, the Argentine military no longer posed a threat to the constitutional order. At the same time, a large unemployed labor force acted as a damper on trade union militancy. Organized labor was no longer likely to paralyze the country by a general strike.

Such a radical transformation was made possible by the hyperinflation Argentina experienced during the last years of Raúl Alfonsín's administration, which became so destabilizing that the entire social order seemed about to collapse. Moreover, the neoliberal reforms initially brought about a phase of economic expansion, fueled by a steady inflow of foreign loans and investments, up through 1995. Since then, however, there has been recession and rising unemployment. Following his reelection in 1995, Menem saw his popularity steadily decline.

Public disillusionment has affected both major parties. The percentage of congressional votes won by the Justicialist Party declined from a high of 45 percent in 1989 to only 36 percent in 1997, while the Radical Party's share of congressional votes went from a high of 48 percent in 1983 to only 22 percent in 1995. Among labor unions, traditionally the backbone of the Peronist movement, Menem was viewed as a traitor to the party's classical principles. Radicals, on the other hand, blame Alfonsín for mismanaging the economy and for making a deal with Menem in 1994 to change the constitution.

There is little likelihood that Argentina's capitalist revolution will be reversed. The system has become so modernized that it is difficult to imagine a return to yesterday's small-scale economy. Nor were Menem's critics able to come up with a credible alternative to his neoliberalism. Old-fashioned paternalistic populism was discredited by the upheavals that finally drove Alfonsín out of office, and the collapse of the Soviet Union equally discredited state socialism.

But if the capitalist revolution seems permanent, what about democracy? In 1989 there was a peaceful transition from the Radical Party administration of Raúl Alfonsín to the Peronist Carlos Menem; it was the first time since 1916 that an Argentine political party had voluntarily surrendered power to its opposition. But the real test of democracy's grounding in Argentine political culture came in October 1999, when Menem's Peronist administration accepted the victory of Fernando de la Rua in the presidential elections. De la Rua had trounced his Justicialist rival, Eduardo Duhalde, by winning nearly 50 percent of the vote in a multicandidate race. Thus, for the second time, an Argentine political party has dutifully handed over power to its opposition—a sign that the country has politically matured.

## Chile

By the end of the twentieth century, Chile had elected three consecutive presidents since the end of the Pinochet dictatorship. The strongest proof that democracy had been renewed in Chile and that the Pinochet era had been left behind came with the presidential elections of December 1999 and January 2000. Ricardo Lagos, a socialist who had been minister of Education and Public Works in the previous two elected governments, won the primaries of the Concertación coalition, resoundingly defeating the Christian Democratic candidate. The rightist Alliance for Chile, made up of the National Renovation Party (PRN) and the more conservative Independent Democratic Union (UDI), nominated Joaquín Lavin from the UDI, who had become nationally visible because of his innovative administration as mayor of an upper-class suburb of Santiago, where he had promoted public works, health clinics, housing for the poor, and centers for the elderly.

Neither Lavin's earlier association with the Pinochet government, nor Lagos's participation in the Allende government was discussed in the campaign, where the principal focus was on issues of education, health care, public safety, and the economy. Lavin pointed to his record as a "doer" and benefited from the dissatisfaction with the incumbent government because of a sudden increase in unemployment to 11 percent. After a well-financed campaign in which he projected an image of youth, vigor, and charisma (and reportedly outspent the Concertación candidate by somewhere between US$50 million and US$10 million), Lavin came within thirty-four thousand votes of defeating Lagos in the elections on December 12, 1999, winning a majority of the women's vote and carrying many of Chile's regions. He lost the January 16, 2000, runoff by 2.6 percent, and political observers attributed Lagos's margin to some or all of the 3 percent who had voted for the Communist candidate in the first round, or to a 3 percent shift to Lagos in the women's vote.

## Costa Rica

Costa Rica has the longest and deepest tradition of democratic governance of any nation in Central America. Indeed, experts in Latin American politics have rated Costa Rica as the most democratic country in all of Latin America for the past decade. Civil liberties, including freedom of press, speech, and assembly, are widely respected and protected. Free and open elections have become the hallmark of Costa Rica's style of politics, with observers throughout the world seeking to copy elements of an electoral system that faithfully guarantees against voting fraud and corruption. Human rights, so often brutally abused in other Central American nations, are carefully respected, and one rarely hears even allegations of their violation.

Costa Rica is a peaceful island in a violent region. It abolished its army in the late 1940s and is constitutionally prohibited from forming another one. Although there have been minor incursions and incidents over the years along Costa Rica's northern and southern borders, border guards and paramilitary units have been adequate to cope with these international conflicts. Although Costa Rica has not been immune to terrorist attacks, their number and severity have been quite limited. Costa Rica would be incapable of mounting a credible defense against a determined aggressor, but Costa Rica's friends in Latin America have often made it clear that they would use their own military forces to deter thoughts of any such move.

*Uruguay*

By the early 1980s military leaders in Uruguay recognized that the restoration of civilian rule was inevitable and began looking for a way to maximize their continuing influence and minimize any retribution to them after leaving power. This change was formally achieved in March 1985 after elections the preceding November, in which two of the major presidential contenders, Wilson Ferreira Aldunate of the Blanco Party and Liber Seregni of the Broad Front, were prohibited from participating as candidates. The victor in 1985 was a Colorado Party candidate, Julio María Sanguinetti. Voting fell largely along party lines, and the resulting legislative representation was very similar to what it had been in 1971, the last election before the total military takeover.

The Colorado regime encountered difficulties and controversies in its quest for normalization, and in the 1989 elections the Blanco Party prevailed for only the third time in history, winning a plurality in the two legislative chambers and electing a president, the moderate Blanco leader Luis Alberto Lacalle. In 1994 the Colorados again won the presidency, but only barely, with the Blancos and the Broad Front closely behind. National politics seemed to have been transformed by that election, perhaps permanently, to a three-party system.

In December 1996 a reform was narrowly approved by the voters in a constitutional plebiscite. This constitutional reform, which passed by the barest margin (50.3 percent) in a national referendum, represents a revolutionary change in the electoral system. Among the most significant features are the following: (1) Although elections will continue to take place every five years, unlike the old system each party can now have only one presidential candidate. (2) A primary system will determine each party's candidate. The successful candidate must obtain at least 40 percent of the primary vote, with at least a 10 percent lead over the nearest competitor. If this mandate is not won by any candidate, a party convention will choose the candidate. (3) To win the presidency, the successful candidate must obtain an absolute majority of the votes. If not, a second round will take place between the top finalists. (4) Local elections are now separated from national elections. Elections for *intendentes* (roughly equivalent to governors) of the nineteen departments and their local legislative bodies take place in the year following the presidential and congressional elections.

These reforms have several major implications. First, the elected president will be able to claim majority support, a result unheard of under the old system. Second, voters may have to choose from candidates not of their party, or even of their liking, in the case of a second round. Third, the primary system may help produce a real party leader as opposed to the historical norm that produced leaders of party factions. Finally, local and national governments will be elected at different times, allowing ticket splitting for the first time in history. This may help generate more power at the local level and with it, more demands on the central government.

## Democratic but Not Fully Consolidated

If the four most democratic countries are fine-tuning their regimes, the nations of the second group still have basic construction to do. The democratic nations that still require reform to reach full consolidation include Brazil, the Dominican Republic, and Panama.

### Brazil

Since the transition to democracy in 1985, Brazilians, regardless of their ideological leanings, have fully participated in vigorous partisan politics, informed by media coverage that reflects a broad range of political views and ideologies. The democratic period started when the first civilian president in two decades, Trancredo Neves, died between his election and the inauguration. His running mate, José Sarney, completed his term of office but was faced by high inflation and a constitutional reform that failed to give sufficient power to the central government.

Elected in 1990, Fernando Collor de Melo had initial success in decreasing inflation, but he faced insurmountable barriers in the Congress, where his party had only 3 percent of the seats. He was impeached before completing half of his term because of corruption in his government, and in 1992 he was replaced by his vice president, Itamar Franco. In May 1993, with chronically high inflation increasing, sociologist and senator Fernando Enrique Cardoso was appointed finance minister.

Convinced that unbalanced public accounts were the principal cause of inflation, Cardoso instituted a fiscal adjustment strategy to prepare for the introduction of a new currency. Cardoso's strategy, the Real Plan, had two parts. First, the value of the new currency, the real, was pegged to the dollar, leading to cheap imports and forcing domestic producers to become more competitive. The second part was fiscal reform, with attention given to changes in social security, the civil service, and the tax system. State-owned companies were privatized and deficit spending was eliminated at all levels of government.[1] Begun on July 1, 1994, the Real Plan brought inflation down from 5,154 percent in 1994 to about 1.7 percent by the end of 1998.

As a result of this success, Cardoso was elected president in the October 1994 elections and won a second term in 1998. While inflation has not returned to the levels before the Real Plan, Brazil did have to devalue its currency in 1999. Institutional resistance has prevented some parts of the plan from being enacted, such as social security reform.

As for the future, one can speculate that the two dozen or so political parties will eventually coalesce into three or four major fronts or umbrella organizations that fit into the pattern of Right, Center, and Left—with Brazil's political Center being considerably to the left of the U.S. Center. Less speculative are polling results from the 1990s that show increasing disenchantment with all political parties and politicians—so much so that those vying for leadership roles are careful to stress their "independent" and nonpartisan credentials.

Brazil has much potential, but its burdens include a chaotic and overly bureaucratized system, constitutional arrangements that are still untried, weak and patronage-dominated institutions, and a fragile democracy. In the 1990s a new order was indeed taking shape, but in spite of more than a decade of democracy, progress was often slow. If anything, the average Brazilian expects more of Brazil, of its leaders and its system, because it is seen as a maturing democracy. However, this average Brazilian also has to deal with the daily indignities of unemployment, corruption among civil servants, a chaotic party system, and inadequate health and educational institutions.

## *The Dominican Republic*

In 1996, Leonel Fernández Reyna became president of the Dominican Republic in the second round of what were the fairest elections in modern Dominican history. In his campaign, Fernández promised "a new way," and in many ways he delivered on his promise. During his term in office, it became evident how much the country had democratized over the last two decades, something that was previously blurred by the presence of three-time president Joaquín Balaguer, Fernández's predecessor.

From an institutional point of view, today democracy looks better and more stable than ever in the Dominican Republic. Although there were four difficult years of gridlock as President Fernández and his minority Dominican Liberation Party (PLN) battled with the Dominican Revolutionary Party (PRD) and the Social Christian Reform Party (PRSC), the president consistently appealed to Congress for support and refused to use his executive prerogatives to force legislation. This provided a contrast to Joaquín Balaguer's presidencies, when the polity had been characterized by the dominance of the executive branch and the Congress's quiescence. President Fernández also began to reform and revitalize the judicial system, attempting to make it a more equal branch of government. Unable to succeed himself in office, Fernández was followed after a democratic election in 2000 by Hipólito Mejía of the social democratic PRD.

*Panama*

After the end of Panama's military government in 1989, there were two successive democratic elections by which power has alternated between populist parties (the Democratic Revolutionary Party and the Panamenistas), creating the impression that the country's political system has matured and that democracy has finally been consolidated. Although the elections of 1994 and 1999 were generally democratic, they also took place within the context of an unstable and highly polarized multiparty system. In sum, the historical tendency to find extreme party fragmentation associated with elitist and/or externally imposed democracy persisted into the 1990s.

In addition, both in Panama and in the United States there is a sense of nervousness about Panamanian democracy in the new millennium. The inauguration of President Mireya Moscoso de Gruber on September 1, 1999, reflects elements of both change and continuity in Panama, which now has its first woman president, and one who came to power as the result of two successive democratic elections. But the fact is that the new president represents a political party that represented the popular classes in their search for radical economic and cultural change.

Currently, elitist and populist forces coexist in an unstable equilibrium that results from an increasing income gap, stubbornly high unemployment, disillusionment with the results of neoliberal economic reforms, and a large national debt. Possibly President Moscoso will be tempted to return to her populist authoritarian roots, or perhaps her failure to do so will result in populist leadership coming from elsewhere in Panama.

## Democratic in the Past but Now Threatened

In northern South America, Colombia and Venezuela, which at least appeared to be among the most democratic countries in Latin America from the late-1950s on, had encountered grave problems by the end of the century.

*Colombia*

During the twentieth century, the resiliency of the Colombian system was remarkable. Party hegemonies came and went; civil wars tore the social fabric; leftist guerrillas called for revolution; Castroist and Maoist groups of university students waged spectacular battles; and drug lords attempted to terrorize politicians into submission. The Colombian population doubled every twenty-four years or so (this rate has now "slowed" to every thirty years), and thousands of landless peasants left the countryside for a life that was little better in the cities. Despite all these challenges, in essence Colombian politics remained the same: elitist, patrimonial, civilian, modified two-party, classist. Although it possessed one of the most liberal-democratic systems in Latin America, Colombia did less for its poor than many other countries. In part this is because of its great problems and complexities, but in part it is because the political system, whether by design or accident, has favored nondecisions.

As the new millennium began, Colombia was in the midst of a "dirty war" among the government, Marxist guerrillas, paramilitary groups, the military, and common criminals. The war had begun in the 1980s, and over time it worsened, despite governmental efforts to contain it.[2] Four major guerrilla groups were active in the war, but by the 1990s two principal groups remained: the Armed Forces of the Colombian Revolution (FARC) and the Army of National Liberation (ELN). Death squads, which became organized nationally only in the late 1990s, called themselves the United Self-Defense Groups of Colombia (AUC).

The FARC, the largest, most militant, best-equipped, and best-trained guerrilla group, had roughly sixteen thousand combatants in 1998. From its origins in armed bands in the 1950s, the FARC has always had close ties with the Communist Party and is still dominated by Marxists. The strength of the FARC in rural Colombia, particularly in remote frontier regions, can be attributed to the national government's lack of presence and a general climate of lawlessness. The FARC has become a de facto state in those areas, acting as a gendarme among squatters and peasants who grow illicit crops. The FARC's stated goal is a popular revolution that destroys the existing social and economic order and establishes a Marxist-Leninist state. Led by Manuel Marulanda Vélez (a.k.a. "Tirofijo"), the organization finances itself partly by selling protection to drug dealers, as well as through ransoms for kidnappings and through extortion from ranches and businesses that operate in FARC-controlled territory.

The FARC entered a cease-fire pact with the government in May 1984. Having strengthened its forces during the truce, the FARC gained territory and combatants during the late 1980s and 1990s. At the close of the decade, the Colombian government had ceded forty-two thousand square kilometers to the FARC in an effort to jump-start peace talks. Flexing its muscles, the FARC delayed negotiations, prompting U.S. alarm about the weak bargaining position of the Colombian government.

The ELN, another rural Marxist movement formed in the 1960s, was originally based in Santander and now controls large tracts of oil-rich lands. Inspired by the Cuban Revolution and supported by Havana, the ELN reportedly had five thousand members in 1998. Like the FARC, it also uses kidnappings and extortion to finance its operations. It has disrupted the Colombian economy, particularly by bombing the pipeline that runs from the eastern plains to the Caribbean and carries most of Colombia's export petroleum. The ELN is apparently staunchly opposed to coca cultivation and to negotiation with the government. In 1998 a jailed leader was quoted as saying, "We'll never disarm or demobilize. In our territory we are the state."[3]

Founded originally by landowners to protect themselves from guerrilla groups in the absence of governmental protection, some death squads were later dominated by drug groups. In 1988 the minister of justice reported there were some one hundred sixty death squads operating in the country. At that time the most notorious was Death to Kidnappers (MAS), set up by the drug dealers to protect themselves from kidnapping by guerrillas; for other groups killing "troublemakers" is the goal. Members of the Patriotic Unity (UP), a legal political party set up by the FARC, have been killed, along with journalists and leftist students, and campesinos making demands for land or other goods have been attacked.

Yet most crime in Colombia has nothing to do with either guerrillas or death squads. The country leads the world in homicides per capita; murder is the principal cause of death, and the country, with 40 million people, has more homicides than the United States. Kidnapping, rape, and robbery are also endemic.

As a result by 1986 Colombia once again was experiencing a "partial breakdown of the state."[4] Simply put, this breakdown meant that with a high probability of impunity, individuals or groups could pursue their goals (land, money, justice, and so on) through violence. There simply was little likelihood that the Colombian law enforcement system would catch criminals or that the court system would try them. The lack of public order has since worsened, despite the efforts of several presidents to restore it. Colombia seems to close observers to be in the "abyss," "screwed," or "at the edge of chaos."[5]

It is no longer certain that the governmental patterns can continue. Further, in early 2000 the U.S. government approved an aid package to Colombia that would provide over US$1.3 billion, clearly meant to be directed against drugs and not against guerrilla groups.

*Venezuela*

On February 4, 1999, former paratrooper Hugo Chávez took the oath that made him Venezuela's ninth consecutively elected democratic president. This ceremony took place one day short of the date, seven years earlier, when Lieutenant Colonel Chávez mounted the abortive military coup in which he almost toppled the government of President Carlos Andrés Pérez (1989–1993) and terminated Venezuela's thirty-two year democratic experiment. Failure was followed by eighteen months in jail for Chávez, a pardon by President Rafael Caldera (1994–1999), and several years in the political wilderness. Hugo Chávez then confounded his enemies by mounting a skillful campaign for the presidency and winning the national elections of December 5, 1998, with 57 percent of the total popular vote. Confident in his triumph and contemptuous of his political opponents, the newly inaugurated president proclaimed the existing 1961 Constitution to be "moribund" and promised a "New Democracy," one that would be honest, responsive, and worthy of the Venezuelan people.

In rapid succession President Chávez organized a referendum on April 25, 1999, in which 85 percent of the voters authorized balloting for delegates to a Constituent Assembly that would draft the new constitution. Another election on July 25 gave Chávez supporters 122 of the 131 seats in the Constituent Assembly. The assembly submitted its draft constitution for approval in a national referendum on December 15, 1999, receiving a "yes" vote from 72 percent of voters. Thus ended Venezuela's four-decade-long experiment with a political regime that President John F. Kennedy once called Latin America's best hope for freedom.

For President Chávez, the old democracy's defenders were "degenerates," "rancid oligarchs," and "squealing pigs"—"Hood Robins" all (Venezuelans use the term "Hood Robin" to describe someone who steals from the people to increase personal wealth—a kind of reverse Robin Hood). The new president charged the leaders of Venezuela's long dominant political parties, AD and COPEI, with being the worst of the Hood Robins. He charged that they robbed, lied, corrupted, and ultimately impoverished what should have been one of Latin America's wealthiest and most advanced countries.

The financial, physical, and economic milieu in which Venezuelans found themselves at the end of the twentieth century supported Chávez's characterization of the post-1958 democratic elites as Hood Robins. Between 1959 and 1999, hundreds of billions of dollars in revenue from the international sale of petroleum flowed into the country. But a myriad of public works projects either remained only half finished or were in a deteriorated state due to lack of maintenance, the social security system was bankrupt, and thousands of abandoned children lived in sewers and contributed to increasing lawlessness in the cities. More than 80 percent of the population lived below the poverty line at a time when Venezuelan elites had demonstrated a lack of confidence in their own leadership by transferring more than US$100 billion in capital to safe havens in Europe, the United States, and the Orient. Outrage over the failure of seven democratically elected governments to make substantial progress in developing the country permeated all aspects of national life.

Not only did Chávez successfully identify himself with the rage of his fellow Venezuelans, but he also promised them that he would mobilize the military to assist in development. Staged appearances at which military units mingled with crowds when the president appeared in public transmitted the new order's distaste for the old democratic politics, which were castigated as the primary cause of Venezuela's economic decline. Over and over again the audience heard the armed forces praised as honorable, patriotic, and competent, an institution that the political parties had used badly for more than forty years.

The Venezuelan Constitution of 1999 resembles the constitution of France's Fifth Republic. It increases presidential power by extending the term of office to six years and by allowing for the immediate reelection of the president to one additional term. In other words, after Chávez won the national election in mid-2000, he could remain president until 2012. The most plausible shape of Venezuela's political system in the first decade of this century will be some variant of limited pluralism—retention of the commitment to liberty, social justice, and equality, but modified by austerity. The New Democracy, despite its founder's preference for the public sector, has little choice but to craft rules that facilitate entrepreneurial activity and attract foreign investment. Of course there is a small but real possibility that some kind of authoritarian military regime could surface. Yet descent into chaotic disorder, while conceivable, is highly unlikely.

As in the past, the international environment will play a major role in shaping Venezuelan politics. Rising petroleum prices allowed the Chávez government to compensate for capital flight in 1998 and 1999 and to make new investments in 2000. Nevertheless, President Chávez must convince Venezuelan businesspeople to repatriate the capital that they transferred out of Venezuela and foreigners to bring new capital into the country. Also, the attitude of the U.S. government will play an important role in determining the fate of Venezuela's new political regime. Washington gave strong backing to Venezuelan democracy during the 1960s, and similar support for the 1999 constitutional order is necessary if that system is to realize its full democratic potential. All sides must be patient and forbearing.

The New Democracy's leftist ideology and military demeanor feeds doubts in Washington and among foreign investors. Conversely, the history of foreign support for previous elites reinforces Venezuela's suspicion of the United States and its multinational corporations. Whether Venezuela's New Democracy can attract the overseas resources it needs to grow economically, while at the same time deepening its democracy, will say a great deal about the viability of democracy throughout Latin America.

## Formally Democratic but with Weak Institutions

The third and largest group of nations in our schema of democracy includes Bolivia, Ecuador, El Salvador, Guatemala, Honduras, Nicaragua, Paraguay, and Peru. These are all formally democratic and usually elect their chief executives, but they all have weak institutions, such as political parties, independent interest groups, congresses, and judiciaries. All have suffered either from recent civil wars or extreme poverty—or both.

### Bolivia

The democratic era dawned in Bolivia in 1982, when the reconvened 1980 Congress selected as president Hernán Siles Zuazo, leader of the leftist Democratic Popular Unity (UDP) coalition. The demands of the UDP's constituency for increased state spending on the poor were unrealistic in light of the urgent need for fiscal austerity. Because of the mismanagement of the regime of Hugo Banzer, the massive foreign debt it contracted, and the massive corruption of the military, the economy collapsed. When Siles took office, debt service totaled 50 percent of export earnings. Declining agricultural and mineral production aggravated the situation, and Siles's poor management and political skills only worsened things further and siphoned credibility from the government. As the government printed money to address the fiscal deficit, annual inflation soared over the 20,000 percent mark. Siles was forced to resign and to call for early elections.

An alliance between the MNR and Banzer's center-right Democratic Action Party (ADN) governed Bolivia between 1985 and 1989, led by Víctor Paz Estenssoro in his fourth term as president of Bolivia. Banzer had won a plurality with 28.5 percent of the vote, just ahead of the MNR's 26.4 percent. The third major party on the scene was the Leftist Revolutionary Movement (MIR), the only significant leftist party to survive the UDP coalition. The MIR earned 8.8 percent of the vote in 1985. Slowly, a more coherent multiparty system was beginning to emerge out of the nearly seventy parties that had competed in 1978.

Banzer and Paz Estenssoro signed a Pact for Democracy on October 17, 1985, committing their parties to work in Congress to pass necessary economic reforms while using the executive's control of force to suppress the capacity of a weakened labor movement to obstruct reform. Unlike the disastrous UDP government, this coalition had a majority in Congress. The government's New Economic Policy reduced inflation to 11 percent in one year, and it reduced a massive fiscal deficit through a shock program that devalued the currency and drastically cut state spending, mainly through slashing state payrolls. The Paz Estenssoro government also liberalized the economy in order to restore international capital flows and took steps to shift the engine of economic growth from the bloated and inefficient state to the private sector.

By 1989, five parties were dominating elections; they would consistently take two-thirds of the vote during the 1990s. In 1989 a populist party, Conscience of the Fatherland (CONDEPA), defeated the three largest parties in the department of La Paz and secured control of city government, which it has dominated since. By 1993 the second populist party, the Civic Solidarity Union (UCS), also had become a significant threat to the traditional parties by building hospitals, schools, and roads and by distributing other scarce goods throughout the countryside. Two additional key players in the 1990s were the leftist Free Bolivia Movement (MBL), with a limited base consisting of highland, middle-class intellectuals, and the Tupaj Katari Revolutionary Movement of Liberation (MRTKL).

The MNR candidate Gonzalo Sánchez de Lozada, in an effort to recapture the indigenous vote, chose as his vice presidential running mate Víctor Hugo Cárdenas, an Aymara linguist who had represented the MRTKL in Congress between 1985 and 1989. The controversial choice capitalized on the popularity of indigenous themes in the early 1990s. In the June 1993 elections, Sánchez de Lozada and Cárdenas won 35.6 percent of valid votes in a field of fourteen candidates—14 percentage points more than the runner-up ADN-MIR ticket and the widest victory margin of any candidate since the military annulled the 1980 elections. Further, the MNR won 17 of 27 seats in the Senate and 51 of 130 seats in the Chamber of Deputies.

In 1997 Banzer was elected president. The MNR and the MBL were shut out of the government when he formed a "megacoalition" with the four other major parties, comprising 80 percent of seats in Congress and enabling the new government to legislate virtually by decree. Nevertheless, Banzer faced serious challenges. In his victory, he had actually placed second to the level of abstention (28.82 percent) in a country where voting is obligatory. The megacoalition was formed in part to counter this paper-thin mandate. But maintaining a large, programmatically incoherent coalition required the equitable distribution of political patronage and the maintenance of legislative loyalty among parties that opposed each other's economic and social policies. Internal disputes over policy and patronage were partially resolved in August 1998, when Banzer expelled CONDEPA, leaving the government with a comfortable 76-seat majority in the 130-seat lower house and with 20 of 27 seats in the Senate.

*Ecuador*

During the period from 1979 to 2000, Ecuador tried to consolidate its democratic system, and presidents with different programs and different political ideologies—populists, conservatives, democratic socialists, or Christian democrats—struggled to legitimize their authority, particularly when they carried out severe austerity measures in violation of their populist campaign promises. Effective presidential rule was hampered by the difficulty of building coalitions among small and fractious legislative parties that were in constant flux as representatives changed their party identification. Elections were relatively free and competitive, but democratic institutions were extremely fragile and often what took place in the public realm was mired in rampant corruption and bureaucratic ineptitude.

Ironically, despite substantial oil reserves, a diversity of agricultural exports including bananas, coffee, cacao, cut flowers, and fish, and a high potential for ecotourism, Ecuador remains one of the weakest countries in Latin America. Between 1996 and 2000 Ecuadorians had to put up with presidents and party leaders who contributed to a political and economic mess, a mess that has fueled the latest insurrection. Banks collapsed, inflation hovered around 60 percent, debt payments were delayed, the GDP was shrinking at alarming rates, unemployment increased to staggering figures, a privatization program faltered, and corruption continued unabated.

During the 1979–1984 period, President Jaime Roldós first confronted the personal animosity of Asaad Bucaram's majority forces; after both men died in 1981, President Osvaldo Hurtado confronted a fragmented political body, which included the vitriolic attacks of the traditionalist opponents led by León Febres. When Febres became president in 1984, he spent nearly two years turning the majority from its initial opposition to his government. Persuasion, browbeating, and behind-the-scenes maneuvering brought temporary success, but Febres subsequently lost control of the CNR and eventually finished his term with a bitter Congress opposing his every move. The fate of President Rodrigo Borja, who began with a progovernment majority in 1988, did not contribute to a more responsible and responsive CNR. Whatever the contributions of the CNR to the Ecuadorian body politic, as a legislative institution it remains erratic in substance and in policy impact.

Despite the inauguration of Ecuador's sixth successive democratic government in August 1998, there was a brief military takeover in January 2000. This was followed by a return to civilian rule with the election of Gustavo Noboa, showing that Ecuador's democratic system remains fragile and strongly dependent upon international economic forces, powerful foreign influences, and even acts of nature over which there can be no control. Many of the central features of Ecuadorian politics are antithetical to the creation of a stable and efficient system, which means that the governing elites face difficult choices as the new century begins. It is hard to imagine how current neoliberal policy guidelines favored by international financial organizations and the United States can help Ecuador deal with its fragile democracy and improve its weak and antiquated economic system.

At the beginning of the new millennium many worried that Ecuador's endangered democracy might succumb to more breakdowns and even to military-authoritarian rule if serious reforms were not instituted. The morass was magnified by the growing authoritarianism in Venezuela and Peru and by escalating guerrilla insurgencies and political violence in Colombia, which are showing signs of having a contagious effect on Ecuador. Given the prospect of more indigenous protests and greater support for military takeovers to "save" the *patria* if national security is threatened, consolidating a set of democratic rules will be even more problematic in the years to come.

## El Salvador

El Salvador experienced two presidential elections between the end of the war in 1991 and the end of the century. In 1994 a president, Assembly deputies, and mayors were elected. The results gave lie to the common wisdom of the previous decade that the FMLN had no popular support. Its candidate, Rubén Zamora, forced a runoff with ARENA's candidate, Armando Calderón Sol, who ultimately won. Meanwhile, the FMLN won twenty-one seats in the Legislative Assembly and thirteen mayoralties.

By the time of the next local elections in 1997, growing unhappiness across the country with ARENA's policies, particularly in the economic area, was reflected at the ballot box. The number of ARENA deputies dropped from 39 to 28, and the number of municipalities it controlled declined from 207 to 162. The FMLN, meanwhile, increased its Assembly seats to 27 and its mayoralties to 48. These results led the former rebels as well as many political pundits to predict that, with a strong candidate in 1999, the FMLN had a real chance of winning the presidency.

It was not to be, however. The FMLN irretrievably damaged itself in a bitter internecine fight over who would be its presidential candidate. The August 1998 party nominating convention began in a spirit of unity but deteriorated into chaos as a relatively small group of radicals without credentials invaded the convention and drowned out the speech of the moderates' candidate, San Salvador mayor Hector Silva. One month later the FMLN nominated as its candidate a former guerrilla, Facundo Guardado. But the election was already lost. In March 1999, U.S.-educated Francisco Flores was elected president on the ARENA ticket in a landslide.

The widespread assumption following the 1999 election was that the FMLN was too deeply divided to put itself back together and that its days as a significant political party were numbered. Many predicted that the former revolutionaries would fade away into electoral obscurity like the M-19 had in Colombia. That prediction, however, did not take into account the continuing and growing disenchantment with ARENA, which had been in power for a decade. To almost everyone's surprise, the FMLN came roaring back in the 2000 local elections, virtually matching ARENA's popular vote, winning for the first time more seats in the Assembly than its political nemesis (31 to 29), and increasing by 30 the number of municipalities it would control for the next three years, to 78. ARENA's hold on municipalities continued to decline, dropping to 124.

In March 2000, elections for mayors and members of the Legislative Assembly brought further gains for the FMLN and further losses for ARENA. The 2000 elections suggested that the FMLN was learning to govern as well as to campaign. The FMLN controlled 78 municipalities, including 8 of 14 departmental capitals, which meant that the former rebels governed well over 50 percent of the Salvadoran population at the local level.

In his victory speech Hector Silva, the reelected mayor of the capital, called for a political pact among the mayors of greater San Salvador, the private sector, and the national government. However, achieving cooperation remained the biggest challenge in the Assembly and municipalities. ARENA has a long tradition of antidemocratic practices, and it views politics as a zero-sum game in which the end, remaining in power, justifies any means. The FMLN's plurality in the Assembly meant that in order to achieve legislative results it would have to govern in coalition with other parties, at times including ARENA.

In San Salvador, accustomed to decades of laissez-faire economic policy, the private sector still finds the FMLN suspect, particularly since Silva has attempted to enforce city taxes on them. Since the 1994 elections when the FMLN first won thirteen mayoralties, the national government has treated opposition-led municipalities more as enemies than as collaborators in serving the people. The executive branch has withheld or delayed the delivery of funds appropriated by the Assembly for FMLN-controlled municipalities. The question following the 2000 elections, with their significant FMLN gains, was whether President Francisco Flores's government would become more cooperative.

The other problems facing the country were equally serious. Common crime had replaced political violence as the number one social problem, and the national police force was still ill-equipped and insufficiently trained to control it. The gap between rich and poor was still vast, and President Flores's rhetoric on this subject was not matched by a coherent government policy to address it.

In short, there is reason to be more optimistic from an electoral perspective and to hope that El Salvador has better prospects for stable democratic governance. However, from a socioeconomic perspective, the horizon is cloudy. Given the country's highly centralized government, the responsibility to provide the necessary leadership lies with the party in national power—ARENA.

## *Guatemala*

In November of 1999, Guatemala held its fourth consecutive presidential election since the Constitution of 1985 was enacted. The electoral campaign was rancorous and social tensions persisted, but there was another peaceful transfer of power from one civilian administration to another after this election. It is not clear how Guatemala has managed to engineer such a transition, from devastating repression to an apparently successful democratic electoral process. Nor is it certain that a true transition to democracy has occurred in Guatemala, given its violent past and its current social and economic conditions. It is not clear that there have been fundamental changes that augur well for a democratic future.

Two related questions confront Guatemala in the new millennium: (1) Will there be satisfactory progress toward solving the nation's worst social problems, including its ethnic divisions, its bitter legacy from the past half-century of violence, and its economic inequality? and (2) Can the new institutions and processes of liberal democracy be strengthened and consolidated?

Within the political process itself, three mostly positive but mixed patterns emerged in the 1990s. First, although political parties and alliances were transitory, the institutionalization of the electoral process itself seemed to be progressing, an important step in a transition to democracy. But it was not clear that democracy could survive in Guatemala without stable political parties. Second, although the democratic election of civilian presidents is necessary for effective public policy and a democratic society to emerge, it may not be sufficient. Which other elements of democratic government Guatemala still lacked remained to be seen. Third, if indeed effective public policy and a democratic society are to emerge from the electoral process, social movements and popular sector groups, in cooperation with moderate elites willing to be responsive and accountable to the democratic majority, must continue to play a major role.

Economic problems and the degradation of urban social life continue to be major obstacles in Guatemala's path to development. The legacy of past human rights violations and ongoing concerns about the impunity of those responsible, as well as social disintegration and urban crime, continue to plague the nation. The new democratic political institutions will suddenly appear fragile if these conditions deteriorate excessively. The institutions again will be assaulted by forces on one side of the spectrum demanding social progress, and by forces on the other side refusing to change.

## *Honduras*

Honduras made impressive democratic strides during the last decade of the twentieth century. The electoral system has become firmly institutionalized. The long-dominant military has been subordinated to civilian control. Most Honduran civilian politicians and military officers appear to have accepted the democratic system, and fears of U.S. reprisals help keep those who resist it in check. Consequently, the chances of a reversion to authoritarian politics in the short term are minimal.

However, Honduras is hardly a model democracy. The performance of elected democratic governments has fallen far short of public expectations. Most public officials have concentrated on capturing the legal and illegal spoils of office for themselves and their political networks rather than on addressing the needs of one of the poorest populations in the Americas. Neoliberal economic reforms have yet to improve the lives of the underprivileged majority. Street crime is raging out of control.

Although presidents Carlos Roberto Reina (1994–1998) and Carlos Flores Facussé (1998– ) won praise from international financial institutions for their efforts to reform the economy, most Hondurans saw little improvement in their miserable living conditions. Nearly half of the population continued to subsist on the equivalent of less than one dollar a day. The economic prospects of the poor majority might have been improved by educational reforms to raise the low quality of Honduran public schools and to increase the average number of school years completed. (In the late 1990s only about 40 percent of Honduran children completed primary school.) Unfortunately, such policies have not advanced beyond the discussion stage. Tax reforms to reduce tax evasion by the wealthy minority might have helped fund these and other programs to reduce deep social inequalities, but few of those with influence in Honduran politics are interested in paying more taxes. Recent governments also have failed to revive the agrarian reform program and to address the still rapid 2.8 percent population growth rate that burdens the rural poor with overly large families. Honduran governments have provided some temporary public work and food assistance to the poor, especially since Hurricane Mitch in 1998; however, these are only stopgap measures.

It is not difficult to understand why most Hondurans have been critical of the economic and social policies of their elected leaders in the 1990s. Hondurans have also been deeply disillusioned by the high level of government corruption, particularly under the Callejas administration. But for many, the greatest disappointment has been their democratic rulers' inability to control the crime wave that has enveloped the country in the last decade. The numbers of bank robberies, homicides, car thefts, and muggings have soared, and new criminal organizations have proliferated. The formerly military-controlled national police has been purged of corrupt and abusive officers and transformed into the National Civilian Police (PNC) and the General Directorate of Criminal Investigations. However, the Flores government has not found the resources to expand these organizations sufficiently to reverse rising crime levels. The underfunded, poorly equipped eight thousand–person PNC is wholly inadequate to police a country of this size.

Hence it is not a surprise that the public is unhappy with the quality of democratic governance in Honduras. If democracy is to be consolidated for the long term, the Honduran mass public must develop a much stronger sense of allegiance to democracy. However, this can only happen if elected officials start to behave in a manner more worthy of public respect and begin to implement governmental policies that tangibly improve the lives of ordinary people. Although Honduran civilian and military elites are gradually learning to abide by democratic rules, most ordinary Hondurans have found democratic governance to be a major disappointment. Neoliberal structural economic reforms required by international financial institutions have yet to reduce poverty or inequality in a country where almost three-quarters of the population still lives below the poverty line. Moreover, widespread corruption has discredited democratic governments. Elected leaders also have failed to stem an explosion in street crime that has placed all Hondurans at risk. Because of these failures, the democratic system has not yet earned the broad, unconditional support necessary to guarantee its long-term survival.

## Nicaragua

A combination of mediation by Central America's presidents and a decision by the Bush administration to pursue negotiated solutions to Central America's conflicts led to internationally supervised elections in Nicaragua in 1990. To the surprise of the revolutionary Sandinista party (FSLN), the elections were won decisively by a fourteen-party coalition headed by Violeta Barrios de Chamorro, widow of martyred journalist Pedro Joaquín Chamorro. The FSLN, however, remained the largest bloc in the legislature. In order to govern effectively, the Chamorro administration made working agreements with the FSLN, including the decision to leave General Humberto Ortega, brother of former President Daniel Ortega, in command of the military; in the process, Chamorro broke up her own coalition and created new problems with the U.S. Congress.

During the Chamorro administration, Nicaragua experienced six years of political turmoil, economic crisis, and citizen insecurity. Determined to "govern from below," the FSLN promoted strikes, obstructed legislation, and resisted military reforms. Conservative elements ultimately gained control of the legislature and engaged in a fierce battle with the administration over constitutional amendments. Jobless and landless, former members of both the Contra forces (antirevolutionary forces left over from the 1980s civil wars) and the Sandinista forces returned to the battlefields, with some rural areas ending up in a virtual state of war.

Despite all this, some progress was made. Annual inflation, which under FSLN rule had passed 30,000 percent, fell to under 20 percent. The strength of the military was greatly reduced, the police were brought under government control, and the draft was ended. Most Contras disarmed, and some refugees returned home. Humberto Ortega was eventually replaced as military commander, demonstrating a loss of FSLN control over the armed forces. After a bitter fight, amendments to the constitution reduced executive powers, protected private property, depoliticized the military, and barred the reelection of the president or the election of any close relative. Finally, in 1996 the Chamorro administration conducted elections that were reasonably fair, if far from perfect, and peacefully transferred power to another party.

In the 1996 election there were over twenty candidates, but it quickly became a race between Daniel Ortega of the FSLN and an alliance of Nicaragua's fractionated Liberals, headed by Managua mayor José Arnaldo Alemán. Alemán was elected president with 51 percent of the vote to 37.7 percent for Ortega. The Alemán administration managed to improve relations with the United States, but the economy remained a disaster and charges of corruption threatened to engulf the regime. In addition, the devastation of Hurricane Mitch further undermined efforts at economic recovery. By the end of the century, Alemán, like his predecessor, was negotiating a political arrangement with the FSLN and was also seeking to ensure his immunity from future prosecution.

As the twenty-first century dawns Nicaragua's future is uncertain at best. While there seems little danger of a return to the open violence of previous decades, armed bands still roam remote areas and both common and organized criminal activity is at near record levels. Politics remain mired in bitter conflict, reflecting both personal rivalries and past disputes. The population seems increasingly cynical about the entire process, seeing little hope in any party's program and believing that corruption and extreme partisanship will continue to be the norm. Social conditions are terrible, poverty is endemic, much of the infrastructure is inadequate and worn out, and both human and financial capital tends to seek foreign prospects.

Yet the situation is far from hopeless. The key is the emergence of a credible, competent political leadership concerned more with national well-being rather than with personal aggrandizement. Unfortunately the nation has little tradition of such leadership, and the most likely prospect seems to be continued suffering and turmoil for the bulk of the population.

## Paraguay

After the military coup that overthrew long-term dictator Alfredo Stroessner in 1989, General Andrés Rodríguez quickly consolidated power, purging the Colorados of high-ranking militants, and the military of potential adversaries. As promised, he released political prisoners, relaxed press restrictions, and allowed Paraguayan exiles to return. Three months following the coup, Rodríguez won elections in May 1989 with a lopsided 74 percent of the vote and was inaugurated on May 15, 1989, for a four-year term.

Over the course of Rodríguez's presidency, Paraguay experienced significant democratic reforms and economic initiatives and began remarkable steps to rejoin the international community after decades of ostracism and isolation. A new constitution, established in 1992, prohibited party membership for new military officers, and Rodríguez's technocratic economists privatized some money-losing state enterprises, reduced government spending, simplified the tax code, and eliminated controls on interest rates and foreign exchange transactions.

The façade of Colorado unity cracked further when Carlos Filizzola, an independent candidate, won Asunción's mayoral race in 1991. Furthermore, corruption showed few signs of dissipating, particularly after 1993 when the country entered a deep recession. Paraguay's enormous black market represents the country's most dynamic economic sector, and ranking officers hold lucrative side interests in narcotics, contraband, prostitution, and money laundering. Rodríguez himself was reportedly involved for his entire professional life in a whole series of ventures involving rake-offs, graft, and cronyism and was not about to tackle the issue. Meanwhile, Paraguay's regional integration into MERCOSUR, the common market of southern cone nations, along with privatization, economic reform, and some U.S. economic assistance, provided some needed momentum for Paraguay's difficult democratic transition.

The Colorados continued to be divided over their presidential candidate into 1993. Construction and ranching magnate and conservative politician Juan Carlos Wasmosy ultimately prevailed, representing a continuing alliance between the military, dominant economic groups, and Colorado Party elites—the triad of the Stroessner dictatorship. Intimidation against opposition parties and open intervention by the military preceded the national elections in May 1993, making it clear that party and military elites would only accept a Colorado victory.

Wasmosy won the presidential election on May 9, 1993, with 40 percent of the vote, beating Domingo Laíno of the PLRA (32 percent) and Guillermo Caballero Vargas of the new, independent EN (23 percent). The failure of both opposition candidates to unite, to unseat the ruling party, and to initiate a practice of party coparticipation reflected a historic opportunity lost.

Wasmosy's inauguration on August 15, 1993, extended the Colorado Party's unbroken hold on Paraguay past the half-century mark. With strong remnants of the military/Colorado alliance still visible, moving from authoritarianism to some form of democracy was problematic in Paraguay. Citizen groups participated more frequently in the process, with strikes and protest marches by peasants, workers, and government employees, and social groups began to network and organize. Yet regime elites, many of whom had also been part of the dictator's coalition, paid only lip service to their demands and remained uncommitted to democracy.

The greatest test of Paraguay's new democracy occurred in April 1996, when President Wasmosy dismissed army strongman General Lino Oviedo, who refused to step down. With Oviedo in revolt and threatening to kill him, Wasmosy was temporarily forced to take refuge in the U.S. Embassy. Crucial to ending the crisis without bloodshed was the unhesitant, massive show of support Wasmosy received from the Clinton administration, the Organization of American States (OAS), and the MERCOSUR governments of Argentina, Brazil, and Uruguay. The renegade militarist Oviedo was finally forced to resign. Paraguay's worst political crisis since 1989 ended in a victory for its shaky democracy, but the barracks revolt of General Oviedo was also a dark reminder that ingrained authoritarian tendencies do not necessarily disappear with the onset of democracy.

Renewed crisis erupted in September 1997, when the Colorados nominated Oviedo as their party candidate for the presidential elections in 1998, despite internal party opposition and a negative reaction from Washington. When President Wasmosy ordered Oviedo's arrest on charges of "insulting" the president, the general went into hiding and campaigned as a fugitive for forty-one days. As Paraguay continued its madcap course to the May 1998 national elections, Oviedo surrendered and campaigned from jail. The MERCOSUR giants of Argentina and Brazil again played the role of guarantor of Paraguayan democracy by threatening the country's membership in the free trade bloc if Oviedo were elected. Business elites and economists, alarmed over the political instability and its impact on the economy, estimated that in 1995 there were over 0.5 million under- and unemployed people in a nation of only 5 million.

By the 1998 elections, politics were so helter-skelter in Paraguay that after General Oviedo was sentenced to ten years in prison for leading his 1996 coup attempt, he continued to run for president and led in the polls until the Supreme Court upheld his conviction and his candidacy was nullified. Oviedo's running mate, civilian engineer Raul Cubas, then became the Colorado Party presidential candidate. The upheaval among the Colorados was still not enough to bring victory to opposition candidate Domingo Laíno, now with the Democratic Alliance (AD), who lost the May 1998 election with 46 percent of the vote to Cubas's 52 percent of the vote. With the campaign slogan "Cubas in government, Oviedo in power," the Colorado Party, like Mexico's PRI, extended its control over national government well past half a century.

By February 1999, when Paraguay had reached a milestone ten years of uninterrupted democracy, President Cubas was locked in a power struggle with his own vice president, and he faced imminent impeachment for defying the Supreme Court and freeing General Oviedo from prison in one of his first acts in office. On March 23, 1999, Vice President Luis María Argaña was assassinated in downtown Asunción. With Argaña's murder, Paraguayan politics crossed an important threshold from vicious rhetoric to actual violence. Argaña's faction of Colorados immediately blamed Cubas and his mentor, Oviedo. Cubas was impeached by Congress a week later, after Asunción's central square became a bloody riot in response to Argaña's murder, with rooftop snipers killing six and wounding hundreds in battling rival blocs. Rumors of a coup swirled in the capital, and total collapse was averted only when the ambassadors of Brazil, the United States, and the Vatican met with Cubas, negotiated his resignation, and arranged a new coalition government.

In the most rapid and complete overhaul of government and politics since Stroessner's 1989 overthrow, the first civilian coalition government in Paraguay's long history of one-party rule emerged, headed by former Senate president and Colorado Luis González Macchi. Together with a cabinet including two members each of the Liberal and EN Parties, González Macchi promised to back a Liberal as the vice president in the upcoming elections.

In his July 1999 report to Congress on the preceding year, which had seen three presidents come and go and a vice president assassinated, President González Macchi spoke openly of Paraguay's economic stagnation and political crises. Weakness in cotton and beef prices and recession in neighboring Brazil implied a continued economic slump that could sap the new coalition government's popularity. Widespread disenchantment with a weak economy and a political class with no experience in the give-and-take of coalition government could help pave the way for a comeback of the populist, authoritarian General Oviedo or another of his kind. In June 2000, Oviedo was arrested in Brazil, and Paraguay requested his extradition.

The new government surely faces heightened expectations and growing demands to respond to Paraguay's enormous social deficit in health care, education, economic and gender inequality, and poverty. Reflecting a narrow view of democracy, the Colorado governments of Rodríguez and Wasmosy encouraged progress in democratization, but they failed to address economic and social concerns. The distribution of land in Paraguay, one of the most skewed ratios in Latin America, might well become the source of Paraguay's version of the Chiapas insurgency in Mexico. Presidents Rodríguez and Wasmosy supported only the interests of large landowners, the business class, and the military in their dealings with land policy. Any meager resources available for rural peoples were given to campesino groups that organized, voted, or threatened—that is, not to indigenous peoples. The continued instability of the government, the absence of an accountable bureaucracy or anticorruption efforts, and the lack of established social policy means that Paraguay is still regarded as high-risk by potential investors.

## Peru

Democracy returned to Peru with the 1980 election of Fernando Belaúnde Terry, the president from the AP who had been deposed by the military in 1968. Then in the 1985 presidential vote the AP candidate was routed, gaining only 6 percent of the total. The largely Marxist IU garnered 21 percent for its candidate, Alfonso Barrantes, and a rejuvenated APRA, with the youthful (thirty-six) Alán García as its standard-bearer, won with 46 percent. The García victory was doubly historic: After a fifty-five-year struggle, APRA had finally gained both the presidency and a majority in both houses of Congress, and for the first time in forty years and for only the second time since 1912, an elected civilian president handed power over to an elected successor. The 1986 municipal elections also saw substantial APRA gains, including for the first time ever the mayorship of Lima.

During the García presidency two major problems arose: hyperinflation (after García refused to pay international debts) and the Shining Path guerrilla insurgency. While rumors of a possible coup abounded, military spokespersons committed their institutions to upholding civilian rule. Parties across the political spectrum competed aggressively for support in the November 1989 municipal elections and the April 1990 presidential and congressional elections. From virtual oblivion, Peru's Right reemerged, taking advantage of the capacity of novelist Mario Vargas Llosa to galvanize popular concern over President García's failures. A new coalition, the Democratic Front, or Fredemo, was formed among conservative and centrist parties, including former President Belaúnde's AP, perennial conservative candidate Luis Bedoya Reyes's PPC, and Vargas Llosa's new Liberty Movement. To the surprise of many, the Fredemo captured a plurality of mayoralties in the 1989 municipal elections.

However, Shining Path also used the elections to step up its campaign of violence and terror by killing over one hundred candidates and local officials and intimidating scores of others into resigning. As a result, about 25 percent of Peru's eighteen hundred district and provincial councils could not carry out their elections at all, and the total number of valid votes cast in other elections was sharply reduced.

Just before the April 1990 national elections, opinion polls made Vargas Llosa the heavy favorite. Many were stunned when another political newcomer, National Agrarian University president Alberto Fujimori, came from less than 2 or 3 percent in the polls a month before the vote to finish second, with 25 percent—just behind Vargas Llosa, with 28 percent. In June Fujimori won easily in the runoff that is required of the top two contenders when no one gets an absolute majority. His victory was explained as the electoral expression of popular frustration with politics-as-usual. There was also the sense that Vargas Llosa was too removed from the economic hardships suffered by most Peruvians and had become too identified with the politicians of the Right.

In 1992, with the support of the armed forces, Fujimori dissolved Congress and the judiciary and began to rule by decree. This *autogolpe* (self-coup) drew immediate and almost universal international condemnation. The United States immediately suspended all assistance save humanitarian and counternarcotics aid. It also used its influence to ensure that the international financial institutions postponed Peru's economic reinstatement and that most of the dozen countries making up the Peru Support Group also suspended new aid to Peru. Fujimori, chastened by the intensity of the international response, agreed immediately to prompt electoral restoration. This was accomplished with national elections for a new, smaller, one-house Congress in November 1992 and municipal elections in January 1993. The result was a substantially different political dynamic: The traditional parties were largely marginalized, the political process was much more concentrated in the presidency, and Fujimori now had a congressional majority. Furthermore, former president García was forced into exile after the *autogolpe* and lost his leadership role in APRA.

The new constitution written by the Congress was narrowly approved (52 to 48 percent) by a referendum in October 1993. It recentralized government authority, set the bases for privatization and economic liberalization, provided the death penalty for terrorism, and allowed for the immediate reelection of the sitting president. As the *autogolpe* worked out, then, Fujimori was very much the winner.

What saved Fujimori's authoritarian gamble was the careful police work of a small, specialized antiterrorist group in the Ministry of the Interior, formed under García, which paid off with the dramatic capture of Shining Path leader Abimael Guzmán and key lieutenants on September 12, 1992. Several hundred other guerrilla operatives were rounded up in the weeks to follow, thwarting what was to have been a massive Shining Path offensive to close out the year. Tougher antiterrorist decrees issued in the aftermath of the *autogolpe* permitted rapid trials in military courts and life terms without parole for some two hundred key figures. More than any other development, the capture of the bulk of the Shining Path leadership legitimated the *autogolpe* and gave the Fujimori government the political space to pursue its ambitious national reconstruction agenda.

President Fujimori had remained in office longer than any elected civilian government in Latin America in recent times. Although his government can be accused of multiple machinations to ensure his continuation in office, he also had a broad base of popular support. Such widespread approval came in part from his government's ability to restore economic and political stability to Peru. Inflation virtually ended by the end of the 1990s, falling from 57 percent in 1992 to 6 percent by 1998. With economic liberalization and Peru's reinsertion into the international financial community, economic growth was restored, averaging over 7 percent from 1994 through 1997. Between 1993 and 1998, Peru received over US$10 billion in new investment and US$8 billion in new loans. A variety of innovative local development initiatives reduced poverty by about 20 percent between 1991 and 1997. Political violence was dramatically curtailed, by 1998 it had fallen to less than 10 percent of the early 1990s levels (or about 300 reported incidents and 150 deaths).

Over the course of the Fujimori decade, political parties have been further undermined by a combination of government initiatives and their own limitations. Independent parties, including the president's own, proliferated and dominated the 1995 national elections and the 1995 and 1998 municipal elections. No traditional party except for APRA received 5 percent of the vote or more in the 1995 national elections, a dramatic turnaround from the 1980s.

After an overwhelming mandate in 1995, with 64 percent of the valid vote and a majority in Congress as well, President Fujimori called for "direct democracy without parties or intermediaries." His administration worked to make this happen by increasing expenditures for local development projects and by providing direct monthly stipends to municipal governments. His government also changed the political rules, often arbitrarily and unconstitutionally, to make it difficult to rebuild a robust political party system and to undermine the opposition's attempts to mount an effective electoral campaign. The media and the opposition were also intimidated through wiretaps, physical assaults, and character assassination campaigns orchestrated by the Peruvian National Intelligence System (SIN), directed by Fujimori's closest ally and confidant, Vladimiro Montesinos. A national referendum on the issue of a third term, supported by 1.4 million signatures, was to be held in 1998, but President Fujimori thwarted the vote by instructing his congressional majority not to accept its validity. Obviously, direct democracy was being defined selectively to include programs that were perceived to benefit the Fujimori government and to exclude those that might pose a risk to its continued dominance. At the same time, many of the programs carried out in the government's name served to lift Peru's poorest out of the most abject poverty.

Having set up the electoral machinery and procedures in his favor, President Fujimori surprised no one by deciding to run for a third, constitutionally dubious term in the national elections of 2000. Unlike 1995, however, this time he came close, with over 49 percent of the valid vote. But he did not secure an absolute majority in the first round, nor did his supporters win a majority in Congress. He was forced into a runoff with second-place finisher Alejandro Toledo, a U.S.-educated economist without political experience.

The international community, led by the OAS Election Observer Mission, did its best to ensure a free and fair voting process for the runoff. But it was not successful. Toledo withdrew in protest, international and domestic official observers declined to oversee the vote, about one-third of all ballots cast were spoiled in protest, and the incumbent won with 52 percent of the valid vote. President Fujimori's tainted victory undermined his legitimacy both at home and abroad and made it much harder for him to govern effectively. Later he announced his resignation.

All of this became more confusing and bewildering on September 16, 2000, when Fujimori announced that he was calling new presidential elections in 2001, in which he would not be a candidate. He also announced that he would deactivate SIN, whose powerful head, Vladamiro Montesinos, had been accused of offering bribes to a opposition member of Congress. In the weeks that followed, Montesinos fled to exile in Panama and then returned to Peru, where he was sought for arrest—the pursuing troops led at times by leather-jacket-clad President Fujimori. No one seemed to know what was going on, what the military was likely to do, and how long the dubiously elected Fujimori would be able to hang on to the presidency.

## In Transition from Authoritarianism to Democracy: Mexico

Ernesto Zedillo became president of Mexico in 1994 after the PRI candidate was assassinated and as his nation became one of the three participants in NAFTA. He inherited an overvalued peso, necessitating a devaluation that took his country to the brink of disaster. Zedillo deserved praise for pulling Mexico's economy from the brink, but the PRI would pay a big political price for the 1995–1996 recession.

In 1995 the PAN scored three gubernatorial victories. The following year both the PAN and the Democratic Revolutionary Party (PRD) registered impressive gains against the PRI in municipal contests in three states. Yet the PRI endured its most stinging setbacks in 1997, when the PAN added two more statehouses to its column. At the same time, the PAN, the PRD, and two minor parties captured 261 seats in the Chamber of Deputies, compared with 239 seats for the PRI, taking control of the Chamber away from the revolutionary party for the first time since the PRI's formation. Even more dramatically, Cuauhtémoc Cárdenas won the highly visible post of mayor of Mexico City, which afforded him a launching pad for a third presidential bid in 2000.

In the face of resounding electoral defeats, the PRI entered 1998 without a president who would chart the party's course. The once mighty party, its corporatist sectors in shambles, appeared even more directionless after arrogant leaders in Mexico City quashed the candidacy of a popular activist for governor of Zacatecas. This short-sighted act drove the rejected *priísta* candidate into the arms of the PRD and set the stage for the loss of yet one more PRI stronghold to opponents.

Amid much soul-searching came the need to select a PRI nominee in Chihuahua, a huge, PAN-controlled state. Instead of having party leaders choose the candidate, a move that would have spelled defeat, midlevel operatives proposed an open primary in which all Chihuahuans could participate. The risk succeeded when a well-liked moderate defeated an old-timer to gain the party's nomination and went on to win the general election. Thus, in one fell swoop, the PRI involved a quarter-million people in the selection process, recruited a winner, and conveyed a startling message to both the country at large and its own militants: the party could embrace inclusiveness and transparency and still come out on top. The Chihuahua results endowed the rambling PRI with a mission—namely, holding primaries wherever possible to improve the quality of candidates and to enhance the legitimacy of a party long identified with fraud and corruption. Animated by the introduction of primaries, the PRI captured seven of the ten gubernatorial elections held in 1998 and five of seven statehouse contests in 1999.

The experience with primaries convinced the PRI to employ a primary to select its presidential nominee. Despite the healthy distance that he had pledged to maintain from the PRI, Zedillo thrust himself into the nominating process, selecting the president and secretary-general who would run the governing party during this historic event. In addition, he named a traditionalist intensely loyal to the PRI to referee the intramural contest as chair of the Committee for the Development of the Internal Process. Zedillo also gave a thumbs-down on two prospective contenders.

As a result, four party leaders vied for the party's nomination, instead of a single candidate chosen by the president. PRI hard-liners argued that throwing open this critical choice would wreak havoc on the party. They warned of an embarrassingly low turnout, pointed to the impossibility of recruiting party members to staff sixty-four thousand voting places nationwide, and predicted that a bare-knuckled internecine battle might rupture the faction-ridden party. The upshot, naysayers insisted, would be a victory by the PAN or the PRD. As late as mid-October 1999, the party's old-timers, accustomed to top-down control over decisionmaking, urged Zedillo to cancel the primary process. Indeed, it had turned into an expensive, acrimonious, and freewheeling slugfest between Francisco Labastida Ochoa, the former government secretary who had held three key cabinet posts and an ambassadorship, as well as being governor of Sinaloa, and Roberto Madrazo Pintado, who had held seats in the Chamber of Deputies and Senate before being elected governor of Tabasco.

But the primary took place. On November 7, 1999, 10 million Mexicans went to the polls, awarding the lion's share of their votes to Labastida. Few serious irregularities marred the balloting. The primary not only boosted the fifty-seven-year-old Labastida's credibility, but it also ensured that future presidential aspirants would stress issues, popular appeal, and organizational ability rather than skill at flattering the incumbent. It also furnished the PRI with evidence of its strength and weakness in three hundred districts from which members of Congress would be elected in July 2000, and it buried forever the old, authoritarian device for selecting a chief executive in which the president chose his own successor.

By supporting the primary process, Zedillo snatched the PRI from underdog status, weakened the ability of future presidents to arbitrarily select successors, and involved almost one-fifth of the 57.5 million voters in a decision that used to be made by one man. Provided the party's election-night unity endured, the process also invested Labastida with a solid advantage over the PAN and PRD nominees.

The resurgence of the revolutionary party spurred PAN and PRD officials to examine the possibility of a joint presidential candidate to remove the PRI from the presidential mansion. After several months of parleys, the negotiations broke down in September 1999 because neither PRD nominee Cuauhtémoc Cárdenas nor PAN candidate Vicente Fox would step aside in favor of the other. Cárdenas had been battling for the presidency since

1988. Fox was a fifty-six-year-old businessman, rancher, and former president of Coca-Cola in Mexico who in 1995 had won the governorship of Guanajuato; he had been barnstorming the country for two years in pursuit of *panista* support. In late 1999, public opinion polls showed Fox running well ahead of Cárdenas, whose unimpressive record as Mexico City's mayor had diminished his popular appeal. The chances of the Left representing a united, responsible alternative to the PRI and the PAN remained slim as long as Cárdenas and Muñoz Ledo continued to clamor for center stage.

The 2000 election in Mexico was different from past elections for several reasons besides the presidential primary. First, an independent electoral commission was in charge, rather than the PRI-packed group that had monitored the vote in the past. Second, the media was more independent, not being limited to covering the PRI candidate. The candidates even participated in televised debates. Divisions of the electorate were examined and analyzed by pollsters and newspapers, the results suggesting that younger, middle-class voters supported PAN while older, poorer voters tended to be for the PRI. Yet the power of the PRI bureaucracy was clearly behind Labastida. It was alleged that jobs were threatened, higher child support payments promised, and refrigerators given, all to help the PRI candidate.

On July 2, 2000, Vicente Fox won the presidency with 42 percent of the national vote. Labastida received 36 percent, and Cárdenas came in a distant third with 17 percent. For the first time in Mexican history a president elected by one political party turned power over to one elected by another party.

## Some Fragile Democratic Institutions but Lacking a Democratic Base: Haiti

Haiti is a country with almost no democratic tradition. There was an elected president in the last years of the twentieth century, but when he dismissed the Parliament (which he had the right to do), he failed to call new elections to replace it. When the elections were finally held in mid-2000, the head of the national election commission had to flee the country in fear for his life, international observers doubted the veracity of the vote count, and members of the apparent majority party staged riots that closed down the national capital and other major cities.

A nation in desperate socioeconomic condition with almost no record of decisive government faces limited choices. Haiti has a reservoir of individual skills and political shrewdness, but the democratic challenge is to pool these human resources and to develop relevant economic and political organizations. Although there are egalitarian and cooperative features in the nation's peasant environment, Haiti's traditional political culture and its variety of language groups are serious obstacles to the development of a modern democratic government. In addition, portions of the elite have little interest in collaborating in the economic, political, and cultural integration of the nation, rendering near-term national development problematic at best.

This absence of modern institutions does not mean that Haiti's large rural peasantry and marginal population are politically inert. In fact, occasional outbursts from groups that represent the majority of the population have given Haiti its complex character. These outbursts, such as the one that led to Duvalier's ouster in 1986 and the one in the 1990s that represented what was to became Aristide's power base, have represented very real political frustrations. But with no institutional channels, these frustrations remain unstructured. Disconnected from elite political agendas, these violent expressions have not resulted in any institutional changes.

## The Nondemocracy: Cuba

Cuba's political development following its independence was characterized by U.S. intervention, clientelism, strongman rule, and military intervention in politics. The legitimacy of the early regimes seldom rested on popular consent. In the 1940s and 1950s democratic reformism failed to develop viable ruling institutions, and corrupt governments undermined public support for political democracy. Authoritarian regimes alienated the rising middle sectors and relied on coercion rather than on consent, seldom ruling with popular support. Economic dependency made national development difficult and resulted in a social system without cohesion.

The Castro revolution uprooted capitalism, allied itself with the Soviet Union, and reordered the political system through mobilization and charismatic rule because the revolutionary elite believed that development could be achieved only through political and economic centralization. Egalitarianism, unity, and social militancy became the supreme values of the new Marxist order, and pluralism, representative democracy, and a mixed economy were consciously rejected. Private education was abolished, and the state reshaped the entire educational system, expanding health services as well. State control of industry, commerce, telecommunications, agriculture, and even small-scale production created a large bureaucracy, which led to a new technocracy composed of administrators, planners, managers, and "producers of culture and information." A new class with its own vested interests thus appeared.

The economic crisis that followed the disappearance of the Soviet Union speeded up the process of cultural decay and definitively demonstrated that revolutionary socialism will never produce prosperity or freedom. None of the policy directions attempted since then have worked: Neither an expanded tourist industry, new developments in microbiology, liberalized rules for foreign investment, nor the partial "dollarization" of the economy will reverse the economic debacle. In fact, these "concessions to capitalism" indicate just how desperate the regime is for any economic respite. Unanticipated social and psychological effects of these concessions are already evident, as are confrontations between regime supporters and opponents.

Finally, even the minimal satisfaction of some material needs is jeopardized by incompetence and corruption in the management of an economy that is spinning out of control. The political impact of this failure is evident in increasing disaffection, the flight of thousands to the United States in perilous journeys, and the defection of hundreds of erstwhile regime supporters and members of the professional, military, cultural, technocratic, and sports elites. Losses of human capital aggravate the economic crisis and are a clear sign that millions of Cubans have reached the end of the line and see no way out of a national calamity. Meanwhile, U.S. policy wavers between being tough on the only Marxist-Leninist regime in the Western Hemisphere and relaxing the embargo as a way of encouraging liberalization.

## Notes

1. Amaury de Souza, "Cardoso and the Struggle for Reform in Brazil," *Journal of Democracy* 10, no. 3 (July 1999): 53–54.

2. See Harvey F. Kline, *State Building and Conflict Resolution in Colombia, 1986–1994* (Tuscaloosa: University of Alabama Press, 1999).

3. *Time*, September 28, 1998, p. 16.

4. Paul Oquist, *Violence, Conflict, and Politics in Colombia* (New York: Academic Press, 1980), chap. 5.

5. The metaphors are from, respectively, former President Misael Pastrana, quoted in Andrés Oppenheimer, "Rising Violence Rips Colombia," *Miami Herald*, June 12, 1988; *En qué momento se jodió Colombia* (Bogotá: Editorial Oveja Negra, 1990); and Francisco Leal Buitrago and León Zamosc, eds., *Al Filo del Caos: Crisis Política en la Colombia de los años 80* (Bogotá: Tercer Mundo Editores, 1990).

# 9

# Conclusion: Democracy in Latin America

In the preceding chapter, we reviewed the recent experience with democratization in Latin America and concluded that most of the Latin American countries are becoming more democratic. We conclude this book by drawing attention to the main characteristics of democracy and to the difficulties that Latin American countries have had in achieving and maintaining constitutional governments.

## Democracy: A Complex Concept

By 2000 all twenty Latin America countries except Cuba had an elected chief executive, suggesting that democracy had finally arrived as the dominant political regime in the region. But although elections are necessary if a country is to be called a democracy, they are not sufficient. Various Latin American dictators, including Anastasio Somoza Debayle in Nicaragua, had already shown that a nice electoral facade can make a country appear to be democratic, even when fraud makes it far from that.[1]

The history of elected governments in Latin America surely warns against assuming that elections in themselves indicate that there is a democracy. Elections are often a good first step but they are not the whole story. With a cultural tradition that has favored strong leadership more than institutional constraints on power, the region has many times had elections without having democracy. This came about for four basic reasons: (1) the limitation of suffrage on gender, educational, economic, or racial grounds; (2) restrictions on the voting rights of members of opposition parties; (3) the qualification of the power of the elected executive by some other body, usually the military or foreign governments and multilateral institutions; and (4) excessive executive power.

First, in the years after independence, suffrage was determined by either literacy or property ownership. Of course in many countries the landless and uneducated tended to be Indians and Blacks, but there were also many Whites who had the misfortune to fall into that category. Female suffrage in Latin American countries tended to be granted later than in the United States. However, by the 1960s there were few, if any, Latin American countries in which suffrage was not at least theoretically open to all.

Second, there have been many instances in Latin America in which the vote was denied on the basis of political loyalty. At times this has been done by not allowing members of one political party to vote, while allowing members of another to vote more than once (e.g., Colombia in the 1950s). In other cases the ability to vote as one pleases was constrained when the voting process was watched closely by the military (e.g., Venezuela in the early 1950s). Likewise, there have been instances when press freedoms were so restricted that opposition parties could not effectively get their views out to the electorate (e.g., Nicaragua and El Salvador in the 1980s).

Third, there were countries in which all citizens apparently had the right to vote and there were few constraints on any candidate during the electoral process. However, afterward the elected president was greatly restricted in his policy options by the military. Hence, in the 1960s, the Guatemalan military allegedly informed President Julio César Méndez Montenegro that he could do anything as long as it did not affect either the military or the large landowners. The Sandinistas in Nicaragua placed similar restrictions on Violeta Barrios de Chamorro, requiring that she protect Sandinista labor unions and the military in return for agreeing to let her take the presidency after her election in 1990.

Sometimes the constraint might come from some foreign government or international organization. The 1960s were filled with events in which Latin American governments were constrained in their economic policies, especially those having to do with foreign businesses, by either the United States government, the World Bank, the IMF, or all three. Perhaps the most notable instance was the pressure put upon the government of Salvador Allende in Chile. However, since the early 1990s, outside constraints have had more to do with ensuring the continuation of democracy. In 1992, for example, the United States reduced aid to Peru after President Alberto Fujimori suspended the Congress and the judicial system, and it threatened to do the same after the controversial presidential election of 2000.

A fourth limitation of democracy has been the excessive power of the president in systems with no real separation of powers or checks and balances. Hernando de Soto and Deborah Orsini could have been describing any number of Latin American countries when they described Peru before the presidency of Alberto Fujimori: "The only element of democracy in Peru today is the electoral process, which gives Peruvians the privilege of choosing a dictator every five years. Rule making is subsequently carried out in a vacuum, with the executive branch enacting new rules and regulations at a clip of 134,000 every five years (an average of 106 each working day) without any feedback from the population.[2]

The gridlock of this system led President Alberto Fujimori to disband Congress and the courts in 1992, leading to international condemnation for ending "democracy." Guatemalan president Jorge Serrano tried to do the same in 1993. In this case, the president's effort failed for lack of support from the armed forces, who removed him from power. Both cases show that even though excessive executive power detracts from democracy in Latin America, on occasion the chief executive has attempted to increase his already overwhelming power.

Traditionally almost all Latin American countries have had *constitutional* ways by which the president might acquire more power. The power to declare a "state of siege" or a "state of emergency" allows presidents to decree policy, in many cases without conferring with the congress or having the decrees subject to judicial review. So while the democratic idea of limited power is found in Latin American constitutions, so also are means for the chief executive to rule with almost unlimited authority.

Let us be explicit about the concept of democracy. As we have said, although elections are a necessary condition for democracy, they are not sufficient. Although scholars disagree on what other characteristics a regime must have to meet that standard, we would suggest that the following conditions must be met:[3]

- Constitutionally elected officials must control government decisions. They must be able to govern constitutionally without the veto power of unelected agents such as the military and must be able to act independently without outside constraints.
- Elections must be frequent and fair.
- Almost all adults must have the right to vote.
- Almost all adults must have the right to become candidates for public office without fear for their lives or their property.
- Citizens must have the right to express themselves about politics without the fear of punishment.
- Citizens must have the right to seek alternative sources of information, and such sources must exist and be protected by law.

- Citizens must have the right to form independent organizations and groups, including political parties and interest groups, and the government should not favor certain interest groups over others.
- Political power should not be concentrated in one person or group; rather, there should be separation of powers.
- Human rights, especially the right to life, must be respected.

All of these constitute *institutional* characteristics of democracy. However, some argue that a full democracy should also have a considerable degree of egalitarianism, a sense that all people are full citizens and not the victims of class, racial, or gender discrimination. All people should feel that they are free to participate; social and economic programs should be more or less just, and there should be a certain civic consciousness, an understanding that people generally deal with each other in fair, impartial, and just ways. Accepting these additional requirements for democracy, we can see that although some of the Latin American countries may have the institutional apparatus of democracy, in many respects they are still far from having democratic societies.[4] Indeed, it is doubtful that *any* political system meets even the above institutional requirements perfectly. Below we show how close the political systems of the Latin American countries come to fulfilling them.

## Challenges to Democracy

Constructing and maintaining a democracy is not an easy matter anywhere. As the Latin American countries face a possible democratic future, difficulties are likely to arise from a political tradition unfavorable to limited government, serious inequities of income distribution, the aftereffects of recent civil wars, and the absence of governments that can effectively implement policies for the nation as a whole.

### *The Political Tradition*

In Chapter 4 we talked about the traditional Latin American political system. It was authoritarian, elitist, patrimonial, and corporate. It was not based on the idea of the equality of all individuals.

It might logically be anticipated that the groups that benefited from the old system would be resistant to democracy. If Latin American history of the 1970s and 1980s is any guide, we can predict that the two major groups most likely to be uncomfortable with the new rules of the game will be the military and the economic elite. Although evidence suggests that the civilian elites now see democracy as the best hope for stability, if elected governments in Latin America face serious economic difficulties, it is likely that some members of the military will consider the traditional way of disposing of misbehaving governments, the military coup. Recent history has borne this out: There were two attempts to overthrow the elected president of Venezuela in the early 1990s; the *New York Times* reported in January 1994 that many Brazilians were ready for the military to return to power because of economic problems and rampant corruption among civilian politicians; and Ecuador and Paraguay each had a military coups in early 2000. Yet with the passing of each year, the probability of a military coup seems lower.

## Pockets of Underdevelopment

Although very modern in many ways, all Latin American countries have large pockets of people living in abject poverty. The neoliberal economic changes that have been occurring in the area since the early 1990s—the end of protective tariffs, the privatization of state-owned industries, the reduction of support for the poor—are likely, at least in the short run, to increase the number of poor people through the unemployment caused when previously protected industries go bankrupt. In addition, some people with slightly higher living standards, such as owners of small businesses and bureaucrats, may oppose further change because they once benefited from the traditional state-capitalist economic system.

Even before the recent changes, socioeconomic inequalities seemed to some to make democracy unlikely in Latin America. Robert Wesson is only one of the scholars who conclude that inequality makes it difficult to achieve democracy. After listing the problems of ethnic divisiveness, low standards of living, disdain for politics, a weak or unfree press, poorly organized and narrow parties, unfair elections, politically powerful armies, weak institutions of higher education, traditions of strong leadership, the paternalistic state, and clientelist politics, he argued that "one basic condition may account for most of the rest, and it is probably a sufficient condition to explain the difficulty of democracy in Latin America, although no means the sole cause. This is inequality, the separation of the rich from poor or top from bottom, of educated from ignorant or illiterate, or refined and proud elite from despised masses."[5] The difficulty that this inequality creates for democracy is that "to expect the cultured and well-off would accede to major social changes because they are outnumbered and outvoted in elections of dubious honesty by the ignorant and impoverished—many of whom are undernourished and diseased—is unrealistic. That would require a society of saints with an unlikely degree of loyalty to democratic principles."[6] Abraham Lowenthal, for his part, points out that economic inequality has increased, leading to an even greater gap between "the 'fast caste'—with their cellular phones, Internet connections, walled homes, and private security guards—and those mired in deprivation."[7]

The neoliberals see democracy and economic reform as interdependent, but ironically the poor and those who benefited from the mercantilist system may use the new democratic political regime to elect presidents and members of national congresses who are opposed to neoliberalism. This seems to have happened in Venezuela in the 1993 election of Rafael Caldera and the 1999 election of Hugo Chávez. Alternatively the poor may turn to guerrilla violence, as Indians did in the post–Cold War revolutionary Zapatista National Liberation Army in early 1994 in Chiapas, Mexico.

The paradox of democracy lies in the fact that it pits *representativeness* against *governability*. Democracy implies an unwillingness to concentrate power in the hands of a few, and so it subjects leaders and policies to mechanisms of popular representation and accountability. To be stable, however, a democracy must be able to act, sometimes quickly and decisively. Representativeness requires that parties and leaders speak to and for these conflicting interests; to be able to govern, parties must have sufficient autonomy to rise above them.[8]

A related contradiction of democracy likely to be important in Latin America is that between *consent* and *effectiveness*. Democracy means literally "rule by the people." To be stable, a democracy must be deemed legitimate by the people; they must view it as the best, most appropriate form of government for their society. This legitimacy requires a profound moral commitment and emotional allegiance, but these develop only over time and partly as a result of effective performance. Larry Diamond describes this requirement: "Democracy will not be valued by the people unless it deals effectively with social and economic problems and achieves a modicum of order and justice."[9] This has been a problem in many Latin American countries as the neoliberal removal of customs barriers leads to large-scale unemployment of individuals who had jobs under the old, protected economies. The 2000 presidential elections in Mexico, for example, demonstrated how acquiring popular consent to such reforms, however effective they might be, can be a political issue. Even within the party in power there was opposition to the neoliberal changes as their effects on the poor of the country became clear.

## The Legacy of Civil Wars

In many Latin American countries, thousands have died in recent civil wars. The tension between *conflict* and *consensus* exists in any democracy—

by its nature a system of institutionalized competition for power. As Diamond argues, "Hence the paradox: Democracy requires conflict—but not too much; competition there must be, but only within carefully defined and universally accepted boundaries. Cleavage must be tempered by consensus."[10] Many Latin American countries have suffered years of war before learning this lesson. Nowhere has the problem of conflict been more serious than in Mexico and Colombia, where there have been long and bloody civil wars. Other countries have had civil wars at the beginning of their independent history but then moved on to less violent modes of competition. In the 1960s Marxist guerrilla groups chose armed conflict instead of electoral competition, and the resulting civil wars created a series of related problems for Latin American democracies.

It is especially difficult for a democratic government to deal with revolutionaries with different ethical standards. As Gustavo Gorriti has argued about countries with guerrilla challenges,

> The authorities in the threatened countries must confront the nightmarish realities that any Third World democracy faces when battling a determined group of ruthless insurgents. A well-planned insurgency can severely test the basic assumptions of the democratic process. While they provoke and dare the elected regime to overstep its own laws in response to their aggression, the insurgents strive to paint the very process they are trying to destroy as a sham. If ensnared in such perverse dynamics, most Third World democracies will find their legitimacy eroding, and may eventually cease to be democracies altogether.[11]

Democracy is abandoned altogether when a government under this pressure becomes involved in a "dirty war." A number of Latin American countries have had such wars, in which thousands of people have been murdered or simply "disappeared." In Argentina and Chile in the 1970s, in El Salvador in the 1980s, and in Colombia and Peru in the 1980s and 1990s, the government or at least the military has been involved in such wars. Once the dirty war is over and democracy is restored, the nation is left with the challenge of deciding to what extent violators of human rights in the previous period should be punished. Punishing the guilty (from the military, predominantly) may in turn threaten the democracy. Some may prefer justice, but that threatens a military takeover. As did Raúl Alfonsín in Argentina, many civilian presidents may pardon alleged violators of human rights rather than risk making the military so angry that it intervenes again.

During the 1960s most Latin American countries had guerrilla threats, but by 2000 only Colombia was still burdened with a significant guerrilla movement. The Shining Path still existed in Peru, albeit with much less importance than before; and guerrillas still existed in the southern part of Mexico. In countries where civil wars have only recently ended, the difficult task is to achieve consensus among erstwhile enemies. As has become apparent in El Salvador and Colombia, a government may grant amnesty to guerrillas, but the people who suffered at their hands may not be ready to forgive and forget.

*The Inability to Govern*

As relatively poor countries with serious problems of transportation and communication, many Latin American countries have never been able to ensure the rule of law for the entire nation. Although their electoral and legal processes might be quite democratic, their governments actually govern only the major cities, at best. This weakness of government was exacerbated in Latin American countries by the emergence of the drug trade. Especially affected in this regard were Colombia, Peru, Bolivia, and Mexico. María Jimena Duzán, herself a personal victim of the drug trade, has described the distortion of democracy in her native Colombia: "Today in Colombia . . . [there] is a terrorized political class that has delivered itself to the designs and money of the drug dealers. Those who stand up to the bosses and challenge them have fallen victim."[12] In Peru, the Marxist Shining Path and the drug interests of the Upper Huallaga Valley destabilized politics for ten years, and in Bolivia one military dictator had very close connections to the coca-growers syndicate. Mexico, given its size and apparent stability, has at times seemed less affected. However, its location has made it a key transit point to the United States, and some think that drug interests have infiltrated its government as much as they have in Colombia.

## Change and Continuity

Although the main structures and institutions of Latin American society and politics remained remarkably stable through three centuries of colonial rule and even on into the post-independence nineteenth and early twentieth centuries, in recent decades the process of change has been greatly accelerated. In Chapter 2 we identified six broad areas of change: the political culture and values, the economy, social and class structure, political groups and organizations, public policy, and the international environment.

Latin American political culture is undergoing transformation. New values and ideologies—democracy, participation, liberalism, capitalism, and socialism—have challenged the traditional belief system of fatalism, elitism, hierarchy, and resignation. New communications and transportation networks are breaking down traditional beliefs and isolation. The hold of traditional Catholicism on Latin America is also loosening as Protestantism, secularism, a changed Catholic Church, and other belief systems make serious inroads. In a process that varies from country to country, the older authoritarian assumptions are being questioned and the older bases of legitimacy are being undermined. Latin American political culture is changing rapidly.

And yet many of the old beliefs linger on, particularly in the undeveloped rural areas and in the more traditional and poorer countries but by no means not exclusively there. For example, although in general people in Latin America prefer democratic rule, some define democracy as "strong government." Some want regular democratic elections but also want spoils, patronage, and government favors in return for the vote. Some believe in separation of powers but would still vest strong authority in the all-powerful executive. Hence, while formal democracy has been established throughout the region (except in Cuba), genuinely egalitarian and participatory democracy is still weak in most countries. Most of the countries lack a "civil society"—a network of independent interest groups that mediate between the citizen and the government.

One bright light on the horizon is economic reform. Even though many problems remain, the economic structure has been dramatically changed in recent decades. These are no longer sleepy, traditional, backward "banana republics"; rather, the Latin American economies have become much more dynamic and diversified. The older subsistence agriculture and one-crop economies are increasingly giving way to industry, manufacturing, commerce, business, tourism, and services. Latin America is now far more integrated into the world economy; feudalism and semifeudalism have given way to capitalism and neoliberalism. All these changes have put more money into the economies of the area, have provided new jobs, including jobs for women, and have quickened the way of life and increased general prosperity for many.

And yet these changes are very uneven. Much of Latin America remains poor, backward, and undeveloped. Some countries and some people are "making it" into the developed world; others lag behind. Moreover, even with the new wealth, Latin America has the worst distribution of income of any area in the world. In addition, some markets have been freed up, but the temptation to return to the older mercantilism and statism is still powerful. So even though there has been economic progress, many problems remain.

One of the most serious problems is a continuing social dualism, with a few very wealthy people and a large number of abjectly poor people. The wealth gap in Brazil engendered the nickname "Belindia"—one part modern and wealthy like Belgium and another part traditional and poor like India. This dualism exists in all Latin American countries, with the possible exception of Cuba, and in some countries—Peru, Bolivia, and Guatemala, most notably—it is accentuated by the fact that the traditional, poor sector also contains Indians who do not even speak Spanish.

Economic development has given rise to widespread social changes in all the countries of the region. Latin America has gone from 70 percent rural to 70 percent urban, from 70 percent illiterate to 70 percent literate. Life expectancy has risen from 60 years to 70, and per capita income has significantly increased. In addition, the once feudal, two-class societies of Latin America now have business, industrial, commercial, banking, and other elites in addition to the traditional landholding oligarchy. All the societies now have sizable middle classes, ranging from 20 to 40 percent of the population. Trade union movements, peasants, women, indigenous elements, and the urban poor are all being organized for the first time. There are new community groups, social movements, and NGOs. These social changes have made Latin America far more pluralistic than in the past, thus providing a more solid base for democracy.

But these general figures are often deceiving. Poverty, malnutrition, illiteracy, and disease are still endemic in Latin America in many areas, both rural and urban. Most of the wealth has remained in the hands of the elites and middle classes; little has trickled down to the poor. In most countries these same elites still rule; despite elections, power is still mainly in the hands of the social, economic, and political elites. Traditionally, interest groups could exist only if given permission by the elite or the state. Today this seems to be changing, as new groups can survive even if the government does not grant them recognition. Yet the social system is still unbalanced: The trade unions, peasant leagues, women's groups, indigenous movements, and other mass organizations tend to be weak and divided as compared with the elites.

It is unclear how completely the Latin American nations have changed from systems of government control and regulation of groups to new systems of de facto liberal, pluralist legitimacy. Latin America is undoubtedly more pluralist than before, but the mass of the population is still excluded from effective participation in decisions that affect them most closely because organized groups tend to have a middle- and upper-class bias. Nor does Latin America, despite its greater pluralism, have the kind of counterbalancing interest-group competition and lobbying activities characteristic of U.S. democracy.

Many of the same problems are characteristic of Latin American political institutions. Nineteen of the twenty Latin American countries hold elections regularly and are at least formally democratic, and that is encouraging. Similarly, the human rights situation is significantly better in most countries than it was twenty years ago. But the cultural and institutional bases of many of these new democracies are still fragile. Polls indicate that democracy's popularity is actually declining in Latin America, that the public doesn't think democracy has delivered on its promise. Cronyism and patrimonialism are still widely practiced, often more prominent than egalitarianism and merit-based promotion. Corruption, violence, and crime are increasing. At the same time, political parties, local government, and political institutions in general are not held in high esteem by the public. Latin America seems to practice democracy at election time, but in the intervening years presidents rule as almost constitutional dictators.

Many of the same disclaimers apply to public policy: The national economies are growing, but the gaps between rich and poor are widening. Liberalization, privatization, and economic reform are going forward, but only ever so slowly. Agrarian reform is all but dead as an issue, and where there is urban reform, the problems seem to mount up faster than the solutions. There are new social reforms, but they seldom seem to reach those most in need. In the areas of education, housing, health care, and employment, important steps have been taken, but the difficulties seem to outstrip government's capacity to cope with them.

The final area of major change in Latin America is in the international realm. It is clear that Latin Americans no longer live in isolation. Globalization has come to the region. Television and movies from around the globe bring in new styles of taste and comportment: blue jeans, dating, McDonald's, Coca-Cola, freedom, consumerism. Globalization also brings with it the requirements of democracy and human rights, and if these are abused, international sanctions are likely to follow. Globalization also means economic competition, requiring that Latin America lower its protective tariffs and be prepared to compete with the world's most efficient economies. Competition has major political implications as well, requiring state downsizing, privatization, changes to the patronage system, and the likely failure of thousands of small, inefficient, "mom-and-pop" stores and businesses.

So the balance sheet on Latin American politics and development is still a mixed one: lots of progress on economic growth, social change, and democratization, but major weaknesses and problems in all of these areas as well. The gross figure on democratization sounds wonderful—nineteen of twenty countries are democratic—but the deeper we probe into the individual countries, the more problems we see.

What overall conclusions emerge from these considerations? First, most of Latin America is now in a transitional stage: It is in the process of breaking the chains of the past but is not yet fully modern or developed either. Second, we need to recognize that sustained development, whether in Africa, Russia, or Latin America, requires several generations to occur, not just a few years. Third, modernization is uneven: Urban areas are affected more rapidly than rural ones. Fourth, the benefits of development are also uneven: Some groups benefit more than others, and there is always a trade-off between growth and equity. Fifth, it is clear that those countries that have ample resources, strong institutions, and good public policy—Argentina, Brazil, Chile, Costa Rica, Mexico, Uruguay—are doing better than those that lack these features.

Latin America today represents a dynamic, ever-changing mix of traditional and modern. Abject poverty exists alongside gleaming skyscrapers and the most modern, high-tech industry. Widespread corruption and patronage coexist with efficient firms and new public policy agencies. Latin America has embraced democracy, but it is concerned about instability, chaos, and ungovernability and so it retains authoritarian features. The countries, their businesses, their governments, and their unions all recognize the need to streamline and eliminate waste, but that is hard to do if one's administration, business, agency, job, or family will be hurt in the process. Given these conditions, it is probably no accident that we get such leaders as Chávez in Venezuela, Fujimori in Peru, or the PRI in Mexico. Many governments combine democratic with authoritarian and populist tendencies. It is in the bridging of these gaps between traditional and modern, authoritarian and democratic, statism or mercantilism and liberalism that the genius of Latin American politics and politicians often shines through.

## Conclusion: Latin America in the New Millennium

Note that very few of the countries described in this book are fully consolidated democracies; most are in transitions where democracy is still weak and may still be precarious. Remember what we stated at the beginning of this chapter: Elections are a good start on the route to democracy, but to be considered truly democratic, a country must meet many other criteria—human rights, civil liberties, genuine pluralism, freedom and equality, civic consciousness and participation, civilian supremacy over the military, and separation of powers.

Most countries of Latin America made an impressive transition to electoral democracy during the 1980s, when the region's economies were in severe recession and plagued by foreign debt. In the 1990s most of the economies of the area began to recover, showing positive growth and able to begin a process of economic reform to go along with the earlier political reforms. Just as democratization had challenged the older authoritarianism, economic reform helped to free up systems that had been overly statist and inefficient. Liberalism in the economic sphere was increasingly seen as related to democracy in the political sphere. More recently, globalization has become another factor; participation in the global markets requires that Latin America continue with both political and economic reform if it wishes to be a significant player in the world of the twenty-first century.

The future looks brighter in Latin America than it has in the past. On both the political and economic fronts, the region seems to be doing better than at any time in its history, even with all the problems here enumerated. Although there may be reversions to authoritarianism in some of the poorer, weakly institutionalized countries, the possibility of a continent-wide reversion to authoritarianism as in the 1960s and 1970s seems unlikely. Over time, the social, economic, and political base for authoritarianism is being eroded by greater literacy and affluence, a growing middle class, and stronger democracies.

Among the most important questions still to be answered are the following: Which Latin American countries can succeed in consolidating and institutionalizing their still-fragile political systems? Can they adapt rapidly enough to globalization? Can they combine economic growth with equity and social justice? and finally, Can they reconcile their recently renewed democratic precepts with their own past historical traditions, which are often authoritarian, corporatist, and patrimonialist? Attempting to answer these and other important questions not only allows us to explore the possibilities for Latin America's future success but also illustrates why Latin America remains such a fascinating area.

Latin America has made great strides in recent decades, but many problems and uncertainties remain. Both the progress and the problems provide good reason for students of the area to remain intrigued by it. We hope that some of our enthusiasm for Latin America, maintained even in bad times over the past forty years, has rubbed off on you for the better times ahead.

## Notes

1. Classifying as democracy anything with elections, however fraudulent, was called "electoralism" by Philippe C. Schmitter and Terry Lynn Karl, "What Democracy Is . . . and Is Not," *Journal of Democracy* 2, no. 3 (Summer 1991): 78.

2. Hernando de Soto and Deborah Orsini, "Overcoming Underdevelopment," *Journal of Democracy* 2, no. 2 (Spring 1991): 106.

3. These characteristics are stated quite clearly in Schmitter and Karl, "What Democracy Is," p. 81, quoting Robert Dahl, *Dilemmas of Pluralist Democracy* (New Haven: Yale University Press, 1982), p. 11.

4. One study of Latin America that added other criteria to the institutional requirements of democracy was Jorge I. Domínguez and Abraham F. Lowenthal, eds., *Constructing Democratic Governance: Latin America and the Caribbean in the 1990s* (Baltimore: Johns Hopkins University Press, 1996).

5. Robert Wesson, *Democracy in Latin America: Promise and Problems* (New York: Praeger, 1982), p. 125.

6. Ibid., pp. 130–131.

7. Abraham F. Lowenthal, "Latin America at the Century's Turn," *Journal of Democracy* 11, no. 2 (April 2000): 43.

8. Larry Diamond, "Three Paradoxes of Democracy," *Journal of Democracy* 1, no. 3 (Summer 1990): 49.

9. Ibid.

10. Ibid.

11. Gustavo Gorriti, "Latin America's Internal Wars," *Journal of Democracy* 2, no. 1 (Winter 1991): 86–87.

12. María Jimena Duzán, "Colombia's Bloody War of Words," *Journal of Democracy* 2, no. 1 (Winter 1991): 105.

# Suggestions for Further Reading

Alba, Victor. *Politics and the Labor Movement in Latin America.* Stanford: Stanford University Press, 1968.

_____. *The Latin Americans.* New York: Praeger, 1969.

Alexander, Robert J. *Organized Labor in Latin America.* New York: Harper and Row, 1965.

_____. *Agrarian Reform in Latin America.* New York: Macmillan, 1974.

Ames, Barry. *Political Survival: Politicians and Public Policy in Latin America.* Berkeley and Los Angeles: University of California Press, 1987.

Anderson, Charles W. *Politics and Economic Change in Latin America: The Governing of Restless Nations.* Princeton: Van Nostrand, 1967.

Augero, Felipe, and Jeffrey Stark, eds. *Fault Lines of Democracy in Post Transitional Latin America.* Miami, Fla: North-South Center Press, 1998.

Bushnell, David, and Neill Macaulay. *The Emergence of Latin America in the Nineteenth Century.* New York: Oxford University Press, 1988.

Camp, Roderic Ai. *Democracy in Latin America: Patterns and Cycles.* Wilmington, Del.: Scholarly Resource, 1996.

Cardoso, F. H., and E. Faletto. *Dependency and Development in Latin America.* Berkeley and Los Angeles: University of California Press, 1978.

Chalmers, Douglas, et al., eds. *The New Politics of Inequality in Latin America: Rethinking Participation and Representation.* New York: Oxford University Press, 1997.

Chevalier, Francois. *Land and Society in Colonial Mexico.* Berkeley and Los Angeles: University of California Press, 1970.

Collier, David, ed. *The New Authoritarianism in Latin America.* Princeton: Princeton University Press, 1979.

Collier, David, and Ruth Berins Collier. *Shaping the Political Agenda: Critical Junctures, the Labor Movement, and Regime Dynamics in Latin America.* Princeton: Princeton University Press, 1991.

Cortes Conde, Roberto. *The First Stages of Modernization in Spanish America.* New York: Harper and Row, 1974.

Dahl, Robert. *Dilemmas of Pluralist Democracy.* New Haven: Yale University Press, 1982.

De Soto, Hernando. *The Other Path: The Invisible Revolution in the Third World.* New York: Harper and Row, 1989.

De Soto, Hernando, and Deborah Orsini. "Overcoming Underdevelopment." *Journal of Democracy* 2, no. 2 (Spring 1991).

Dealy, Glen. *The Public Man: An Interpretation of Latin American and Other Catholic Countries.* Amherst: University of Massachusetts Press, 1977.

Diamond, Larry. "Three Paradoxes of Democracy." *Journal of Democracy* 1, no. 3 (Summer 1990).

Diamond, Larry, Juan J. Linz, and Seymour Martin Lipset, eds. *Democracy in Developing Countries: Latin America.* Boulder: Lynne Rienner, 1989.

Dominguez, Jorge I., and Abraham F. Lowenthal, eds. *Constructing Democratic Governance: Latin America and the Caribbean in the 1990s.* Baltimore: Johns Hopkins University Press, 1996.

Eisenstadt, S. N., F. Bronner, R. Kahane, and B. Siebzehner, eds. *Social Change in Latin American Societies.* Jerusalem: Magnes Press, 1986.

*En qué momento se jodió Colombia.* Bogotá: Editorial Oveja Negra, 1990.

Falcoff, Mark. *A Culture of Its Own: Taking Latin America Seriously.* New Brunswick, N.J.: Transaction Books, 1998.

Fitch, John Samuel. *The Military Coup d'Etat as a Political Process: Ecuador, 1948–1966.* Baltimore: Johns Hopkins University Press, 1977.

Freyre, Gilberto. *The Masters and the Slaves.* New York: Knopf, 1964.

Fuentes, Carlos. *The Buried Mirror: Reflections on Spain and the New World.* Boston: Houghton Mifflin, 1992.

Gibson, Charles. *Spain in America.* New York: Harper and Row, 1996.

Glade, William P. *The Latin American Economies: A Study of Their Institutional Evolution.* New York: Van Nostrand, 1969.

Gorriti, Gustavo. "Latin America's Internal Wars." *Journal of Democracy* 2, no. 1 (Winter 1991).

Grindle, Merilee. *State and Countryside: Development Policy and Agrarian Politics in Latin America.* Baltimore: Johns Hopkins University Press, 1986.

Gwynne, Robert N., and Cristobal Kay, eds. *Latin America Transformed: Globalization and Modernity.* New York: Oxford University Press, 1999.

Halperin Donghi, Tulio. *The Aftermath of Revolution in Latin America.* New York: Harper and Row, 1973.

Haring, Clarence. *The Spanish Empire in America.* New York: Harcourt Brace, 1963.

Hirschman, Albert O. *Journey Toward Progress: Studies of Economic Policy-Making in Latin America.* Garden City, N.Y.: Doubleday, 1965.

Jimena Duzán, María. "Colombia's Bloody War of Words." *Journal of Democracy* 2, no. 1 (Winter 1991).

Johnson, John J. *Political Change in Latin America: The Emergence of the Middle Sectors.* Stanford: Stanford University Press, 1958.

―――. *The Military and Society in Latin America.* Stanford: Stanford University Press, 1964.

Karst, Kenneth, and Keith Rosen. *Law and Development in Latin America.* Berkeley and Los Angeles: University of California Press, 1975.

Klaren, Peter, and Thomas J. Bossert, eds. *Promise of Development: Theories of change in Latin America.* Boulder: Westview Press, 1996.

Kline, Harvey F. *State Building and Conflict Resolution in Columbia, 1986–1994.* Tuscaloosa: University of Alabama Press, 1999.

Kryzanek, Michael J. *Latin America: Change and Challenge.* New York: Harper Collins, 1995.
Lagos, Marta. "Latin America's Shining Mask." *Journal of Democracy* 8, no. 3 (July 1997).
Landsberger, Henry A. *Latin American Peasant Movements.* Ithaca: Cornell University Press, 1969.
Leal Buitrago, Francisco, and León Zamosc, eds. *Al Filo del Caos: Crisis Política en la Colombia de los años 80.* Bogotá: Tercer Mundo Editores, 1990.
Leeds, Anthony. "Brazilian Careers and Social Structure: A Case History and Model." *American Anthropologist* 66 (1964): 1321–1347.
Levine, Daniel. *Religion and Politics in Latin America: The Catholic Church in Venezuela and Colombia.* Princeton: Princeton University Press, 1981.
Lipset, Seymour, and Aldo Solari, eds. *Elites in Latin America.* New York: Oxford University Press, 1967.
Loveman, Brian. *For la Patria: Politics and the Armed Forces in Latin America.* Wilmington, Del.: Scholarly Resources, 1999.
Lowenthal, Abraham F. "Latin America at the Century's Turn." *Journal of Democracy* 11, no. 2 (April 2000).
Lowenthal, Abraham F., ed. *Armies and Politics in Latin America.* New York: Holmes and Meier, 1976.
Malloy, James, ed. *Authoritarianism and Corporatism in Latin America.* Pittsburgh: University of Pittsburgh Press, 1997.
Mander, John. *The Unrevolutionary Society: The Power of Latin American Conservatism in a Changing World.* New York: Knopf, 1969.
Martz, John D. *Colombia: A Contemporary Political Survey.* Chapel Hill: University of North Carolina Press, 1962.
McCoy, Terry, ed. *The Dynamics of Population Policy in Latin America.* Cambridge, Mass.: Ballinger, 1974.
McDonald, Ronald H., and J. Mark Ruhl. *Party Politics and Elections in Latin America.* Boulder: Westview Press, 1989.
Mecham, J. Lloyd. *Church and State in Latin America.* Chapel Hill: University of North Carolina Press, 1966.
Mercier Vega, Luis. *Roads to Power in Latin America.* New York: Praeger, 1969.
Needler, Martin. *The Problem of Democracy in Latin America.* Lexington, Mass.: Lexington Books, 1987.
Oquist, Paul. *Violence, Conflict, and Politics in Colombia.* New York: Academic Press, 1980.
Oxhorn, Philip D., and Graciela Ducatenzeiler, eds. *What Kind of Democracy? What Kind of Market? Latin America in the Age of Neoliberalism.* University Park: Pennsylvania State University Press, 1998.
Peeler, John. *Building Democracy in Latin America.* Boulder: Lynne Rienner, 1998.
Pike, Frederick B. *Spanish America, 1900–1970.* New York: Norton, 1973.
Pike, Frederick B., and Thomas Stritch, eds. *The New Corporatism.* Notre Dame, Ind.: University of Notre Dame Press, 1974.
Schmitter, Philippe C., and Terry Lynn Karl. "What Democracy Is . . . and Is Not," *Journal of Democracy* 2, no. 3 (Summer 1991).

Sigmund, Paul. *Multinationals in Latin America*. Madison: University of Wisconsin Press, 1980.
Silvert, Kalman H. *The Conflict Society: Reaction and Revolution in Latin America*. New York: American Universities Field Staff, 1966.
Skidmore, Thomas E., and Peter H. Smith. *Modern Latin America*. New York: Oxford University Press, 1997.
Smith, Peter H. *Latin America in Comparative Perspective: New Approaches to Methods and Analysis*. Boulder: Westview Press, 1995.
Souza, Amaury de. "Cardoso and the Struggle for Reform in Brazil." *Journal of Democracy* 10, no. 3 (July 1999).
Stepan, Alfred. *The State and Society: Peru in Comparative Perspective*. Princeton: Princeton University Press, 1978.
Tannenbaum, Frank. *Ten Keys to Latin America*. New York: Vintage, 1962.
Tokman, Victor E., and Guillermo O'Donnell, eds. *Poverty and Inequality in Latin America: Issues and New Challenges*. Notre Dame, Ind.: Notre Dame University Press, 1998.
Urrutia, Miguel. *The Development of the Colombian Labor Movement*. New Haven: Yale University Press, 1969.
Veliz, Claudio. *The Centralist Tradition in Latin America*. Princeton: Princeton University Press, 1980.
Veliz, Claudio, ed. *The Politics of Conformity in Latin America*. London: Oxford University Press, 1967.
Vernon, Raymond. *The Dilemma of Mexico's Development*. Cambridge: Harvard University Press, 1963.
Wesson, Robert G. *Democracy in Latin America: Promise and Problems*. New York: Praeger, 1982.
Wesson, Robert G., ed. *Coping with Latin American Debt*. New York: Praeger, 1988.
Wiarda, Howard J. *Corporatism and Development in Latin America*. Boulder: Westview Press, 1981.
———. *The Democratic Revolution in Latin America*. New York: Holmes and Meier, 1990.
———. *Latin American Politics: A New World of Possibilities*. Belmont, Calif.: Wadsworth, 1994.
———. *The Soul of Latin America: Culture and the Political Tradition*. New Haven: Yale University Press, 2001.
Williams, Edward J. *Latin American Christian Democratic Parties*. Knoxville: University of Tennessee Press, 1967.
Worcester, Donald E., and Wendell G. Schaeffer. *The Growth and Culture of Latin America*. New York: Oxford University Press, 1970.
Wynia, Gary W. *The Politics of Latin American Development*. New York: Cambridge University Press, 1990.
Zea, Leopoldo. *The Latin American Mind*. Norman: University of Oklahoma Press, 1963.

# Index

agencies
  autonomous state, 145–146
  decentralized, 162
agrarian reform, 67, 145, 152–154,
    162–163, 211. *See* farming; land
    reform
Alliance for Progress, 25, 156
anarchy, 21
Argentina
  business in, 91–92
  class structure of, 168–169
  democracy in, 168–169
  economy of, 151–152
  federal government of, 143
  military in, 80
  political parties of, 169
  unions in, 95
Army. *See* military
attitudes, 47–48, 48*t*3.2
authoritarianism, vii, 2, 14, 16, 17, 34,
    39, 63, 65.
  bureaucratic, 26, 79–80
  current attitudes of, 39–49
  democratic hybrid of, 24, 45–46,
    48–49, 64, 77–78, 121, 123–124,
    132–133, 135, 182, 190, 191,
    193–194, 202–203, 212
  overthrow of, 39
  *See also* dictatorships

Blacks, 3–5, 33, 35
  bottom of social scale for, 51
  slavery of, 15, 16, 52–53
  slavery revolt by, 19, 20, 54
Bolivia
  democracy in, 179–181

indigenous groups in, 104
narcotics in, 158–159
political party in, 158–159, 179–180
revolution of, 72–73
Brazil
  Blacks in, 3–4
  Catholic Church and, 86–87
  democracy in, 172–173
  federal government of, 142–143
  government of, 138
  indigenous groups in, 103
  judiciary in, 140
  military in, 76, 81
  monarchy of, 19–21
  other interest groups of, 108
  *panelinha* in, 109–110
  political parties in, 119, 121–123, 123
  slavery and, 52–53
bureaucracy, 64
  underdevelopment of, 160–161

*campesinos*, 97, 153
capitalism, 2, 8–9
Cárdenas, Lázaro, 127–128
Caribbean, xvi
  slavery of, 52–53
Catholic Church, 20, 28, 29, 35–36,
    37–38, 64, 69, 102, 167
  changes in, 209
  colonial policy and, 17
  converting to, 14, 52, 53–54, 82
  decline of, 84–85
  divorce and, 87
  interests of, 84
  liberation theology of, 83–84, 87
  as major power group, 82

new effect of, 85–86
other churches challenge to, 17, 86–87, 88
political involvement of, 83–88
upper class and, 83–84
*caudillos,* 75, 77
Central America, xvi
conquest of, 15
support for democracy in, 40, 42*f*3.3, 44*f*3.6
Chávez, Hugo, 45, 162–163, 177–179
Chile, 19
business in, 90–91
Catholic Church and, 87
democracy in, 169–170
economy of, 151
military in, 80
oligarchy of, 21
political parties in, 115–116, 169–179
unions in, 96
Christianity. *See* Catholic Church
civil service, 326
class structure.
caste system for, 53–54
economic/social change of, 66–68
egalitarianism and, 66
elite in, 58, 83–84
government influence of, 131–132
indigenous groups and, 62–63, 64–65
industrial workers in, 59–60, 63, 64–65
interest groups in, 57
middle class in, 58–59
peasantry and, 60, 63, 64–65
regional/national variations of, 55–57
state-society relations of, 63–65
two, 51, 54
urban poverty and, 61, 63
widening gaps in, 209–211
women's groups and, 61–62, 63
*See also* middle class
Colombia, 19, 70–71
Catholic Church and, 83

democracy in, 174–177
government of, 138–139
indigenous groups in, 104
industrialization in, 90, 92
judiciary in, 141
law enforcement in, 160, 176–177, 182
narcotics in, 157–158, 159
military in, 78–79, 81
other interest groups of, 107, 108
political parties in, 112–113, 175–176
racial mixture of, 5
evolution in, 175–176, 207–208
unions in, 95–96
unitary government of, 143–144
colonial rule, 13–21, 18*t*2.1
communism, 24, 99, 116, 120, 164, 169, 175. *See also* Marxism
Conservatives, 38, 112–115, 126
constitution, 132–134, 136, 138–139, 141, 143, 177–178, 189, 193
corporatism, 35–36, 39, 64, 127
Costa Rica
democracy in, 170–171
political parties in, 119
coup d'état, 8, 23, 46, 78, 79, 81–82, 85, 86, 93, 116, 164, 182, 188, 190, 193, 205
Creoles, 18, 20, 54, 75
Cuba, 19, 24
conquest of, 15
economic diversification in, 149
Marxism in, 153, 198–199
political parties in, 119
revolution of, 25–26, 73–74
survival against U.S. by, 164
Venezuela guerrillas and, 176
culture
pluricultural/multiethnic, 104
separation of, 53

debt, 9, 150–151
democracy, vii–viii, 1–3, 17, 20, 24–25, 33–34.
changes in, 208–213

# INDEX

civil war legacy against, 206–208
disillusionment with, 40–44, 41*f3.1*, 42*f3.4*, 43*f3.5*, 44*f3.6*
electoral, 26–27
elite and, 58, 124
ethnic populations and, 56
fragile but lacking in, 198–199
inability to govern in, 208
institutional characteristics of, 203–204
middle class and, 55–56
fullest, 168–172
non, 199–200
not fully consolidated in, 172–174
past but now threatened, 174–179
pluralism and, 29–30
political tradition against, 204–205
ranking of, 167–168
revolution and, 70
social imbalance and, 63
support for, 39–40, 41*f3.1*, 41*f3.2*, 42*f3.3*, 423.4, 43*f3.5*, 44*f3.6*
transition from authoritarianism to, 65, 195–198
underdevelopment and , 204–206
U.S. for, 164–165
voting and, 201–203
weak institutions and, 46, 51, 179–195
*See also* authoritarianism; political parties
dictatorships, 21, 22, 23–24, 25. *See also* authoritarianism
Dominican Republic, 14–15
democracy in, 173–174
political parties of, 174
drugs. *See* narcotics

economy, 1, 5–6, 9.
barter, 21
centralized government and, 149–150
changes in, 28
crisis of, 23–24, 102, 150–151
development of, 147–152
diversification of, 5, 148–149
dominance of international political, 165–166
globalization of, 2, 8, 10–11, 151–152
GNP of, 156
growth of, 22
neoliberalism in, 149–151
public sector influence on, 146, 161
reforms of, 209–213
single crop/product, 147–149
*See also* industrialization
Ecuador, 19
democracy in, 181–182
government of, 138
political parties in, 119, 126, 182
women and politics in, 106
egalitarianism, 27, 66, 199
El Salvador
democracy in, 182–184
guerrillas and, 208
law enforcement in, 184
political parties in, 119–121, 183–184
women and politics in, 106
elite, 20, 22–25, 33–34, 39, 58, 155, 167, 205
commercial/industrial, 89–92, 124
political parties by, 111–112, 124
England, 14, 17, 21–22
equality, 83
Europeans, 5, 51
executive, chief
choosing of, 111
power of, 133, 135–136, 142, 194, 197, 202–203
exports, 8–9, 22, 26, 148

family planning, 87, 106, 156
farming, 5, 7–8, 9, 14–15, 21, 53, 60, 88, 91, 97, 107, 153. *See also* agrarian reform
federalism, 141–143
feudalism, 7–8, 9, 13, 15, 16, 17, 20, 28, 33, 38

collapse of, 27
  quasi, 51, 54, 67, 167
foreign aid, 2, 30, 100–102, 149, 165
Fujimori, Alberto, 45, 193–195

geography, 6, 34
globalization, 2, 58, 66–67, 91, 151–152,
    211, 213
government, 20–21.
  autonomous state agencies of,
    145–146
  centralization of, 3, 131, 136,
    143–144, 145–146
  change in, 29, 66
  class structure and, 131–132
  constitution of, 132–134, 136,
    138–139, 141, 143, 177–178, 189,
    193
  dilemma of political systems in,
    162–164
  disillusionment with, 44–45
  distributive policy of, 162–163
  elite running of, 20, 22–24, 25
  executive/legislative/judicial
    relations in, 3, 133, 135–136, 142
  federal, 142–143
  globalization effects on, 67, 211, 213
  hierarchical interests in, 134
  independence of Congress in, 138
  interest groups and, 64–65, 131
  judicial branch of, 133–134, 139–141
  legislative branch of, 136–139
  local, 142–144
  real demands on, 66–67
  single party, 23–24
  unitary, 143–144
  weakness of, 208
  women and, 62, 105–106
  See also democracy; public policy
Guatemala
  democracy in, 184–185
  economy of, 152
  guerrillas, 39, 45, 73, 79, 108, 118,
    153, 158, 160, 175–176, 182,
    192–194, 207–208

Haiti, 19–20
  Catholic Church and, 87–88
  conquest of, 14–15
  lacking democracy in, 198–199
  law enforcement in, 161
  military in, 76–77
  slavery revolt in, 19–20
hierarchy, 34–35, 39, 134
Honduras
  business in, 90
  democracy in, 185–187
  government of, 137–138
  human rights in, 102
  law enforcement in, 186
  military in, 80–81
  political parties in, 113–114
  underdevelopment of, 161–162
human rights, 26–27, 83–84, 87, 99,
    102, 133–134, 158, 185, 207, 211

immigration, 55
Import-Substitution-Industrialization
    (ISI) model, 9, 26, 90, 148, 149
independence
  fragmentation after, 20–21
  movement for, 18–20
Indians, 3–5, 8, 14, 16, 22, 33, 35, 54.
  deaths of, 52
  large population of, 52
  Mexican reform for, 54
  organizing of, 55, 62–63, 64–65
  as peasants, 51–53
  slavery and, 15, 17
  See also peasantry
indigenous groups.
  Bolivian, 104
  Brazilian, 103
  as interest groups, 102–105
  narcotics use by, 158
  Nicaraguan, 104
  organizing by, 102–104
  Peruvian, 104
  political parties and, 180
  See also Indians
industrial workers, 59–60, 63, 64–65

industrialization, 8, 17, 24, 38, 59, 90, 147–148
inequality, 33, 34, 153, 205–206
inflation, 150, 172–173, 188, 192, 194
Inter-American Development Bank (IADB), 100–101, 165
interest group(s), 57
  Catholic Church as, 82–88
  coercion vs voting by, 70–71
  commercial/industrial elite as, 89–92
  co-optation of, 70–71
  corporatist, 64–65, 69
  emergence of new, 75
  government coordination of, 131
  indigenous groups as, 102–105
  labor unions as, 94–97
  large landowners as, 88–89
  mediation abilities of, 209
  middle class as, 92–94
  military as, 74–82
  non-governmental organizations (NGO) as, 107–108
  other, 107–108
  peasants as, 97–98
  regional effect on, 109–110
  state controlled, 64–65, 69–70
  United States as, 98–102
  women as, 105–107
international environment, 30
International Monetary Fund (IMF), 00–101, 165, 202
investments, 2, 21–22

judiciary. *See* legal system

land reform, 67, 89. *See also* agrarian reform
landowners, 20, 25, 53, 75, 88–89, 91, 97–98, 153, 167, 176, 191
languages, 1, 3, 21
*latifundios*, 88, 153
Latin America
  support for democracy in, 39–40, 41*f*3.2, 42*f*3.4

law enforcement, 160–161, 176–177, 184, 186, 193–194
legal system, 133–135, 139–141
legislature, 136–139
liberalism, 37–38, 132
Liberals, 112–115, 123, 125, 126, 127
literacy, 38, 54, 55, 66

macho, 34
Marxism, 2, 25, 98, 118, 131, 175, 198–199, 207.
  collapse of, 39–40
  *See also* communism
mercantilism, 7–9, 16–18, 28, 36, 151
mestizo, 4, 5, 53–54, 57, 58
Mexico, 19
  *camarillas* in, 109–110
  conquest of, 15
  corporatism in, 127–128
  democracy in, 40, 41*f*3.2, 43*f*3.5, 195–198
  federal government of, 142
  guerrillas and, 108, 153, 158, 208
  law enforcement in, 160
  narcotics in, 159–160
  political parties in, 69, 126–128, 196–198
  revolution of, 71–72, 127
middle class, 23–24, 25, 28, 54–55
  Colombian, 107
  democracy and, 55–56
  increase of, 58–59
  industrialization fostering of, 93
  as interest group, 92–94
  military and, 59
  weakness of, 51
  working class *vs.*, 93
military, 4, 13, 25–26, 64, 69, 167.
  academies for, 76
  Brazilian, 81
  bureaucratic authoritarian, 79–80, 82
  chief executive and, 111
  Colombian, 78–79
  constitutional, 80–82

counterinsurgency by, 79
democracy and, 121, 123–124, 202
Ecuadorian, 81
fight against narcotics by, 159
governmental control by, 20
Honduras, 80–81
intervention by, 133
Mexican, 127
middle class and, 59
national *vs.* regional, 75–76
para, 108
Paraguay, 77–78, 188–190
political parties and, 171
professional, 75–76, 78–79
Uruguay and, 171
Venezuelan, 81, 86
*See also* authoritarianism; coup d'état; revolution
minerals, 6, 7, 9
modernization, 17, 21–23, 27, 10*1.1t*, 212
monarchy, 16, 18–21, 35, 132, 135, 144
mulatto, 4, 53–54, 57, 58

narcotics, 108, 156–160, 176–177, 189
neoliberalism, 9, 28, 132, 146, 149, 162, 169
Nicaragua
  democracy in, 187–188
  indigenous groups in, 104
  law enforcement in, 160
  political parties in, 188
  revolution in, 73–74
non-governmental groups (NGO), 107–108

oligarchy, 21, 23–24, 25, 28, 38, 57–58, 72, 111 . *See also* landowners
organicism, 35, 39

Panama
  democracy in, 174
  government of, 137
  political parties in, 123–125

Paraguay
  Catholic Church and, 87
  democracy in, 188–192
  law enforcement in, 160
  military in, 77–78, 188–190
  political parties in, 125–126, 188–191
patrimonialism, 36–37, 39
Peace Corps, 25
peasantry, 60, 63, 64–65, 66, 199.
  Colombian, 70–71
  as interest group, 97–98
  Mexican, 69, 127
  *See also* Indians
*peninsulares*, 18, 54
Perón, Juan, 24, 168
Peru
  democracy in, 41*f3.2*, 43*f3.5*, 45, 182, 192–195
  indigenous groups in, 104
  law enforcement in, 193–195
  narcotics in, 158
  nationalization by, 164
  political parties in, 116–118, 128, 192–194
  *See also* Shining Path
petroleum, 9, 150, 179
plantations, 7–8, 14–15. *See also* farming
pluralism, 29, 51, 63–64, 210
policymaking
  political system's dilemma and, 162–164
  underdevelopment and, 161
  U.S. dominance and, 164–166
political culture
  attitudes in, 31, 47–48, 48*t3.2*
  authoritarianism and, 39–49
  changes in, 27–28, 37–39, 208–209
  country's composite view in, 31
  democracy and, 39–49
  historical aspects of, 32–37
  lack of trust of, 46–47, 47*t3.1*
  stereotype avoidance for, 32

political parties, 66, 167, 169–170, 171, 175–176, 179–180, 182, 188–191, 192–194, 196–198
  chief executive and, 111
  Conservatives in, 112–115, 126
  co-optation of, 29, 128
  disillusionment with, 44–45
  Liberals and, 112–115, 123, 125, 126, 127
  new, 115–119
  other, 119–129
  narcotic influence in, 158–159
population, 3
  control of, 155–156
  indigenous, 14, 52
  racial/ethnic breakdown of, 5, 56
populism, 24
Portugal, 3, 7, 33, 37, 52, 144. *See* colonial rule
  conquest by, 13–16
  monarch in Brazil for, 19–20
  slavery and, 53
poverty, 1, 5, 9, 28, 97, 168, 178, 186, 205–206, 209–210.
  urban, 61, 63, 102, 109, 156
  *See also* proletariat; urban reform
presidency. *See* executive, chief
primogeniture, 52
proletariat, lumpen, 61, 63, 109
property rights, 54
public policy, 146, 212
  changes in, 29
  economic development and, 161
  narcotics and, 156–160
  population and, 155–156
  urban reform and, 154–155
Puerto Rico, 15, 19

race relations, 3
  Creoles/peninsulares, 18
  ethnic integration of, 5, 57
  European elite and, 56–57
  mixture of, 4–5, 53
reform, 206.
  financial, 173, 209–213

Mexican, 163–164
neoliberal, 132, 146, 149, 162, 186
political, 169, 171–172
popular, 206
urban, 154–155
Venezuelan, 162–163
*See also* agrarian reforms
revolution
  American, 18
  Bolivian, 72–73
  Columbia and, 175–176, 182
  Cuban, 25–26, 73–74
  democracy and, 70
  Mexican, 8, 71–72, 127
  Nicaraguan, 73–74, 188
  social, 23
  *See also* coup d'état; independence

Sandinistas (FSLN), 73–74, 153, 164, 187–188
Shining Path, 108, 118, 158, 192–194, 208
slavery, 15, 16, 52
  Aristotle and, 33
  revolt against, 19, 20, 54
social change, 1–2, 28–29
social structure. *See* class structure
socialism, 24, 38
society,
  civil, 102
  conflict, 38
South America, xvii
  conquest of, 15–16
  support for democracy in, 40, 41*f*3.2, 43*3.5*
Soviet Union, 25, 39, 149, 169
Spain, 3, 7, 33–34, 37, 52, 75, 144, 133. *See* colonial rule
  conquest by, 13–16
  slavery and, 53

trade, 9
  free, 11, 101–102, 151
  foreign, 91
transformations, vii-viii

trust, 46–47, 47*t*3.1

underdevelopment, 160–161, 205–206
unions, 23, 25, 28, 168
   Argentinean, 95
   Chilean, 95–96
   disillusionment with, 44
   as interest group, 94–97, 102
   Mexican, 69, 127
   organizing of, 55, 64–65
   politics and, 94–95
   state-controlled, 95
   Venezuelan, 96
unitary systems, 143–144
United States (U.S.)
   anti-communism of, 25–26, 99
   business and, 100, 102
   concerns of, 75
   democracy fostered by, 39
   dominance by, 22, 99, 164–166
   foundations of, 18*t*2.1
   government of, 99–100
   interest groups and, 57, 65, 98–102
   international agencies of, 100–102
   investment by, 21–22
   Latin America contrast to, vii-viii
   legal system of, 134
   minority population of, 56
   modernization and, 13, 17
   narcotics opposition by, 156–160
   political culture of, 32
urban reform, 154–155. *See also* poverty
urbanization, 38, 55, 66, 89, 93, 166

Uruguay
   democracy in, 171–172
   government of, 136
   political parties in, 114–115
U.S. Agency for International Development (USAID), 100–101, 153–165

Venezuela, 19
   Catholic Church and, 85–86, 139
   democracy in, 41*f*3.2, 43*f*3.5, 45, 177–179, 182
   distributive revenues of, 162
   government of, 138–139
   judiciary in, 140–141
   military in, 86
   nationalization by, 164
   political parties in, 85, 118–119, 128
   unions in, 96
voting, 39–40, 48*t*3.2, 54, 171–172, 181, 187–188, 195, 197–198, 211
   limitations and, 20, 70
   right to, 54
   without democracy, 194, 201–203

Whites. *See* Europeans
women
   achievement of groups of, 61–62, 63
   as interest group, 55, 102, 105–107
   politics and, 62, 105–106
   *See also* family planning
World Bank, 100–101, 107, 165, 202

Zapatista Front of National Liberation, 108, 153